MW01252783

Indeterminate Bodies

Also by Naomi Segal:

ANDRÉ GIDE: Pederasty and Pedagogy

COMING OUT OF FEMINISM? (*coeditor with Mandy Merck and Elizabeth Wright*)

FREUD IN EXILE: Psychoanalysis and its Vicissitudes (*coeditor with Edward Timms*)

LE DÉSIR À L'ŒVRE: André Gide à Cambridge 1918, 1998

NARCISSUS AND ECHO: Women in the French *récit*

SCARLET LETTERS: Fictions of Adultery from Antiquity to the 1990s (*coeditor with Nicholas White*)

THE ADULTERESS'S CHILD: Authorship and Desire in the Nineteenth-Century Novel

THE BANAL OBJECT: Theme and Thematics in Proust, Rilke, Hofmannsthal and Sartre

THE UNINTENDED READER: Feminism and *Manon Lescaut*

Indeterminate Bodies

Edited by

Naomi Segal

Lib Taylor

and

Roger Cook

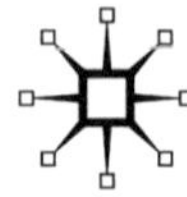

First published 2003 by
PALGRAVE MACMILLAN
Houndmills, Basingstoke, Hampshire RG21 6XS and
175 Fifth Avenue, New York, N. Y. 10010
Companies and representatives throughout the world.

PALGRAVE MACMILLAN is the global academic imprint of the Palgrave Macmillan division of St Martin's Press, LLC and of Palgrave Macmillan Ltd. Macmillan® is a registered trademark in the United States, United Kingdom and other countries. Palgrave is a registered trademark in the European Union and other countries.

ISBN 0–333–94969–2

This book is printed on paper suitable for recycling and made from fully managed and sustained forest sources.

A catalogue record for this book is available from the British Library.

Library of Congress Cataloging-in-Publication Data
Indeterminate bodies / edited by Naomi Segal, Lib Taylor, and Roger Cook.
p. cm
Includes bibliographical references and index.
ISBN 0–333–94969–2
1. Body, Human–Social aspects. 2. Body, Human (Philosophy) 3. Body, in literature. 4. Human figure in art. 5. Gender identity. I. Segal, Naomi, 1949– II. Taylor, Lib, 1950– III. Cook, Roger, 1940–
HM636.I53 2002
306.4–dc21 2002074814

10 9 8 7 6 5 4 3 2 1
12 11 10 09 08 07 06 05 04 03

Printed and bound in Great Britain by
Antony Rowe Ltd, Chippenham and Eastbourne

Contents

List of Plates

Second plate section

Acknowledgements

Please note that bibliographical details of all secondary texts are to be found at the end of the chapter in which they have been used. The date given within the chapter for a text which has been cited in translation or in a re-edition is the original date of publication, though page-numbers refer to the translation or re-edition used.

We are pleased to acknowledge two generous grants which have enabled this book to appear in its illustrated form. A University of Reading Research Endowment Trust Fund grant and a Research Grant from the British Academy were used, respectively, towards production costs and the costs of reproduction and copyright permissions.

We also acknowledge with gratitude the following permissions – see List of Illustrations: the Becker Collection, Syracuse University Library Department of Special Collections, New York, for 'Madam Meyers' (ca. 1885) and 'Priscilla the monkey girl' (ca. 1926); Regen Projects, Los Angeles, for Lari Pittman's *Once a Noun, Now a Verb*, # 2 1997 (private collection, New York), *Headhunter*, 1982 (Collection William Weidner, Los Angeles), *Untitled # 1 (A Decorated Chronology of Insistence and Resignation*), 1992 (Collection Rachel and Jean-Pierre Lehmann) and *Like You, Hoping and Wanting But Not Liking,* 1995 (Eli Broad Family Foundation), *Santa Monica*; HVG (Hungarian Economics Weekly), Szerkesztöség, Hungary, for the front-page image of May 1998; the Ministero dei Beni e delle Attività Culturali of Italy for Pieter Bruegel, *The Parable of the Blind*, 1568. Museo Nazionale di Capodimonte, Naples; the Ministerio de Educación, Cultura y Deporte of Spain for Diego Velázquez, *Las Meninas* (*The Maids of Honour*), ca. 1656. Museo Nacional del Prado, Madrid; Werner Herzog Filmproduktion, Munich for a still from *Land des Schweigens und der Dunkelheit* (*Land of Silence and Darkness*) (dir. and prod. Werner Herzog, West Germany, 1971); Locus Solus Inc, New York, for a still from *Night on Earth* (dir. Jim Jarmusch, prod. Locus Solus, USA, 1991); Twentieth Century Fox Film Corporation for a still from *Gentlemen Prefer Blondes* (Howard Hawks, 1953); the photo-archives of the Tyrš Museum of Physical Education and Sports, National Museum, Prague, for *Oath to the Republic*. Men's routine. 10th Sokol Festival, Prague, June–July 1938, *No obstacle prevents the task from being fulfilled*. From the Svazarm Day. 1st Spartakiáda,

Prague, July 1955, and *Routine for Working Class Youth*, 6th Czechoslovak Spartakiáda, Prague, June 1985.

This book would have been impossible without stimulus of the MA on *The Body and Representation* at the University of Reading, in which all the editors are actively involved. We wish to express our gratitude to past and present colleagues and students on the course, with whom it has been our pleasure to work over the past seven years, and without whom our lives as university teachers would have been much less colourful and inspiring.

We dedicate this book to the memory of Rex Stainton Rogers.

Notes on the Contributors

Ajamu is a self-taught photographer, SM/cultural activist and black queer arts festival producer. Through experimentation and risk-taking his work has set out to extend, transgress and push the boundaries of contemporary theoretical debates, specifically in relation to race, sexuality and representation. His work has been exhibited in solo and group shows in galleries and alternative spaces throughout the world. He has also participated in numerous talks and his work has appeared in a wide variety of publications and journals worldwide. Ajamu lives and works between London and Holland; he is at present a theory researcher at the Jan van Eyck Akademie, Maastricht.

Jonathan Bignell is Reader in Television and Film in the Department of Film, Theatre and Television at The University of Reading. He is author of *Media Semiotics: an Introduction* (1997) and *Postmodern Media Culture* (2000), editor of *Writing and Cinema* (1999), and joint editor of *British Television Drama: Past, Present and Future* (2000). He is joint General Editor of Manchester University Press's 'Television Series'.

Roger Cook teaches Lesbian and Gay Studies in the MA on The Body and Representation and is a Lecturer in the Department of Fine Art at the University of Reading. He has published articles and conference papers relating the work of Pierre Bourdieu to the field of contemporary art and is completing a PhD thesis in the Department of the History of Art and Architecture at Reading. He made brief appearances in some of the films of the late Derek Jarman, notably in *The Garden* in which he appeared as Jesus Christ.

Márta Csabai is a postdoctoral Research Fellow in the Research Institute of Psychology of the Hungarian Academy of Sciences, Budapest; and a lecturer on medical and health psychology at the University Medical School, Debrecen. She is a member of the teaching staff of the doctoral programme in theoretical psychoanalysis at the University of Pécs. Her research and publications are related to themes of gender and psychoanalysis, hysteria, and representations of the body and health.

Sherril Dodds is a Lecturer in Dance Studies at the University of Surrey. Her book, *Dance on Screen: Genres and Media from Hollywood to Experimental Art,* examines images of dance in the screen media and she has written chapters on female striptease in *Dance in the City* (edited by Helen Thomas), on postmodernism and popular culture in *Dancing Texts* (edited by Janet Adshead-Lansdale) and on music video in *Music, Sensation and Sensuality* (edited by Linda Austern).

Ferenc Erős is Deputy Director and Head of the Department of Social and Cultural Psychology of the Research Institute for Psychology at the Hungarian Academy of Sciences, Budapest, and Professor of Social Psychology at the University of Pécs, where he codirects a doctoral programme in theoretical psychoanalysis. His research areas include: authoritarianism, prejudice and discrimination; minority identity and coping with threatened and traumatised identities; and the relationship between psychoanalysis and social psychology. He has published several books and essays on these topics.

David Forgacs is Professor of Italian at University College London. His research areas are modern Italian cultural history and history of the media. His recent publications include *L'industrializzazione della cultura italiana, 1880–2000* (2nd edn 2000) and *Rome Open City* (2000).

Francesca Froy attended the MA in The Body and Representation at The University of Reading from 1995–6 following a degree in anthropology. She specialised in the social impacts of Internet communication and has since co-authored an article on computer-mediated communication use by the deaf and hard of hearing with J. M. Bishop and K. Taylor. She has worked for four years in urban policy in the UK before doing a traineeship with the City of Tomorrow and Cultural Heritage Unit at the European Commission. She is currently working in urban and public policy research for a consultancy based in Brussels.

Sander L. Gilman is Distinguished Professor of the Liberal Arts and Medicine at the University of Illinois in Chicago and the director of the Humanities Laboratory. A cultural and literary historian, he is the author or editor of over sixty books, including *Seeing the Insane* (1982, repr. 1996) and *Jewish Self-Hatred* (1986). Both his most recent monograph, *The Fortunes of the Humanities: Teaching the Humanities in the New Millennium,* and his most recent coedited book, *A New Germany in the New Europe,* appeared in 2000.

Karín Lesnik-Oberstein is a Lecturer in English Literature at the University of Reading, and the Deputy Director of the University's Centre for International Research in Childhood: Literature, Culture, Media (CIRCL). Major publications include her books *Children's Literature: Criticism and the Fictional Child* (1994, repr. 2000), and (as editor and contributor) *Children in Culture: Approaches to Childhood* (1998), and she is currently working on a book on the topics of the article in this volume.

Anna McMullan is Director of the MPhil in Irish Theatre and Film at the School of Drama, Trinity College Dublin. Her main areas of research and publication include contemporary Irish theatre, gender and performance, and the drama of Samuel Beckett. She has coedited with Caroline Williams the contemporary drama section of the fourth volume of the *Field Day Anthology*, devoted to Irish women's writing (forthcoming 2002). Her book *Theatre on Trial: Samuel Beckett's Later Drama* was published in 1993.

Michelle Meagher completed the MA on The Body and Representation at The University of Reading in 1997. She currently lives in Virginia, USA, where she is studying towards a doctorate in Cultural Studies at George Mason University. For the moment, she is studying twentieth-century philosophies of embodiment and working on the intersections of feminist theory and cultural studies.

Libora Oates-Indruchová teaches literary theory and gender studies at the Faculty of Humanities, Pardubice University, Czech Republic. She edited a reader of classic feminist texts in Czech translation *Dívčí válka s ideologií* [The Girls' War against Ideology]. Her research interests include gender in Czech society and effects of state-socialist ideology on cultural discourses.

Vanda Playford is an artist and doctor living and working in London. Her art practice employs video and photography. She has investigated issues relating to the family, identity, time and memory. She has exhibited in the UK and Europe. She is currently working on a doctorate at the Royal College of Art, looking at bodily symptoms and their relationship to medical practice and visual representation. Her latest work, *Serving Time*, a sound and video installation, was shown at the One 2 Nine Gallery in New York in September 2001.

Ann Scott is Senior Lecturer, School of Integrated Health, University of Westminster, London, and Editor, *British Journal of Psychotherapy*. She is also Series Editor of the Palgrave Psychotherapy Series and author of *Real Events Revisited: Fantasy, Memory and Psychoanalysis* (1996). At the University of Westminster she is currently running an innovative programme in partnership working, bringing together officers from the Metropolitan Police Service in London and their statutory partners, to understand organisational dynamics and cultures.

Naomi Segal is Professor of French Studies at The University of Reading, where she founded and directs the MA in The Body and Representation. She has published numerous articles and is the author or editor of nine other books, including *Narcissus and Echo* (1988), *Freud in Exile* (1988), *The Adulteress's Child* (1992), *Scarlet Letters* (1997), *Coming Out of Feminism?* (1998), *André Gide: Pederasty and Pedagogy* (1998) and *Le Désir à l'œuvre* (2000). She is currently researching *Consensuality: the Sense of Touch and the Hydraulics of Gender.*

Rex Stainton Rogers was, until his death in 1999, a Lecturer in the Department of Psychology at The University of Reading. He was an influential scholar of enormous charisma – a true maverick who devoted his life to 'making trouble' as a critical psychologist. He was particularly critical of traditional developmental psychology and its narrow-minded construction of children. He was the lead author of a number of published works, including *Stories of Childhood* (1992), *Textuality and Tectonics* (1994) and *Social Psychology: a Critical Agenda* (1995). His forte, however, was as a public speaker – in his teaching, conference papers and public lectures.

Wendy Stainton Rogers is currently the head of the Open University's Research School. Her research interests and publications have mainly been in the areas of children's welfare, child protection and critical approaches to health psychology. As a critical psychologist she contributed to Beryl Curt's *Textuality and Tectonics* (1994) and *Social Psychology: a Critical Agenda* (1995). Together with Rex Stainton Rogers she has recently completed *The Psychology of Gender and Sexuality* (2001).

Lib Taylor is a Senior Lecturer in theatre in the Department of Film, Theatre and Television at The University of Reading. She has published on women dramatists since 1958, the theory and practice of women's theatre, contemporary performance and deaf sign languages in theatre. She has also edited several volumes of plays including some by Caryl Churchill. She is a theatre director and some of her research takes the form of performance practice.

Carolyn D. Williams is a Lecturer in the English Department at The University of Reading, and has written *Pope, Homer, and Manliness* (1993); she has also written and broadcast on many body-related topics, including drama, sexuality and the history of medicine, with particular interests in reproduction and resuscitation. She is an active member of university and local drama societies, and is the Departmental First Aider. She is currently writing on literary treatments of Boadicea.

Introduction

Lib Taylor, Naomi Segal and Roger Cook

> Yes or no: do we have a body – that is, not a permanent object of thought, but a flesh that suffers when it is wounded, hands that touch? We know: hands do not suffice for touch – but to decide for this reason alone that our hands do not touch, and to relegate them to the world of objects or of instruments, would be acquiescing to the bifurcation of subject and object, to forgo in advance the understanding of the sensible and to deprive ourselves of its lights. We propose on the contrary to take it literally to begin with. We say therefore that our body is a being of two leaves, from one side a thing among things and otherwise what sees them and touches them; we say, because it is evident, that it unites these two properties within itself, and its double belongingness to the order of the 'object' and to the order of the 'subject' reveals to us quite unexpected relations between the two orders. It cannot be by incomprehensible accident that the body has this double reference; it teaches us that each calls for the other. For if the body is a thing among things, it is so in a stronger and deeper sense than they: in the sense that, we said, it *is of them*, and this means that it detaches itself upon them, and accordingly, detaches itself from them.
>
> (Merleau-Ponty 1968: 137)

'Bodies are good to think with', writes Lynda Birke in an article recently anthologised in a reader on *Feminist Theory and the Body*, 'only when we think of indeterminacy or transformation' (Birke 1998: 48). It was in order to think with bodies that an interdisciplinary Master's degree on The Body and Representation was set up in 1995 by Naomi

Segal at The University of Reading. Twenty-five lecturers from twelve departments teach for the course, and its students come from a wide range of academic and national areas. This book is edited by a team of lecturers from the MA, and includes among its contributors three more staff and two former students, in addition to colleagues from the USA, Ireland, Hungary and the Czech Republic and two London-based visual artists. The idea for the book arose a few years into the course: the title came a little later.

The central issue was always indeterminacy – the radical doubleness of the body standing at boundaries of gender, age, sex or virtuality. But during some intensive discussions at a Writers' Workshop held in 1999 for the contributors to discuss and mutually edit their work in progress, more questions began to be asked of the title and its leading concept. Like Freud with the term *unheimlich*, we found the concept turning around on its base. If 'indeterminate' in the eyes of another, is a body more free of or more subject to social and other determinations? And does that same body, by remaining in a state of in-betweenness or dual 'belongingness', prove itself to be uncertain or, on the contrary, determined to hold its ground? There are good reasons – and not just in the sugar-cloud world of a movie like *Ma Vie en Rose* (Berliner, 1997) – to think that a boy who resists the masculinisation process long enough to be called a 'sissy' is showing himself to be stronger, not weaker, than his rowdy contemporaries. Being determined and showing determination(s) are arguably the reverse – and uneasy consequences – of each other. For a while, the title carried a slash between the first and second syllables. Our final title, *Indeterminate Bodies*, still aims to encapsulate the ambiguities and contradictions inherent in the term.

At the turn of the twenty-first century, even more than in the 1970s, 1980s and 1990s, the body is a locus of avid debate. New medical and technological developments which have advanced the potentiality of body modification, both through surgical intervention and new forms of drugs and through the cultivation of computerised prosthetics, have been the subject of intense disputation. The functioning of cyborg bodies as intrinsic to a technologically advanced society and the operation of virtual bodies as a significant part of its social networks of exchange extend the limits of corporeality. At the same time, in social science and the humanities, questions concerning identity and 'selfhood' have centred on the biological body as a *relatively* indeterminate socially constructed site. In the arts, interest initiated by the intensification of bodily experience challenges fixed forms of representation and proposes new ways of seeing and becoming. This creative work increasingly intersects with science, as technological processes of body modification transgress corporeal limitations and definitions, prompting new images, new forms of representation and performativity – like the video dancer seemingly untrammelled by the limits of what the body can do.

It seems that developments in both arts and sciences are ready to replace the determinism provided by the materiality of the body with an indeterminacy, multiplicity and plurality made possible by, for example, virtual beings, cyborgs, surgical reconstruction, drug therapy, role-play and cultural performance. Yet, at the same time, contingent developments in science imply increasing levels of determinism of the body, as recent research suggests that the body's future is mapped out in advance. The definition of the human genome with its implications of an inescapable bodily and possibly psychological destiny and, it has to be said, with its potential for political, commercial and social exploitation, proposes a determinacy previously resisted by theories of culture. On the one hand, from the 1960s, theories of education have valued nurture over nature as a dominant force in a child's development. Cultural discourses since then have perceived social identities as plurally constructed in however an involuntary and unconscious a way. Against this, the more rigid circumscription of the body made possible by gene research implies far less fluidity across the field of identities. Yet, paradoxically, as we define the genome, new possibilities for disturbing the determined material body have opened up. One might say that in the interests of a desire for indeterminacy, fluidity and instability, science has developed ways of combating the determined body by medical intervention: gene therapy can challenge biological determinism, cosmetic surgery can 'reshape nature' and technological advances can overcome genetic malfunction. So in opening up questions about the biological structure of the body, science has inaugurated new ways of destabilising its determinations and through gene therapy the body seems to have become changeable and repairable, implying that biology may not be our total destiny.

Institutionally and intellectually, the study of the body has proved the ideal motif for linking different areas of research expertise and encouraging different disciplines to share their insights, so that fields as diverse as sports studies and French literature can be brought into productive relationships with each other. The essays in this collection make connections between work on representations (art or text), elements of physical life (visceral corporealities), politics (gender, age, nation, race) and theories of identity through reference to theories of the body. It is not by chance that they repeat or revisit issues from a range of perspectives, and that a question of gender raised, say, in the context of a child's toy will reappear on the Weimar operating table or in the trial scene of *Gentlemen Prefer Blondes*. We want to forge links between the public (what can be seen, external appearances) and the personal (what is concealed, the internal sense of self), and to ask questions about how the body functions as a boundary between these two modes of determination: the outer and the inner, the material and the psychical, the biological and the socio-cultural. Our discussions focus on the body not as a defined palpable object but as the intersection of the materiality of bones, skin and flesh and the dreams, imagination and memories that act as determinants of psychical and social identity.

The first four texts in the volume look at marginal states in relation to childhood and youth, challenging assumptions regarding rights over and responsibilities for children and examining the construction of childhood in a modern, technologically advanced world. The prefatory piece is a short parable by Rex and Wendy Stainton Rogers, a story which is at once a science fiction and the Kaspar Hauser-like tale of a wild child for our century. 'The Tale of Nema' makes strange the notion of childhood and suggests ways of blurring the definition of maturity. By suggesting that contemporary notions of childhood arise out of a post-Enlightenment interest in the socialisation of a child, it contests current assumptions about children and their place in the world. The child of the future, in an imagined world determined by advanced technology, where notions of family and community have been transformed, is repositioned and repositions us as we imagine her.

Karín Lesnik-Oberstein's 'On "Wanting" a "Child" or: an Idea of Desire' continues to question assumptions about childhood by focusing on another version of the 'future child': the idea of a child prior to its conception. Taking a psychoanalytic approach, the essay analyses how the fetishisation of childhood and notions of the child impel the determination to give birth, whether in a natural or technologically assisted way. It examines how the desire for a baby is imbued with ideological drives which construct the child itself as a determinate being, while critiquing the ways in which languages and discourses induce meaning in relation to the wished-for or 'not-yet' child.

Further deliberations on the child as simultaneously determinate, determined and indeterminate are presented in 'Where is Action Man's Penis? Determinations of Gender and the Bodies of Toys' by Jonathan Bignell. Focusing on the material bodies of Action Man and Barbie, the essay examines the nexus of meanings produced by their lack of genitalia, combined with the over-determination of the secondary physical signs of gender: exaggerated musculature, facial scarring and chin stubble for the male doll and large breasts, endless legs and long hair for the female doll. Bignell argues that these secondary corporeal signs, rather than reinforcing the child's narrow gender identifications, allow the activity of play with the dolls to disrupt the gendered positions they appear to encode. Through forms of oppositional play, the child is able to adopt multiple subject positions in relation to the doll and narratives played out around it; as in the adult world, a negotiation of sex and gender is performed across the field of the body through masquerade, role-play and fantasy.

The impulse to embody youthful nationhood in corporeal 'appearance' is also central to Libora Oates-Indruchová's 'The Ideology of the Genderless Sporting Body: Reflections on the Czech State-Socialist Concept of Physical Culture'. This essay analyses pre-1989 Czechoslovakia's policy of 'physical culture', a concept that combines physical education, sports and leisure pursuits. In this context, it is not gender appearance that takes precedence in determining the body or its significance for representing a nation, but rather the display of an equilibrium produced by the synthesis of physicality and disposition. While acknowledging that the Czech policy of physical culture was ideologically driven and that the state-socialism it supported was patriarchal in effect, Oates-Indruchová argues that it can offer a model of theory and practice for disrupting the binary antitheses of gender. She asserts that by an approach to the physical body which emphasises the development of the internal qualities of integrity and virtue through physical activity, neither body nor mind is privileged and the visual elements of masculine or feminine gender become correspondingly less important. The male/female division is superseded by the advocacy of body/mind unity and, despite the ambiguities inherent in the policy and the cultural contexts which determined its implementation, its theoretical focus on performance capability allied to mental equanimity suggests a way of reducing gender hierarchies.

Issues of masquerade and disguise connect the next two sets of essays, which are concerned with attempts to escape the limits of the material body. While the essays of Sander Gilman and Carolyn Williams analyse bodies that transgress the physical determinations of sex and gender, Ann Scott, Roger Cook and Naomi Segal look at transformations and transpositions achieved through the mobilisation of fantasy. But while masquerade becomes a way of concealing difference and guaranteeing coherence, however fictive, for Gilman and

Williams, it is a means of engaging with difference and dislodging coherence for Scott, Cook and Segal. Francesca Froy's work goes further still in proposing that in virtual reality masquerade has displaced the material body, making it both possible and necessary for us to renegotiate notions of 'embodiment' and 'appearance'.

Bret Easton Ellis's *American Psycho* depicts a monstrous figure residing in a monstrous world, and the basic element of both its protagonist Patrick Bateman and the space he inhabits is indeterminacy. Just as historically the hermaphrodite has been compelled to do everything in her/his power to appear coherent despite secret bodily contradictions, Patrick Bateman's appearance of excessive conformity betrays a disturbed, fragile psychic identity. It is Ellis's delineation of this disjuncture between surface appearances and forms of experienced reality, whether lived or imagined, that Ann Scott analyses in '"Lying beneath me she is only a shape": *American Psycho* and the Representation of Madness'. Focusing on the way in which the deliberate indeterminacies of the text function to represent Patrick Bateman's instabilities and psychosis, the essay proposes that rather than being a satire on greed, as commonly defined, the novel is an evocation of both personal and collective madness.

In contrast with the appalling insecurities created by the capriciousness of Ellis's text, the celebration of plural identity which impels much of the work of the American painter Lari Pittman is exhilarating and life-affirming. Roger Cook's assessment of Pittman's position within the contemporary avant garde in 'Determined Indeterminacy in the work of Lari Pittman' focuses on the artist's resistance to the binary polarities which delimit gender and ethnic identities. Within the framework of Bourdieu's notion that art practice can carve out a kind of utopian space relatively free from social determinations, the essay examines how Pittman challenges dimorphic gender classification by reappropriating painting as a radical avant-garde form. As a racially mixed, gay man, Pittman has experienced exclusion and difference. From his position on the margins of cultural and gender identity he has developed his eclectic mix of visual languages in which he not only resists the established aesthetic forms that inscribe binary division, but also distances himself from what might be considered the elitist postmodernist reaction to those forms. His paintings thus enact a masquerade of polymorphic identities which defy the determinations of social categorisation.

The imaginative functioning of inversion and displacement is also explored by Naomi Segal in '"Then some had rather it were *She* than *I*":

Sexing the Textual Body', a comparative examination of ways in which fictions by Rose Macaulay, Marcel Proust and André Gide upset and complicate reader identification. The essay looks at three first-person narratives whose textual figures raise questions of how we read bodily indeterminacy in language. By reference to the Aristophanes of Plato's *Symposium*, Segal defines the three writers in terms of three kinds of desire. The existential bargain between the virtual author and the implied reader whereby the latter agrees to 'embody' the text depends on a complicated and mutually conditioning set of assumptions about sex, gender and sexuality.

If the practice and consumption of fictional play can free up the 'real body', what happens when desire and its material context appear to conflict? Sander Gilman's analysis of the early history of transsexual surgery, 'Not from Adam's Rib: the Origins of Transgender Surgery in Weimar Culture', might be said to connect back to the first three essays, and Bignell's work in particular, in its concern with the primacy of the signs of gender in determining identity – signs which are intended to compensate for genital lack. The essay traces the shift in post-World War One Weimar from a focus on reconstructive surgery, developed out of the operations performed on mutilated soldiers, to aesthetic surgery, a practice closely allied to modern-day cosmetic surgery. Intended to resolve a felt disconnection between an uneasy body and the desires of the psyche and to establish a notion of unitary identity, transsexual surgery posits the body as a set of readable signs, while the 'real' or 'authentic' identity resides within the psyche, and seeks to make the body conform to the psyche by securing the outward signs appropriate for the desired sex.

For transsexuals, 'passing' is a significant achievement since it signals a triumph of will or desire over biological determinism. For hermaphrodites, at specific points in history, 'passing' as a discernible member of a defined sex was essential if they were to avoid being detected as sexually ambiguous and subject to the death penalty. Again visibility regulates gender definition. While Gilman's argument focuses on questions of the right to sexual self-determination by the surgical manipulation of bodily appearance, Carolyn Williams's account of the cultural and symbolic significance of hermaphrodites, '"Sweet Hee-She-Coupled-One": Unspeakable Hermaphrodites', observes that for much of history occupying a classified sex-gender status was fundamental to maintaining a legitimate position in society. Because of this, successfully masquerading a 'norm' for a hermaphrodite becomes as significant as 'passing' for the transsexual. There are, however, strong paradoxes in the representation of hermaphrodites and through her analysis of myth, history, literature and film, Williams traces the contradictions between the flesh-and-blood hermaphrodite, who is reviled and outlawed, and the symbolic or mythic hermaphrodite who is revered and venerated. The hermaphrodite is caught between symbolising idealised divine wholeness and embodying unnatural grotesque monstrosity.

The confines and contradictions of the physical body are potentially erased by the advent of cyberspace, where the body is implied rather than materialised and where the unreliability of identity is valorised rather than punished or condemned. For the virtual body, visual signs alone no longer define self, and appearances relinquish their deterministic meanings in favour of an interplay of texts and fictional avatars. Francesca Froy's essay, 'Indeterminacy in Cyberspace', sees virtual reality not as a mode in which we become disembodied but as a space in which we mediate the boundaries of bodily experience in order to extend the operational sphere of the self. Cyberspace encourages a wealth of self-determinations in its construction as a place of escape from political and cultural categories that limit identities, and by adopting a range of complex and multiple roles, on-line games, chat rooms and email may propose seemingly infinite forms of subjectivity, transcending physical determinations.

On-line gaming environments depend upon an elaborate network of role-playing, and while they inhabit cyberspace, participants impersonate or perform the character/s they choose to adopt. Judith Butler, in her work on gender and identity, proposes that lived identities are also achieved through performance since the sexed self is determined through an endless process of reiteration and citation of the bodily signs that constitute a recognisable gendered subject. However, while the players of MUDs or MOOs may control their virtual personae, Butler argues that the acts which construct quotidian identity are not conscious and voluntary but incorporated into our being through a process of unconscious absorption. Thus, immense difficulties arise in imagining and producing new procedures for reconfiguring the laws that construct the operation of gender in everyday social reality. Froy's essay implies that virtual reality is a space in which desired identities can be tried out in a way that is not possible in the quotidian and that the wilder choices available in cyberspace evoke fresh, fluid forms of identity. Theatre and film performers share with the participants in on-line gaming the opportunity to construct roles intentionally and to exercise control over identities produced within the performance space.

Within these idealised spaces, self-conscious performances might, to use Butler's terms, '"cite" the law to produce it differently', thereby destabilising the regulation of gender circumscription (Butler 1993: 15). The work of both Michelle Meagher and Lib Taylor makes extensive reference to Judith Butler and develops ideas raised by Froy on the notion of performed identities, but shifts the site of investigation from disincarnate cyberspace to the embodied spaces of film and theatre.

Michelle Meagher's essay, 'Flaunting the Feminine', examines the potential of performing gender as a subversive act. The essay engages with the ideas developed by Gilman and Williams in its references to transvestism and cross-dressing, but its critical focus is on drag performances and their theatrical excess. Though once again appearance and visibility are significant, for the drag artist the objective is not to appear authentic and 'pass' but to perform the signs of gender on the body in order to expose their fabrication and adopt their lability. Rather than test the argument against examples of male-to-female or female-to-male cross-dressers, where the disjunction of body and gender draw attention to parodic performance, Meagher asks whether women can use the devices of drag – parody, excess, masquerade – to perform femininity with such extravagance that they produce a subversive bodily act. Through analyses of *Gentleman Prefer Blondes* and *Spice World* she proposes that female/female impersonation might be seen as a more volatile subversive act than traditional forms of drag.

Lib Taylor's essay, 'Shape-shifting and Role-splitting: Theatre, Body and Identity', also examines Butler's ideas of gender formation but this time for an examination of the complex interrelationship of theatre, performance and performativity. Despite Butler's proper insistence that social performativity is not the same as theatrical performance, Taylor argues that since theatre proceeds by a process of performance enacted upon the live body it is a particularly fruitful site for examining the constitution of gender through performativity. The plays of Caryl Churchill provide a ground for interrogating the term 'performance' in all its slippery determinations. By including an account of a piece of theatre she devised and directed herself, Taylor examines how creative arts practice functions as an alternative critical discourse to more traditional forms of scholarly production. The performance of *The cutting up of Mary S* is not only the object of analysis but the discourse by which that analysis proceeds. Traditional academic scholarship is redefined by its collaborative encounter with other, differently determined forms of critical discourse.

In a third discussion of the staging of ambiguities, 'Unhomely Bodies and Dislocated Identities in the Drama of Frank McGuinness and

Marina Carr', Anna McMullan borrows Homi Bhabha's term 'unhomely' – derived from Freud's *unheimlich* – to explore the significance of repressed memories and histories in the work of two Irish playwrights. The plays of McGuinness and Carr are inhabited by damaged bodies haunted by painful recollections and disturbed by the repression of a personal and communal past. McMullan detects similarities in their determination to 'excavate the wounds of history' in their search for identities free of dominant national or gender models. For McGuinness performance becomes the means by which traditional historical discourses are disrupted and renegotiated in attempts to recoup the past with its promise of re-formed identities. For Carr theatre is a space in which the anguish of dispossession is voiced by women alienated from their pasts and unable to determined their own cultural space in the present.

The final group of essays all engage with the ways in which systems of representation affect what the body can be seen – or believed – to do. In his essay 'Blindness and the Politics of the Gaze', David Forgacs reopens the question of 'the gaze' as it has been theorised in visual-art and film studies over the last thirty years. Focusing on a span of aesthetic production from the 1560s to the 1990s, he analyses paintings by Bruegel and Velázquez and films by Werner Herzog and Jim Jarmusch, showing how the representation of blind people can disrupt the assumed circular system of viewing and reciprocity that positions the spectator. When the blind person is the object of the look, the assumptions inherent in theories of voyeurism and specularity which define 'classical' and 'panoptic' paradigms of viewing are undermined and viewers of the blind body are confronted with their intrusive voyeurism, their entry into unnegotiated and undefended space.

In an altogether different context, the notion of revolution in the symbolic sphere is also at the heart of the essay by Márta Csabai and Ferenc Erős, 'Bodies in Transition or the Unbearable Lightness of the "Traditionless" Self'. Their concern is not with the politics of the gaze in artistic representations but with the way that an electorate responds to visual signs at a moment of radical political change. By examining posters and other images from Hungarian election campaigns in the 1990s, Csabai and Erős show how images of the body were used in promoting the transition from state-socialism to democratic capitalism. Arguing from a psychoanalytic perspective, the essay analyses the unconscious ambiguities of images which simultaneously construct and discredit a cultural Other. While, on the one hand, this Other is intended to operate as the abject to be expelled from the body of state in order to strengthen both personal and national desired identities, on the other hand Csabai and Erős suggest that the images, in advocating the expulsion of what is undesirable, encourage acts of discrimination and exclusion based on grounds of ethnic or gender difference.

In each of these instances, the immediacy of spectator identification is routed or rerouted. In the last essay, the playful viewer – like those of Pittman's images, *Spice World* or cyber-fantasy – may be either delighted or disturbed by the sight of bodies loosed from their material limitations. Sherril Dodds focuses on the indeterminacy of form in her analysis of video dance as a new genre of performance in 'Revolution in Video Dance: the Construction of a Fluid Body'. Drawing on Kristeva's notion of poetic language and Bakhtin's theories of the carnivalesque, she explores this fusion of televisual and dance practices, which brings together dancers' bodies transcending their earthbound corporeal capabilities, and televisual forms exceeding conventions by their encounter with post-modern dance. Rather like the cyborg, the dancing body transformed by televisual technologies transgresses the spatial and temporal limitations which restrict both physicality and televisual form. As the semiotic potential of the body is extended to produce revolutionary forms of dance, so the borders of the conventionalised symbolic are opened up.

It was fundamental to the project that this book should ask its questions about determinacy and indeterminacy not only in the form of texts but also in the direct presentation of the work of creative artists. The photographs of Ajamu and Vanda Playford demonstrate the same concern with issues of gender, appearance and performativity as many of the essays. The masculine and the feminine are diffused in Ajamu's photos across images of framed sections of the body. In one series, uncertainties of gender and race prevail as neither the body nor the elements of costume on display offer a secure indication of identity. Appearance here serves only to baffle; signs of gender identification are not encoded conventionally, the light plays tricks with the colour of the skin, and the composition of the posed body, with its focus on fragments and angles, produces deliberate ambiguities. In the other series, a parody of nineteenth-century 'freak photographs' combining racial and gender 'monstrosity', Ajamu highlights the queerness of images of the other with playfulness and wit.

The photographs by Vanda Playford also take as their theme the social and visual codes that determine our gender identity. Her three series focus on the awkward rigidities of the family group photo – always undercut by the fidgeting or baleful child – the unreadably close-up clinical view, and the gender slippage of the balletic art of kick-boxing. While in Ajamu's images one identity seems to dissolve into another, Playford foregrounds, by catching them in their most posed moments, the arbitrariness of social or gender markings. Gesture, position, codes of behaviour are revealed as absurd through an emphasis on the incoherence of body and self. Indeterminacy prevails despite attempts to control and define norms of correct identity.

A few days before this introduction was written, the news broke that the genome project, far from proving the human body to be exceptionally 'rich and strange' in comparison to other bodies, has only 30 000 genes – a mere 17 000 more than the humble and much researched fruit-fly. Perhaps, then, the Darwinian crisis is about to reappear. On BBC radio, science correspondent Pallab Ghosh drew the reassuring conclusion that this simply reminds us how 'complex, subtle and beautiful' the human body is. Both in its determination to *be itself* and in the indeterminate ways in which it allows itself to be seen and felt, the body remains – contained, uncontained, mortal and communal – our first and endlessly fascinating resource.

We hope that these essays will make a contribution to the difficult and ambivalent relation between determinacy and indeterminacy, social determinism and self-determination, and help to explore what Gilles Deleuze and Félix Guattari refer to as the 'zones of indetermination' from which all that is genuinely new and creative emerges:

> It is a zone of indetermination, of indiscernibility, as if things, beasts, and persons [...] endlessly reach that point that immediately precedes their natural differentiation. This is what is called an affect [...] Life alone creates such zones where living beings whirl around, and only art can reach and penetrate them in its enterprise of co-creation. This is because from the moment that the material passes into sensation [...] art itself lives on these zones of indetermination. (Deleuze and Guattari 1991: 173)

Works cited

Birke 1998 Lynda Birke, 'Openings on the Body', in Janet Price and Margrit Shildrick (eds), *Feminist Theory and the Body* (Edinburgh: Edinburgh University Press, 1999)

Butler 1993 Judith Butler, *Bodies that Matter: On The Discursive Limits of Sex* (London: Routledge)

Deleuze and Guattari 1991 Gilles Deleuze and Félix Guattari, *Qu'est-ce que la philosophie?* (Paris: Minuit), translated as *What is Philosophy?* by Graham Burchill and Hugh Tomlinson (London and New York: Verso 1994)

Merleau-Ponty 1964 Maurice Merleau-Ponty, *Le Visible et l'invisible* (Paris: Gallimard) translated as *The Visible and Invisible* by Alphonso Lingis (Evanston: Northwestern University Press, 1968)

AJAMU

Anti-bodies

The only true freak challenges the conventional boundaries between male and female, sexed and sexless, animal and human, large and small, self and other, and consequently between reality and illusion, experience and fantasy, fact and myth.

Leslie Fiedler, *Freaks, Myths and Images of the Secret Self* (1978)

This ongoing project is an attempt to explore an under-theorised arena within popular culture. These images are an attempt to question how the representation of a bearded woman within the context of freak shows raises issues around cultural anxiety, when boundaries of heterosexual norms and gender conventions are transgressed.

1. *Madame Meyers*, oval picture in lace veil, ca.1885.

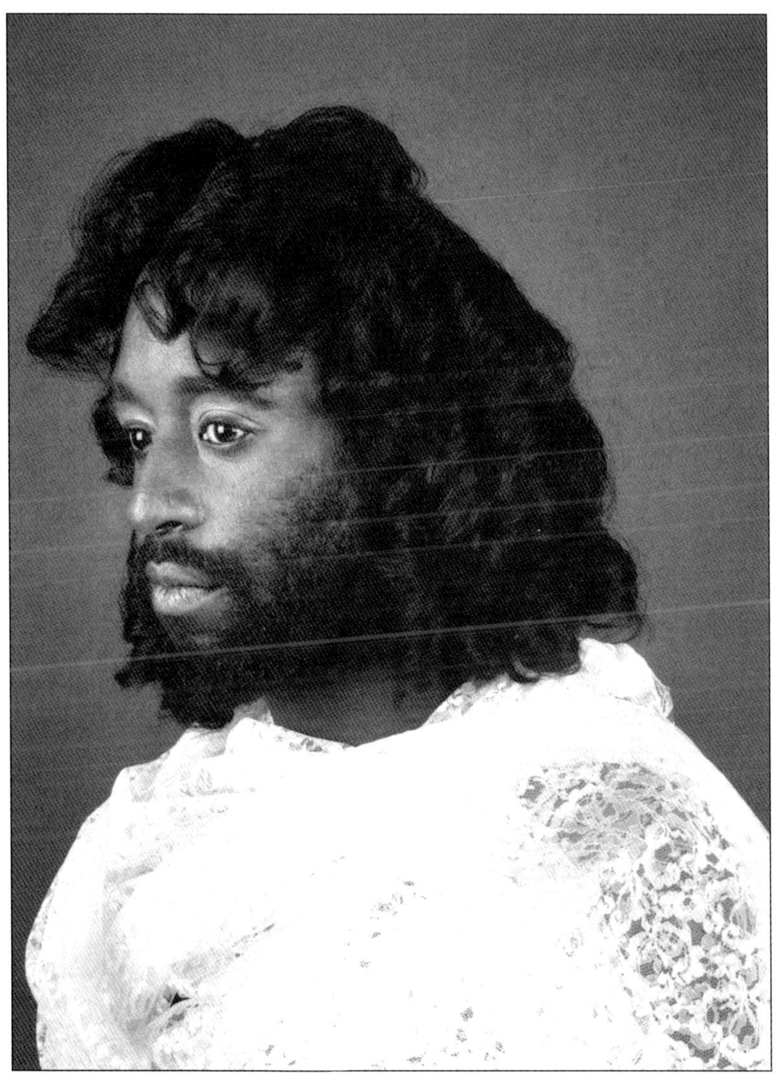

2. Ajamu, *Untitled Self-portrait*, 1998.

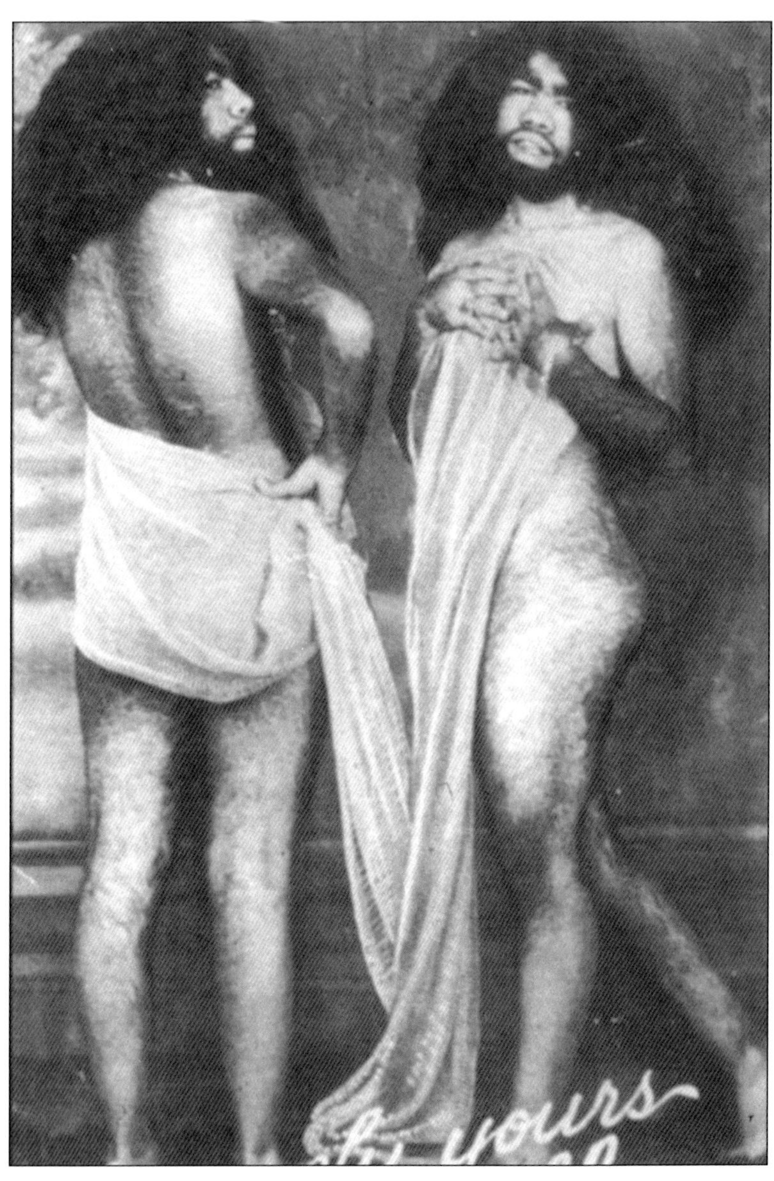

3. *Priscilla Showing Her Hairy Body and Whiskers*, ca.1926.

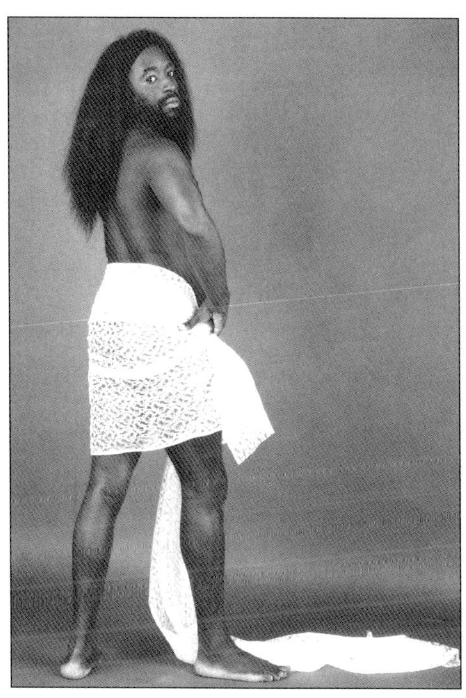

4. Ajamu, *Self-portrait.* 1998.

5. Ajamu, *Self-portrait*, 1998.

6. Ajamu, *Man in Gloves*. 1993.

7. Ajamu, *Man in Gloves*, 1993.

VANDA PLAYFORD

Tutu (photographic stills from the video *Tutu*, 1999)

These images engage with current debates about gender and performance and issues relating to the acceptability of women boxers in sport. Black-and-white, life-sized photographs of a performed and fictitious audience are juxtaposed with the boxers inside the ring, filmed in real time and in colour. The constructed nature of the audience signals their role as both performers and passive observers.

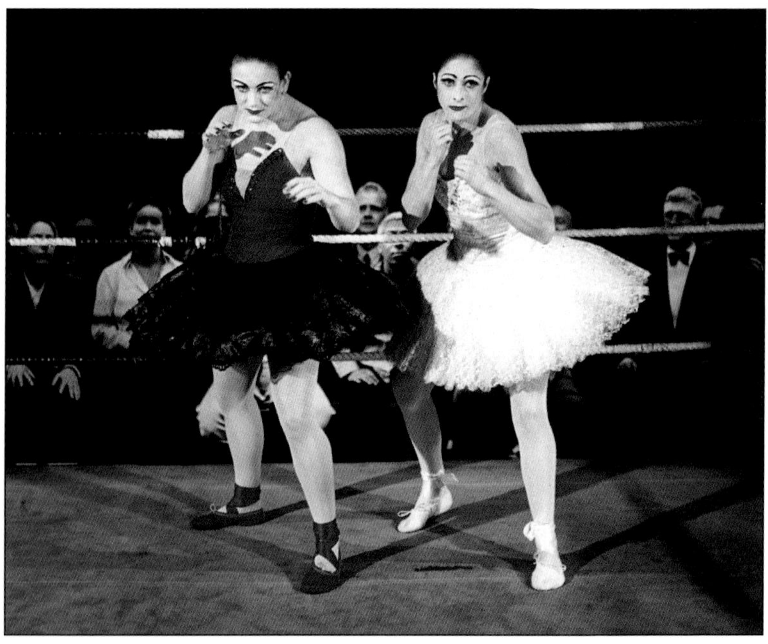

8. Vanda Playford, *Tutu*, 1999.

9. Vanda Playford, *Tutu*, 1999.

10. Vanda Playford, *Tutu*, 1999.

A model family, 1995 (from a series of seven)

These are reconstructions of family photographs, taken mostly by my father in 1965. I was thinking about how to get behind the façade of the 'happy family snapshot' and decided to remake these images with myself acting out the parts of each family member. In this way I was able to reveal some of the emotional dynamics that were going on at the time. The experience of performing each family member was surprisingly real and quite eerie.

11. Vanda Playford, *A Model Family*, 1995.

12. Vanda Playford, *A Model Family*, 1995.

13. Vanda Playford, *A Model Family*, 1995.

A Clinical Examination, 2001 (stills from the video *The Clinical Examination*)

The scientific nature of the clinical examination starts to break down with a process of filming which attempts to relate the doctor's contact with the body to a process of sculpting and painting. The accompanying sound track, fictitious coversations between patients and doctors, further removes the process of understanding the body away from medical knowledge and towards seemingly irrelevant but touchingly personal histories.

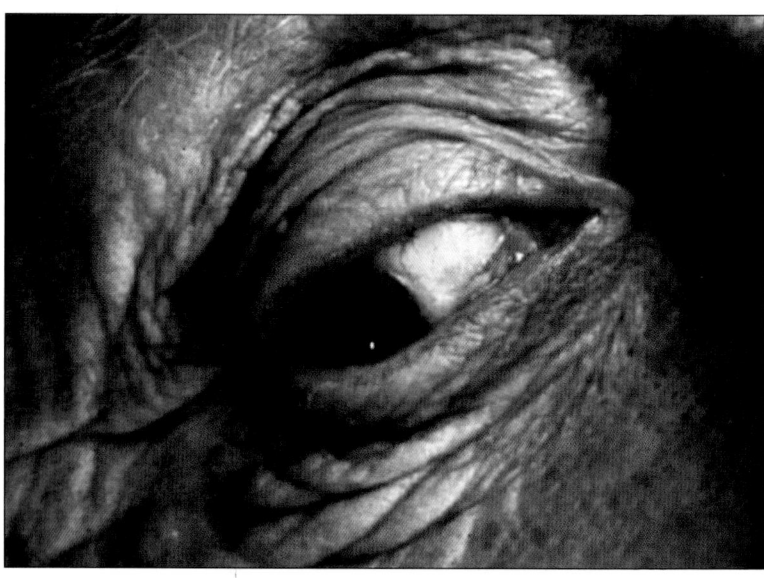

14. Vanda Playford, *A Clinical Examination*, 2001.

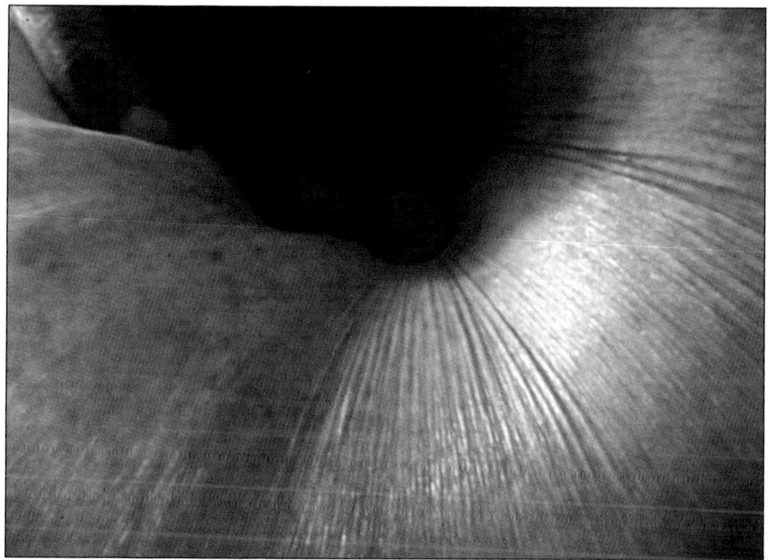

15. Vanda Playford, *A Clinical Examination*, 2001.

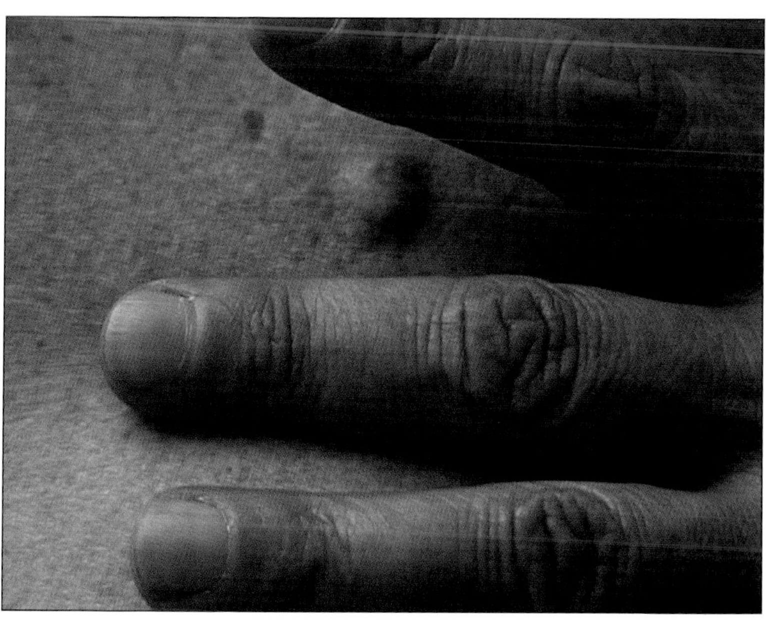

16. Vanda Playford, *A Clinical Examination,* 2001.

The Tale of Nema

Rex and Wendy Stainton Rogers[1]

Are you sitting comfortably? Then we'll begin. One November evening the police are called to a shopping mall by the security staff, to deal with someone they found naked in the women's lavatories at closing time. Wrapped in a blanket and taken to the local police station, 'Nema' (as she gets called by the policewoman who takes charge of the case – it means 'nobody'), appears to have totally lost her memory. She makes no protest when examined by a police doctor, who can find no obvious injuries or possible identifying marks (scars, tattoos, dental work). The doctor is puzzled, and cannot put Nema's age more exactly than somewhere between fourteen and twenty, though she does discover that Nema has borne a child. Dressed in borrowed clothes, Nema sits passively in an interview room while the doctor, the policewoman and the duty inspector debate what to do. With no positive evidence that she is a minor, and faced with someone 'behaving abnormally', they decide to have her admitted to a hospital. Two hours later, Nema is in a psychiatric ward where she rapidly seems to 'come to' and starts talking to the staff in unaccented English. While her amnesia over her personal life remains total, she proves to have an excellent memory, and a voracious appetite both for conversation and for books, magazines, television and radio. Within a week, she seems as normal as anyone could be with a personal memory that is only seven days old and built out of what was available within the psychiatric unit. Trial trips into the outside world reveal that Nema deals extremely competently with ordinary city life – situations such as shopping, sightseeing, ordering a meal, using a taxi. Tested by a clinical psychologist she proves to have an IQ of 148 (on an adult scale), although once the testing is over, Nema gets into a complex argument with the psychologist about whether it makes any sense to try to determine the relative contributions of 'nature' and 'nurture' to measured intelligence! However, problems of a quite unexpected kind soon start to emerge. On her next trip out, Nema wants to take in a movie and a trip to the pub afterwards. She is also beginning to talk about life after her discharge. Sexual relationships, friends, holidays, cars, jobs are starting to occupy her mind.

Interlude: what shall we do with Nema? In British society (and much the same would be true in any industrialised country) the only way of resolving the dilemmas 'Nema' raises would be to legally create an identity, and most crucial of all, an age for her. Only then could we know what to do about her. But how would that be decided? Medically, her body could reasonably be that of any female between fourteen and twenty (depending on 'hereditary' and 'environmental' factors – which, of course, are unknown). Socially, she seems extremely competent, but a lot would depend on her background (nothing exceptional in a city-reared young person but pretty exceptional if she came from an isolated rural community). There is every sign that she is very bright (although how bright would depend on how old she is – she would be judged more intelligent as a fourteen-year-old 'schoolgirl' than as a twenty-year-old university student).

Every clue we try to use turns out to be ambiguous. What about her baby? Nema might be a 'gym-slip mother', or she might have been married for several years. Either way, this would affect who stood as her 'next of kin'. Even if the one thing she could remember was that she was married, it really wouldn't help that much, as she might have married abroad, and in some countries that is possible by the age of fourteen. By the by, in all of this we may have misread her 'sexual identity' altogether. Remember, her knowledge of herself only came from television, papers and from conversations in the psychiatric unit, but prior to her amnesia she might have been a lesbian – for all we know the child was conceived by Artificial Insemination by Donor (AID). Medical and social science, in short, cannot give us an unambiguous answer, and neither can we reason one out from 'common sense'. In the end, we seem to be left with a moral decision – how to do what's right in a situation of uncertainty. Immediately, we come up against a problem – who makes the decision? Do we turn to an 'expert' like a judge or a psychiatrist? Or do we let Nema decide for herself? One solution favoured by moral philosophers would be to ask: who would I want making the decision if I were Nema? The usual answer is *me*, I would want to make that choice. But if Nema chose to be fourteen, would we see that as a sensible choice, or might we find ourselves thinking that anyone who made that choice wasn't rational enough to make it! The notion of 'Nema's choice' also raises awkward questions about actual fourteen-year-olds. If we were to allow Nema to choose to be an adult when she might 'really' only be fourteen, why not allow other fourteen-year-olds so to decide? There is also another cloud in this already murky atmosphere – Nema's child. Suppose this infant were to turn up as mysteriously as Nema. We have every reason to think that the life chances of a baby born to a fourteen-year-old in our society are inferior to those born to a twenty-year-old. Surely then the decision is not Nema's alone but needs must take into account the welfare of her child?

The tale continued: with a pinch of chaos. With everyone around her in a state of self engendered alopecia, Nema herself breaks down under the strain. She blurts out that she is in fact a young woman social history student from the twenty-fourth century. Her amnesia was hypnotically induced prior to her transportation back to our time. These facts were never supposed to emerge under the time travel code of non-interference, but so bizarre did she find our world that her mind-block failed. Now she cannot seem to stop herself talking to her psychiatrist. What emerges in an amazing two-hour recording, prior to her mysterious and instantaneous disappearance, goes roughly like this:

Nema's narrative. Although age doesn't have the meaning in her society that it does in ours, Nema is in fact thirteen. Changes in environmental conditions, diet and health care mean that most young people reach full reproductive sexual maturity at around the age of ten. In her world, quite a lot of young people decide to have children in their early teens, as they are by then physically capable and economically and socially independent. The Equal Rights Law of 2030 substituted the notion of competence for what were previously age-related entitlements. For example, to drive a fuel-cell car all anyone has to do is to pass their driving test – there is no minimum age. The same is true over work. Even before they can talk, children learn to operate touch-controlled robotics, and once they can talk they get into using voice-controlled devices. The result is that appliances that are too dangerous for the young in our world (like cookers) are rendered safe for them in Nema's world. Innovations like new public transport systems and 'clever' cars which can sense possible hazards mean that children of three or four can safely go out alone. Technologies that make learning 'fun' and technologies that make the difficult easy (e.g. robots and waldoes for heavy lifting and very fine work like electronics) mean that by around seven most young people can run their lives more or less independently from adults. Of course, their wrist communicators mean they can always call for help if they need it, and enable tabs to be kept on the very young ones. Nobody has to work for longer than around fifteen hours a week to be financially independent, and once someone has the competence to do a job they have the right to do it. Rates of pay are based on a good job done and cannot by law vary by age. There are still skills which take a 'long time' to develop, but this tends to mean that they are acquired by the age of twelve rather than at nine.

Nema's own life story was fairly typical. When young, her mother had a wide network of friends who by seven or eight tended to move from one person's home to another as a 'gang'. They would save money to take trips together, staying in hostels and learning about the world as they went along. Clannish and mutually supportive to one's 'gang' rather than to 'olders', the peer group was the normal place to which to turn for affection and care. Over time 'gangs' tended to slowly intermingle and change. Both single-sex and mixed gangs existed, and most young people had access to each kind of network. They were places to 'experiment' with interpersonal and sexual relationships (tackling HIV infection was vaguely remembered history at most). There was no 'age of consent' as such; any 'competent' had the right to 'body control' over sex as over anything else. 'Olders' had little to do with the young and little power over them – one result was that physical and sexual abuse across age was virtually unknown. At fourteen, with a lot of both 'homo' and 'hetero' sexual experience behind her (although people didn't tend to make those discriminations), Nema's mother decided she was ready to 'move on', relaxed her ovulation control and became pregnant. She took a residential unit in a family cooperative. Some moved in as couples but Nema's mother had no wish to bond.

Nema was born with the aid of a natal-chine which her mother used to control the birth and deliver the baby. Several members of the 'gang' (including Nema's father as it happened) were around to give encouragement. Although a lot of baby care could be automated, most parents chose to 'do it by hand' in small groups. These groups often attracted 'gangers' and non-parents who also got involved with the infants. By eighteen months, Nema herself was running simple sound-touch machines with other youngsters in the cooperative play area. She tended to go home to her mother to sleep, but also spent time in other units. Her electronic tag meant that both her mother and her other carers always knew where she was. By four Nema had learned to use her interactive terminal to create a 'total personal environment' of furnishings, sound, pictures, and food and drinks dispenser. She could play complex computer-based games with her friends and access libraries of entertainments and information. An interest in electronic music composition brought her first real earnings and by six she was in a 'group'. 'Gang' music was very popular and her income plus her success at 'second go' at the competency test (popularly called the DeTag) meant that by seven she acquired the right to control over her own communicator. Now she could 'switch off' if she chose, enter contracts and be made to pay if she overspent on her credit card! 'Switch off' parties were 'the thing' and, although olders tended to worry, the major 'dangers' tended to be a temporary deafness from the music and the odd recreational drug hangover! Nema managed both. Although 'sex play' was common, her first serious sexual involvements came, as they did for most young people, later during the time of moving between gangs. A far greater 'passion' for her at this time was a powerful interest in twentieth-century history.

Although public transport was good, getting your own fuel-cell car was an important symbolic event. Nema passed her test at ten and at eleven joined a small group working and driving their way along the old trans-Asia highway through Russia to Japan. Treks like this were often the prelude to 'settling down' and she did indeed use the trip to get pregnant. However, back home, she once again developed 'itchy feet' and so she left her baby with a friend-carer and got work with the Time Travel Institute. Work as a vocation was very much left to 'olders' (anyone past sixteen) but there was no age-bar as such, and so at thirteen she got involved in the 'twentieth-century project'. At this point, the psychiatrist had the presence of mind to suspect that such a 'youth culture' must have a down-side. Was it just being young that caused Nema to say so little about 'olders'? Sadly, just at the moment when he was exploring what Nema meant by saying that her mother had never found a vocation and 'elected out' at twenty-six, Nema disappeared back to the future.

Amen to that

Developed into a short story or a novel, Nema's tale would become a speculative or science-fiction story. Not, you may feel, one destined to be a bestseller! The characters are cardboard, the situation grossly contrived. But in the hands of a specialist in the genre – a Doris Lessing, or an Ursula Le Guin – speculative fiction can both entertain us and challenge our taken-for-granted assumptions (see, for example, Haraway 1991; Katz *et al.* 1977; Lefanu 1988). We merely set our sights on the latter, by creating a parable which would make the notion of childhood strange and problematic. First we challenged the idea that childhood is a 'thing' that can be known and defined objectively. Within the confines of our story, it cannot and consequently, all our laws, rules and expectations are suddenly rendered problematic. We then constructed an alternative account of being young, something sufficiently familiar in its technology, social dynamics and culture to be a credible extrapolation of the present. The only development about which we have serious doubts is time travel, but every science-fiction is allowed one 'impossible'. Finding Nema's world in any way believable does not demand that you like or approve of it – our own reactions are highly ambiguous. But any glimmering of plausibility that it has for you serves our purpose – to set the stage for rendering other stories about children less able to be 'taken for granted'. Not every story, of course, has a specific gloss overtly attached – something that tells us where to look and what to look for. Few are so patently didactically located. But every story, we want to argue, gains its meaning through a socially sedimented 'contract' for engaging our regard. One does not just read it, but give it a reading. The reader is drawn into a social process between peruser and perused, which involves the direction and manipulation of attention, both within the material text and between the text and meta-textual understandings. Nema's childhood is a 'fiction', but then so (taking examples from Western cultural experience) are many of the textualised childhoods we know best: Jesus; St Joan; Katy; Tom Sawyer; George from the Famous Five; or Todd from *Neighbours*. Furthermore, while being social fictions, they are also social facts, in the sense of being parts of the fabric from which our understandings of children are woven. In writing Nema as a deconstructive tale, we have deliberately added a key-thread to this tapestry of texts of childhood, something which, if pulled, threatens the stability of the whole cloth. That whole cloth contains not only fictive children but what we may think of as real ones: Victorian 'kids int' mill'; child prostitutes in Bangkok; the child subjects of developmental psychology; the 'children within' uncovered through psychoanalysis; ourselves when young – even our own children!

About such children, it might seem there are real 'facts' that can be established, a 'true knowledge' to be told. This is what we want to challenge. 'Facts', we maintain, are also stories – ones gleaned from our own particular viewpoint and ones that, if believed, help to bring into being the thing we think we see. For example, we may consider 'facts' such as the finding that child prostitutes and some sexually abused children (as does Nema) show 'precocious' sexual development. However, such a 'fact' can only be 'discovered' within certain social regards, in which there is a prescribed appropriate or normal age to be a thing called sexual – it is this which *creates* the reality of 'precocious sexual development', which may then be variously represented, for example: as a personal *pathology* to be treated; a social *problem* to be tackled; or a 'turn on' to be savoured.

The basic thesis of this essay, then, is very simple. We live in a world which is produced through stories – stories that we are told, stories that we recount and stories that we create. Children are drawn into this web of understandings (and their material consequences) from the moment (whenever our stories tell us, that is) they enter the social world. Our stories of childhood largely pre-date and create the locations in the social world for each child, yet each child adds to the story-stock in making their place their own. All this is giving the term 'story' a much broader span than does its day-to-day definition, but it is one which can be found in many recent, post-structuralist treatments of the idea of text (e.g. Shotter and Gergen 1989). What we are attempting to propose in Nema's story fits very much into such a redefinition.

Notes

1 This is a slightly amended version of part of the Introduction to Rex and Wendy Stainton Rogers, *Stories of Childhood: Shifting Agendas of Child Concern* (New York and Hemel Hempstead: Harvester Wheatsheaf, 1992). We are indebted to Wendy Stainton Rogers for permission to reproduce it here.

Works cited

Haraway 1991 Donna J. Haraway, *Simians, Cyborgs and Women: the Reinvention of Nature* (London: Free Association Press)

Katz *et al.* 1977 Harvey A. Katz, Martin Harry Greenberg and Patricia S. Warrick (eds), *Introductory Psychology Through Science Ficion* (Chicago: Rand McNally College)

Lefanu 1988 Sarah Lefanu, *In the Chinks of the World Machine: Feminism and Science Fiction* (London: Women's Press)

Shotter and Gergen 1989 J. Shotter and K. J. Gergen (eds), *Texts of Identity* (London: Sage)

1
On 'Wanting' a 'Child' or: an Idea of Desire

Karín Lesnik-Oberstein[1]

In one of the many places where Freud discusses a mutual implicatedness of 'normality' and 'pathology' he writes:

> A certain degree of fetishism is thus habitually present in normal love [...] The situation only becomes pathological when the longing for the fetish passes beyond the point of being merely a necessary condition attached to the sexual object and actually *takes the place* of the normal aim, and, further, when the fetish becomes detached from a particular individual and becomes the *sole* sexual object. (Freud 1905: 66–7)

Freud is here pondering the very constitutions of desire ('normal love'; 'longing'; 'aim'; '[sexual] object') and their operation as definition, attachment and relatedness. In this article, by looking at the writing of anthropologists on assisted reproductive techniques, I would like to consider what the 'wanting' of a 'child' is constituted by: how are children formulated as 'wanted', or objects of desire? The 'child' not yet born or perhaps even not yet conceived does not, in one sense, exist, and yet is already always subject to multiple processes of determination and definition by the very virtue of being expected, or wanted. In this respect the child is an 'indeterminate body': the very inherent contradiction in that idea – a 'body' by definition constituting a claim to being, to identity, yet somehow apparently without stability or consistency – is explicitly encompassed in the construction of the identity 'child'. Reproductive techniques are most specifically implicated in the ideas of 'wanting' a child: here the child is not seen as produced 'by accident',[2] but must be most explicitly formulated as desired. I will be arguing particularly here that fetishisation, in the terms that Freud is thinking through above, can be formulated as part of 'wanting a child'. This wanting of a child can be divided into separate issues, but in combination the terms can be analysed as modifying and implicating each other. Together they seem to constitute a particular idea of 'desire'.

I am taking the idea of the fetish to mean, then, in this Freudian sense, that which operates as a denial of the absence of the mother's penis, and which can no longer work as fetish if it were to be revealed as having that function or meaning (Freud 1905: 350–7, 352). In other words, the fetish, as Donna Haraway explains, is 'an object human beings make only to forget their role in creating it' (Haraway 1991: 8). I also take the fetishisation of the child (and of 'wanting'), as with all fetishisation, to be produced not 'on top of' or 'out of' a material, object 'reality', but rather as a discourse constituted in interplay and contrast with other discourses. There is, then, here no anterior 'real' 'child' which is misunderstood, perverted, or idealised as fetish, but instead constructions of childhood and the 'child', some of which can come to function, and be formulated, as 'fetish'. As I have argued more extensively elsewhere (Lesnik-Oberstein 2000), I understand this to be Jacqueline Rose's point when she writes in *The Case of Peter Pan or: the Impossibility of Children's Fiction* that she discerns an 'ongoing sexual and political mystification of the child' (Rose 1984: 11).

Theoreticisations of the child as constructed[3] seem to run parallel to a continuing use of languages, both 'popular' and 'academic', of the 'natural' and 'biology' in claiming an essentialised 'real' child.[4] According to some commentators this usage is perhaps even increasing, but this depends on the interpretations of time and history involved. This language of 'naturalness' and 'biology' in relation to the child has a role too in the discussion around 'wanting' or the 'desire for' children. Marilyn Strathern suggests, for instance, that 'there is a subtle shift from regarding naturalness as part of the workings of physiology to attributing it to parental desire' (Strathern 1992: 56).

Both the child and the desire for it are often figured then as *sui generis*: spontaneous, unanalysable, not open to question, *beyond language*. Sarah Franklin, in her 'cultural account of assisted conception', quotes the *Warnock Report*:

> In addition to social pressures to have children there is, for many, a powerful urge to perpetuate their genes through a new generation. This desire cannot be assuaged by adoption. (Franklin 1997: 91)

Franklin cites this as an example of 'many popular representations of infertility [which] [...] draw on the idea that there are natural, biological or genetic pressures to have children which cannot be suppressed' (Franklin 1997: 91). Strathern too points out that

> On the face of it, nothing today seems further from erosion than the concept of nature. Against a background of concern about the natural environment, constant reference is made to what is also natural in human behaviour, and nowhere is it more emphasised than in the debates over the new reproductive technologies. (Strathern 1992: 55)

As Franklin's and Strathern's points indicate, what is simultaneously striking and predictable in many writings on fertility, infertility, assisted reproductive techniques, or the family, is the relative *absence* of discussion of what both the 'child' and the 'wanting' of it *mean*. They are not supposed – in both senses: 'intended' and 'believed' – to 'mean' anything at all: they are supposed simply to be. And this is the nature of the fetish: not open to question; apparently without function; pure presence, desirable in and of itself. The child is represented as wholly determinate: wanted as a self-evidently knowable, recognisable, and separate object/ body. Jacqueline Rose argues that this is about an adult 'demand which fixes the child and holds it in place [...] a conception of both the child and the world as knowable in a direct and unmediated way' (Rose 1984: 4, 9).

Even in books which overtly reflect on what the meanings of 'wanting a child' might be, there seems to be a struggle to develop or find languages of analysis and explanation for this idea in itself. The pieces in Stephanie Dowrick and Sibyl Grundberg's *Why Children?* (1980), for instance – all written from the perspective of engaged and active feminism – thoughtfully and lucidly articulate the idea that this 'wanting' of children can in no way be, politically and ideologically speaking, a ('free') 'choice'. All the writers in the book make explicit a range of social, economic and political pressures to have children. Judith Barrington, for instance, writes that 'I felt a profound shock of recognition when I finally understood that society relies on the nuclear family and the dependence of women on men to maintain the division of labour' (Dowrick and Grundberg 1980: 149). All of the pieces also include comments on the way motherhood and the wanting of children are included in constructions of femininity: 'I "ought to have a child, if I was to fulfil myself as a woman, etc."' (123). Nevertheless, in attempting to account for any final decision to have a child, most of the writers take final recourse to expressions such as 'yearning' (30 and passim), 'urge' (30 and passim), and 'I want to have a child ... to please myself' (67).

Recent anthropological analyses of discourses of reproduction such as those of Franklin and Strathern have diagnosed assumptions and concepts which are implicated in these kinds of formulations of 'natural' desires for a child, but they leave certain issues to one side. My interest here lies in thinking further about the idea of desire they diagnose *as* the discourse of 'wanting' children. Both Strathern and Franklin, as well as, for instance, several of the writers in Sarah Franklin and Helena Ragoné's *Reproducing Reproduction* (1998) or Robbie Davis-Floyd and Joseph Dumit's *Cyborg Babies: From Techno-Sex to Techno-Tots* (1998) see (a language of) desire as being involved both in ideas about 'choice' in reproduction and in the 'wanting' of a 'child'. Strathern, for example, notes, in analysing the implications of new reproductive technologies for anthropological discussions of kinship, that:

> People become parents because parents are said to want children of 'their own'. The colloquialism, an interesting fusion of whom one identifies with and what one owns against the world, points to desire or preference. (Strathern 1992: 25–6)

Similarly, she points out that 'in the language of desire, the question of rights turns on the right to fulfil what one wants [...] This has for long been a significant if unremarkable cultural motivation, in both Britain and Europe, for having families' (32). 'The language of desire' is placed as being implicated in both the 'question of rights' and in ideas of ownership and the child as property and possession, but also remains itself irreducible, or at least descriptively irreducible. This emerges too from the description that:

> On the one hand, desire becomes translated into the choice whether or not to adopt certain procedures, and choice is thereby exercised as choice between different artificial possibilities; in this sense it is limited. But, on the other hand, as a natural dimension to human creativity, desire itself is supposedly without limits. (*Ibid.*, 56–7)

In Strathern this irreducibility, or limitation on analysis, is purposely upheld as within the anthropological paradigm of an attempt at (re-) describing cultural accounts (I will return to this issue in its own right in a moment), but it throws up the question in turn of what – and how

– this desire is itself 'about', and how it relates specifically to the 'child' which is – ostensibly – wanted. What I would like to argue further from here on, then, is that the 'wanting' of the child is not only not about a natural and self-generating desire (as the anthropologists' analyses make clear), but neither is it (therefore ...) about wanting a 'child'. Sarah Franklin points towards, but, like Strathern, does not expand on this issue when she refers to 'everything a hoped-for child had come to represent' (Franklin 1997: 184) for couples undergoing assisted reproduction. For the not-yet 'child' can never be a self-constituted subject, but is an indeterminate space or potentiality, which has definitions mapped onto (or: into) it; definitions moreover which are the result, or compositions, of projections, mappings, appropriations, and (re-) creations. The 'child' as fetish is meant to hide that the 'child' can never be a self-generating presence, but instead is what we might call an assemblage or production.

Moreover, once we 'un-determine' the child in this way, we may see that the anthropologists' texts have to incorporate (embody?) it as an uneasy presence in not being able, or wanting, to take analyses of 'everything a hoped for child had come to represent' further. And this engages difficulties of theory and methodology: in a meticulous effort to (re-) describe the constituents of the languages used the anthropologists are striving also not to 'judge' the IVF participants and 'their' meanings. As Franklin states:

> [*Embodied Progress*] is determinedly a project which moves away from the tendency in legal studies, bioethics, feminist criticism and many strands of cultural and science studies to take a position, or to argue for or against particular techniques. My interest is elsewhere, specifically prior to such judgements, at the level of the effort to make visible the accumulated practices, assumptions and constraints which inform most contemporary assessment and discussion of new reproductive and genetic technologies. (Franklin 1997: 16)

This attempt is framed, as in the case of all the anthropology I am using here, by a foregrounded and well-theorised awareness of the severe limitations, or even impossibility (depending on the specific position taken), of retrieving meanings as 'other'. Inevitably, therefore, even in their own terms, the texts reveal their own investments, and one of these seems to be the uneasiness around the 'child'. Franklin, for instance, explains in a footnote that she prefers to characterise women undergoing IVF as being 'determined' rather than 'desperate', not only because this is 'a more flattering description', but also one that 'correctly identifies her active desires in relation to treatment as opposed to an image of near pathological need' (226–7, note 9). Firstly there must be a question around the qualification 'correctly' here, for it must be at least a possibility that '(near) pathological need' is employed as a definition or description in some cases or at some times.[5] Secondly, and more importantly, however, this is Franklin's footnote to a section of her text in which the very idea under discussion is how 'these women describe themselves as *not* "desperate" initially, and as *becoming* "desperate" *as a result of treatment*' (182–3). Her footnote seems to blur an argument that the women she spoke to do not describe themselves as 'desperate' when they *begin* the IVF, into one defending them against them being 'pathologised' at all while 'undergoing' IVF, even when this seems to be exactly what the women's own narrative seems to endorse: that IVF *produces* a pathology or 'desperation' in them. I am linking this 'desperation' also to the constantly redeferred 'outcome': a child as the hallucinatory and fetishistic resolution to the 'desperation'.

Franklin's footnote touches, then, on the methodological difficulties of coping with investments which inevitably inhabit and direct a text. One aspect of the footnote may be accounted for as produced by a problematic diagnosed by Eve Kosofsky Sedgwick in her 'Epidemics of the Will'. Sedgwick argues in relation to the boom in the language of 'addiction' that:

> so long as 'free will' has been hypostatized and charged with ethical value, for just so long has an equally hypostatized 'compulsion' had to be available as a counterstructure always internal to it, always requiring to be ejected from it. The scouring descriptive work of addiction attribution is propelled by the same imperative: its exacerbated perceptual acuteness in detecting the compulsion behind everyday voluntarity is driven, ever more blindly, by its own compulsion to isolate some new, receding but absolutized space of *pure* voluntarity. (Kosofsky Sedgwick 1994: 133–4)

In the light of this, we may see Franklin's women as deploying a language of 'addiction' in describing 'desperation' as produced in them by the IVF: 'the goal of resolution becomes a receding horizon. "We'll just have a go" soon becomes a preoccupying gambit of tantalising prospects [...] Unforeseen [...] is the extent to which IVF "takes over" and becomes "a way of life"' (Franklin 1997: 11). Franklin's footnote seems, to me, to be produced out of a struggle to differentiate between the use of the word 'desperation' by others about the IVF women, and that use of the word by the women themselves. For Franklin's overall argument, however careful to attempt a 'pre-judgmental' perspective, does, I think, provide a radical critique of many popular, legal and medical ideas of IVF as in any way a 'miracle' technology which produces 'miracle' babies for 'desperate' couples. However, she argues herself too that women participating in IVF also use the *same* discourse about it as that found in many medical and legal texts and the press (as well as using alternative languages of criticism and disappointment): that they too, at least with some, or to some extent, 'believe' and reproduce the 'miracle' story about IVF, *even if* they do not end up with a baby. A problem, then, for Franklin – marked by the footnote – is how to articulate methodologically that the women can neither be placed as purely active and in control of the IVF process (pure voluntarity), but neither can they be described as purely victims ('addicted'). Kosofsky diagnoses this as 'the ugly twisting point of that in the present discursive constructions of consumer capitalism, the powers of our free will are always already vitiated by the "truth" of compulsion, while the powers attaching to an acknowledged compulsion are always already vitiated by the "truth" of our free will' (Kosofsky Sedgwick 1994: 141–2).[6]

Part of this effect is also described by Strathern in a discussion on reproductive technology and consumer society and the 'enterprise culture':

> The enterprising self, as Keat says, is not just one who is able to choose between alternative ways, but one who implements that choice through consumption (self-enhancement) and for whom there is, in a sense, no choice not to consume. Satisfaction is not in this rhetoric the absence of desire, but the meeting of desire. To imagine an absence of desire would be an affront to the means that exist to satisfy it. (Strathern 1992: 37)

One might add that to imagine desire, in this context, as not constituted absolutely somehow *by* the known – and knowable – object, apparently amounts to the same thing as imagining desire as 'absent'. The child is thus (and, again, to some: increasingly) inserted into cultural discourses as the only significant and, moreover, *signifying* fulfilment to desire, legitimising desire in psychological and ideological terms compatible with bourgeois individualist capitalism. The child functions at once as property, to be acquired, as property 'naturalised',[7] and, as one aspect of this naturalisation, as an object which is deployed to *deny*, in an almost unique and prioritised way[8] the idea of it *as* property and acquisition. As Strathern's quotation on the enterprising self suggests, the increasing availability, and types, of assisted reproductive techniques, allows an accrual to reproduction of languages of 'wanting a child' which rely ever more on determinations: or over-determinations and fetishisation (*this* child in *this* way).

Strathern's text, like Franklin's, also becomes involved in methodological anxiety related to her text's necessary 'inhabitation' when, in her argument that '[h]owever one looks at it, procreation can now be *thought about* as subject to personal preference and choice in a way that has never before been conceivable', she adds that '[t]he child is literally – and in many cases, of course, joyfully – the embodiment of the act of choice' (Strathern 1992: 34) Strathern's almost offhand introjection that the child of IVF is 'in many cases, of course, joyfully' chosen also alerts us to the difficulties around the 'wanting of the child' for the anthropological analyses referred to here. The 'joyfully' seems to operate as a defensive measure, upholding, in the midst of the analyses and deconstructions of assisted reproductive techniques, a 'core' of motivation, validity and justification articulated as 'natural' emotion (and emotion as the 'natural'): in Sedgwick's terms, voluntarity and consumer satisfaction retrieved. Michelle Stanworth inserts a similar qualification in her article on 'Reproductive Technologies: Tampering with Nature?', when she argues that '[t]o call "natural" the energy and commitment involved in achieving a wanted pregnancy, in carrying it safely to term and in creating a sense of relationship with the child-that-will-be, is to deny the very human investment that some women make in "my baby"' (Stanworth 1997: 487). In the midst of this anti-naturalisation argument we find the 'investment that some women make in "my baby"' defended as 'very human'. 'My baby', apparently reinstated as an object with pathos, effectively *renaturalises* the woman and her 'energy and commitment' under the guise of the 'very human'.

With reference too to Strathern's argument quoted above, that 'the child is the embodiment of the act of choice', and her added question: 'What do we do with the idea that a child embodies its parents' wishes ...?' (Strathern 1992: 34), we might add the further questions: how can a child be 'literally' an embodiment?[9] What might that, in itself, mean? 'Literalness', after all, is a concept that precisely defies the necessary metaphoricity of 'embodiment'. And, indeed, what do we do with the idea 'that a child embodies its parents' wishes'? Or, to accept the terms of

Strathern's question for the moment, (how) can a child ever *not* be the 'embodiment' of its parents' wishes (albeit not 'literally')? In other words, taking Strathern's point from a slightly different angle, her argument actually allows us to think, in contrast to what she and Franklin describe as the prevalent discourses, that the not-yet offspring is *unwantable*. It is impossible to desire an indeterminate subject/object; the creation of the potential object involves investing it with an already-known determination, which is then denied as 'creation', and defended as 'discovery'. Determined as a 'child', for instance, 'childness' constitutes an already operating fetishisation. As Freud writes: 'the fetish becomes [pathological when] detached from a particular individual and [when it] becomes the *sole* sexual object' (Freud 1905: 67). Or, as Rose puts it:

> what is at stake [...] is the adult's desire for the child. [...] I am using desire to refer to a form of investment by the adult in the child, and to the demand made by the adult on the child as the effect of that investment [...] What we constantly see [...] is how the child can be used to hold off a panic, a threat to our assumption that language is something which can be simply organised and cohered, and that sexuality, while it cannot be removed, will eventually take on the forms in which we prefer to recognise and acknowledge each other. (Rose 1984: 3–4, 10)

A further question is, then, how, through fetishisation, an object is created which splits 'desire' into a desire 'for'.[10] Object relations is here one area of consideration. As Winnicott argues in discussing the difference between relating to and using an object:

> the central postulate in this thesis is that, whereas the subject does not destroy the subjective object (projective material), destruction turns up and becomes a central feature so far as the object is objectively perceived, has autonomy, and belongs to 'shared' reality [...] It is generally understood that the reality principle involves the individual in anger and reactive destruction, but my thesis is that the destruction plays its part in making the reality, placing the object outside the self. (Winnicott 1971: 106–7)

Winnicott's analysis leaves the way open for a not-yet offspring to become an object that can be used, not just related to, and which therefore may become also an object 'outside the self'. This would constitute the idea of a baby which is created, but not – ultimately –

fetishised. And which may be destroyed as creation, but survive to become reconstituted as an 'object outside the self'. But where the child is insisted upon as an already present and already known entity, whether defined as 'natural' or as property or acquisition, this constitutes an over-determination and possible fetishisation.

The problem of desire as linked to supplementarity and deferral is also obscured in an insistence on the child. Freud, of course, discusses this issue when he analyses the connection 'faeces-money-gift-baby-penis'. In accounting for the idea of wanting to have a baby *at all*, Freud makes his well-known argument that

> It is also easy to follow the way in which in girls what is an entirely unfeminine wish to possess a penis is normally transformed into a wish for a baby, and then for a man as the bearer of the penis and giver of the baby; so that here we can see too how a portion of what was originally anal-erotic interest obtains admission into the later genital organization. (Freud 1933: 134)[11]

What is relevant here is not just linked and sliding significations, but why there are ideas of lack or the need for supplements at all, and how a baby is slotted into the idea of fulfilment for this. When the child moreover becomes 'fixed' as the predetermined and only possible fulfilment, as we saw the anthropologists diagnose in writing about much of the discourse of assisted reproduction, this is part of a struggle to absolutely defend against any other possible meaning of, and for, the desire than the necessity of the possession of that 'child'.

In this discussion I have attempted to suggest, then, two, intimately enmeshed, aspects of one argument: firstly, that the child is itself determined, over-determined, and fetishised in order to construct and maintain it as a separate, self-generated object, which both creates – invokes and constitutes – desire, and which therefore is also seen to justify that desire and any actions supposedly motivated by it. Apparently it is sometimes seen as a serious threat to allow the child to remain at all unstable, if not indeterminate.

This is made very apparent – in what is only a superficial paradox to the idea of the child as 'self-generated object' – in the obsessive use of formulations (as described by the anthropologists) which insist on the desired child as in some way 'part of the self', however that 'partship' is configured. Charis Cussins, for instance, describes how '[i]n donor egg in-vitro fertilization ... the overlapping biological idioms of blood and genes come apart' (Davis-Floyd and Dumit 1998: 42) 'Blood' and 'genes' here form the 'part' of self which (pre-)determines the baby. Similarly, Helena Ragoné claims that it 'is of fundamental importance to IVF surrogates to circumvent the biogenetic tie to the child' (Franklin and Ragoné 1998: 121) as this means to them that the child is not 'their own'. She reports Lee, an IVF surrogate, as saying that:

> Yes, it's [the fetus] inside my body, but as far as I am concerned, I don't have any biological tie. The other way [artificial insemination], I would feel that there is some part of me out there. (Franklin and Ragoné 1998: 122)

Besides 'biogenetics', Ragoné also sees race, ethnicity and 'personal relationship' as mediating ideas of the 'own' child. Linda, a Mexican-American IVF surrogate pregnant with a Japanese couple's baby, is reported as saying that:

> No, I haven't [thought of the child as mine], because she is not mine, she never has been. For one thing, she is totally Japanese. It's a little hard for me. In a way, she will always be my Japanese girl; but she is theirs. (Franklin and Ragoné 1998: 125)[12]

The anthropological kinship studies referred to here may, in this context, be reformulated as being about the structurings of ideas of the me/not-me.

The second emphasis of my argument has been that the maintainance of the self-constituted child in texts affects ostensibly unrelated arguments and forces them in certain directions, as we saw in Franklin's, Strathern's and Stanworth's texts. This is part of further complex theoretical questions to do with ideas of how discourses operate, compose and decompose and how they become visible. Equally, related questions remain concerning the terminology I have used with regard to determination, over-determination and fetishisation. (When) can a meaning become a 'fetish'? And how can we think further about the levels of discourse in relation to one another? In this sense what this discussion has gestured towards is an idea that the ultimate indeterminacy is that of the end – or limit – of meaning. *Any* meaning – 'offspring' in every sense – is the first 'determination'. The child as 'fetish' has here been used, then, as meaning at a most extreme opposite polarity, as a complete saturation of determination instituted as a denial of ambivalence, instability and multiplicity: the word as object.

Notes

1 With thanks to Harriet Kline for formulating the subtitle, and to Dani Caselli and Esther Beugeling for finding, and supplying me with, several texts important to my arguments.

2 It may be argued that there are languages of the 'accidental' production of children involved in reproductive techniques too, for instance when too many fertilized eggs are implanted and develop, but this has to do with the specificities of the process. I am interested here in the overall justification involved in the development, use and application of these techniques in the claimed service of providing the much-desired child.

3 See for instance: Philippe Ariès, *Centuries of Childhood: a Social History of Family Life*, trans. Robert Baldick (New York: Vintage Books, 1962); Chris Jenks (ed.), *The Sociology of Childhood: Essential Readings* (London: Batsford Academic and Educational Ltd., 1982); Chris Jenks, *Childhood* (series: Key Ideas, series ed. Peter Hamilton, London: Routledge, 1996); Martin Barker, *Comics: Power, Ideology, and the Critics* (Manchester: Manchester University Press, 1989); Allison James and Alan Prout (eds), *Constructing and Reconstructing Childhood: Contemporary Issues in the Sociological Study of Childhood* (London: Falmer Press, orig. pub. 1990, second edition 1997); Erica Burman, *Deconstructing Developmental Psychology* (London: Routledge, 1994); Jane Pilcher and Stephen Wagg (eds), *Thatcher's Children? Politics, Childhood and Society in the 1980s and 1990s* (London: Falmer Press, 1996); Allison James, Chris Jenks and Alan Prout, *Theorizing Childhood* (Oxford: Polity Press, 1998); Robbie Davis-Floyd and Joseph Dumit (eds), *Cyborg Babies: From Techno-Sex to Techno-Tots* (London: Routledge, 1998).

4 See for an extended version of this argument: Karín Lesnik-Oberstein, 'Childhood and Textuality: Culture, History, Literature', in Karín Lesnik-Oberstein (ed.), *Children in Culture: Approaches to Childhood* (London: Macmillan, 1998), pp. 1–28.

5 It should be noted that Franklin is elsewhere scrupulous in her disclaimers of any straightforwardness of generalising representation, for instance when she warns that '[e]thnically, the interview pool was not representative of the wider IVF consumers' (Franklin 1997: 81).

6 Franklin and Sedgwick's accounts had already suggested to me that accounts of women becoming 'addicted' to techniques of assisted reproduction must either already be circulating somewhere, or that there was a strong likelihood that these would emerge (more fully), and I subsequently indeed came across several mentions of the idea of women 'addicted' to reproductive technologies.

7 All the anthropologists mentioned in this article discuss the 'naturalisation' of 'wanting a child' as well as of the assisted reproductive techniques themselves.

8 Pets might sometimes be considered in the same light.

9 Franklin uses exactly the same phrase: 'Women who successfully give birth to IVF babies will feel in their relationship to those children the sense of achievement that child literally embodies' (Franklin 1997: 193).

10 Post-Freud theoreticisation of 'desire' usually refers to the work of Jacques Lacan, but it is neither my interest here to pursue a further dissection of 'desire' in its own right, nor have I, personally, found Lacan's work to be more helpful than Freud's own in this respect.

11 For further psychoanalytic discussion of 'faeces-money-gift-baby-penis' see especially the work of Melanie Klein, for instance in *The Psychoanalysis of Children* (London: Virago, 1994).
12 The sentence in square brackets is inserted by Ragoné.

Works cited

Ariès 1957 Philippe Ariès, *Centuries of Childhood: a Social History of Family Life*, tr. Robert Baldick (New York: Vintage Books, edn of 1962)

Barker 1989 Martin Barker, *Comics: Power, Ideology, and the Critics* (Manchester: Manchester University Press)

Burman 1994 Erica Burman, *Deconstructing Developmental Psychology* (London: Routledge)

Davis-Floyd and Dumit 1998 Robbie Davis-Floyd and Joseph Dumit (eds), *Cyborg Babies: From Techno-Sex to Techno-Tots* (London: Routledge)

Dowrick and Grundberg 1980 Stephanie Dowrick and Sibyl Grundberg (eds), *Why Children?* (London: Women's Press)

Franklin 1997 Sarah Franklin, *Embodied Progress: a Cultural Account of Assisted Conception* (London: Routledge)

Franklin and Ragoné 1998 Sarah Franklin and Helena Ragoné (eds), *Reproducing Reproduction: Kinship, Power, and Technological Innovation* (Philadelphia: University of Pennsylvania Press)

Freud 1905 Sigmund Freud, 'Three Essays on the Theory of Sexuality', tr. James Strachey, in *On Sexuality* (Harmondsworth: Penguin, edn of 1977), 39–169

Freud 1933 Sigmund Freud, 'Anxiety and Instinctual Life', tr. James Strachey, in *New Introductory Lectures on Psychoanalysis* (Harmondsworth: Penguin, edn of 1991), 113–44

Haraway 1991 Donna Haraway, *Simians, Cyborgs, and Women: the Reinvention of Nature* (London: Routledge)

James, Jenks and Prout 1998 Allison James, Chris Jenks and Alan Prout, *Theorizing Childhood* (Oxford: Polity Press)

James and Prout, 1990 Allison James and Alan Prout (eds), *Constructing and Reconstructing Childhood: Contemporary Issues in the Sociological Study of Childhood* (London: Falmer, 2nd edn)

Jenks 1982 Chris Jenks (ed.), *The Sociology of Childhood: Essential Readings* (London: Batsford)

Jenks 1996 Chris Jenks, *Childhood* (London: Routledge)

Klein 1932 Melanie Klein, *The Psychoanalysis of Children* (London: Virago, edn of 1994)

Kosofsky Sedgwick 1994 Eve Kosofsky Sedgwick, 'Epidemics of the Will', in *Tendencies* (London: Routledge), 130–42

Lesnik-Oberstein 1998 Karín Lesnik-Oberstein, 'Childhood and Textuality: Culture, History, Literature', in Karín Lesnik-Oberstein (ed.), *Children in Culture: Approaches to Childhood* (London: Macmillan), 1–28

Lesnik-Oberstein 2000 Karín Lesnik-Oberstein, 'The Psychopathology of Everyday Children's Literature Criticism', *Cultural Critique*, 45, Spring 2000, 222–42

Pilcher and Wagg, 1996 Jane Pilcher and Stephen Wagg (eds), *Thatcher's Children? Politics, Childhood and Society in the 1980s and 1990s* (London: Falmer)

Strathern 1992 Marilyn Strathern, *Reproducing the Future: Essays on Anthropology, Kinship and the New Reproductive Technologies* (Manchester: Manchester University Press)

Rose 1984 Jacqueline Rose, *The Case of Peter Pan or: the Impossibility of Children's Fiction* (London: Macmillan)

Stanworth 1997 Michelle Stanworth, 'Reproductive Technologies: Tampering with Nature?', in Sandra Kemp and Judith Squires (eds), *Feminisms* (Oxford: Oxford University Press), 482–7

Winnicott 1971 Donald Winnicott, *Playing and Reality* (Harmondsworth: Penguin, edn of 1988)

2
Where is Action Man's Penis? Determinations of Gender and the Bodies of Toys

Jonathan Bignell

The first problem which arises in the study of the gender determinations of toys is to determine the object of analysis. Perhaps the most obvious place to begin is with the physical bodies of toy figures, where the critic would undertake a descriptive account of the size, proportions and tactility of Barbie or Action Man. The account would move on to outline the ranges of limb movement, skin pigmentation, hair and eye colour, and the dispositions of musculature and sexual organs. This material body could then be critiqued as a representation determining the ways in which gender identities circulate and are commodified and perhaps challenged in children's play (Attfield 1996). But this approach is too distant from the ways in which toys have their being in culture. The bodies of toys are very rarely found in their naked state, separated from the ensemble of other material objects like clothes, accessories, playsets, television programmes, computer games, books and comics which set them in place as part of a commodity system. So the critic might then shift the determining instance of the toy's meaning onto one or more of these other textual objects, perhaps regarding the body of the toy as a spin-off from a narrative product which enables and constrains its meaning (Bazalgette and Buckingham 1995). However, there is no agency in either of the two approaches outlined so far, and either the body of the toy, or a text associated with it, becomes the abstracted generator of a cultural effect.

Shifting the instance of determination once again, the analyst of toys might then consider that the institutional agency producing toys and associated products is the originary source of their meanings (Fleming 1996: 109–23). Toys like Barbie and Action Man are produced by multinational conglomerates, and sold into diverse national and regional markets. The objective of profit and the effective organisation of production and sales, together with the establishment of brand identity, differentiation from related products, and the possibilities for creating spin-off products, could be regarded as determining the form that toys' bodies take. The body of the toy is likely to become, perhaps, simple to produce, resilient, easy to recognise, and as acceptable as possible to consumers from a wide range of races and cultures. In short, the toy will become normative, unthreatening and cheap, and its gender identity will rest on highly coded and clearly signalled characteristics distributed not only on its body but also in the supporting products and narratives which accompany it. But again, this economic and industrial determination is potentially monolithic, and leaves no room for the agency of the children who play with toys. To remedy this insufficiency, the analyst might consider the determinations of the toy's meaning in a psychoanalytic framework, as a complex interaction between children and objects, where the dynamics of the interaction will reveal the conscious and unconscious gendering functions that playing with toys serves (Kline 1993). This relational approach, focusing on the agency of individual children, might also involve ethnographic work, and could stress the openness of toys to multiple appropriations. The determination of the meaning of toys might even dissolve into a catalogue of the different ways in which they are played with in particular situations by particular individuals.

This issue of determining the object of study is a familiar one in Cultural Studies, but gains a particular pertinence in the study of toys because of the instability and contested status of childhood itself (Bignell 2000b: 114–38). Debates about sex and gender representation in toys reflect the diverse and contradictory ways in which childhood is constructed in discourse. Arising from psychoanalytic perspectives on the importance of play, and linked with the promotion of educational toys, it has been argued since the 1930s that representational toys inhibit a child's imaginative play (Dawson 1989: 98–100). In a different use of pyschoanalytic perspectives, it is claimed that the fantasy worlds of Barbie's kitchen or Action Man's adventures distort the child's perceptions of 'real life', leading to maladjusted behaviour. From a feminist perspective, strong gender differentiations in toys are critiqued as perpetuating bad gender stereotypes, since toys are regarded as functional in securing a child's gender identity through identifications (Miedzian 1992). Advice to parents about toys has been based on developmental psychology's model of learning as the active acquisition of adult skills and reasoning (Goldstein 1994), so that the supposed passivity of play with representational mass-marketed toys like Action Man or Barbie has been critiqued, while the activity of play with them has been stigmatised as non-educational.

The strategy adopted in this essay is to link and counterpose different critical discourses about toys. Action Man and Barbie, the two most enduring and familiar toy figures, are the objects of analysis, and are considered as material objects, enveloped by related products and texts in an industrial and commercial system, which attain cultural meanings through practices of play in varied forms that are open to modification and appropriation for a range of functions. A further mode of study, placing Action Man and Barbie in their historical processes of change and development, also appears. The determinations of gender in toys, it is argued, are partly a result of the additive effect of the cultural meanings of the toys' material bodies, institutional contexts, play practices etc., but the essay is concerned to stress the ways in which gender determinations also conflict with each other, or are constructed on an unstable or even absent foundation. Without succumbing to the temptation to relativise or collapse the determinations of gender difference, this essay argues that, finally, the culture of toys is characterised by a simultaneous insistence on and dispersion of gender signification. Barbie and Action Man, in their different ways, perform a simultaneous instantiation and displacement of the certainties of gender identity.

According to the British Association of Toy Retailers, Action Man and Barbie were Britain's best-selling toys in 1997. The paradigmatic male toy figure, Action Man (GI Joe in the United States), was introduced in Britain in 1966, and initially there were only three costumed figures in the range: soldier, sailor and pilot. Since then there have been more than 350 variants of Action Man, the majority being military figures, but also heroic masculine identities like polar explorer, footballer, space ranger or lifeguard (Bignell 2000a). Action Man's body shape has remained basically the same during his lifetime, though gripping hands were introduced in 1973, directable Eagle Eyes in 1979, and other physical functions have periodically been incorporated including a cord-operated voicebox. The period of highest sales of Action Man was the late 1960s and early 1970s, when between three and four million Action Man figures were sold per year. But Action Man has never had a penis. His pink flesh-toned pubic area was simply organless for the first thirty years of his life, but since the relaunch of the figure in the 1990s his lower torso has been made of blue vinyl. He is still castrated, but his lack appears to covered by dark blue underpants.

Barbie was the first fashion doll, launched by Mattel in 1959, and over one billion dolls have since been sold, in more than 150 countries (see Birkett 1998). The average British girl has five Barbies, and in the United States there are more Barbies than people. Barbie Millicent Roberts was created by Elliot and Ruth Handler after they saw the German doll Lilli in Switzerland, a doll based on a newspaper cartoon and sold as a sex toy to adults. Barbie's success is largely due to the range of clothes and accessories sold with doll figures: since 1969 over 910 million items of clothing have been produced, and each year she is given about 150 new outfits. The first Barbie wore a striped swimsuit and high heels, and had stigmata-like holes in her feet for a stand, since her feet, shaped to fit the shoes, prevent her from standing unaided. She has had thirty-five pets, has younger sisters and brothers, several female friends, and a penisless boyfriend, Ken Carson. Although Barbie's scaled-up measurements would be 36-18-33, and despite the erotic heritage of Lilli, significant marks of sexual and procreative capacity are absent (though this lack has been remedied by adults on unofficial pornographic websites). Barbie's prototype had nipples, but these were filed off and the doll remodelled without them. She has a mound of Venus but no vagina, and no belly button. Barbie has no penis, unsurprisingly, but she is also short of female sexual organs.

The absence of male genitalia on the body of Action Man occurs despite the overdetermination of gender characteristics in secondary forms. Similarly, the absence of a visible signifier of sex in Barbie's pubic region coexists with the overdetermination of secondary gender characteristics including breasts, long hair, large eyes and a small nose. While there are dolls representing babies of each sex which are anatomically complete, and where the doll will urinate and defecate from the appropriate organs, there are no dolls representing adult bodies which perform these functions, or where adult genital organs are denoted. The indeterminacy of Action Man's and Barbie's genital sex coexists with the overdetermination of gender identity elsewhere, and derives from the displacement of sex into gender when the adult body is represented by toys. For Judith Butler, sexual difference is not simply a function of material differences, for these differences are marked and formed by discursive practices. The regulatory force of sex has a productive power in that it demarcates and differentiates bodies; sex 'is not a simple fact or static condition of the body, but a process whereby regulatory norms materialize "sex" and achieve this materialization through a forcible reiteration of those norms' (Butler 1993: 2). The reiteration of sexual norms is a sign that the materialisation of sex is never fully complete, and that the physical organs of bodies will never be sufficient to stabilise sexed identity. The absence of a penis for both Action Man and Barbie is a recognition that the symbolisation of sex does not rest on the presence or absence of a penis.

In the Freudian account of the child's acquisition of a power to symbolise, the phallus is the signifier of sexual difference, at the centre of the system by which one thing can stand for something else. The phallus is not the penis, and in order to play the role of signifier the phallus must be different to that which it symbolises. The ability of Action Man to function as a signifier of a male and masculine body comes not from his penis, but from the displacement of phallic symbolisation on to other bodily attributes. Sex, like gender, becomes visible as a cultural construct, and both sex and gender become evident as norms by which Action Man and Barbie are imaginable as subjects in play, with bodies which qualify them for intelligible roles. The recognition of Action Man and Barbie as male or female is thus part of what Butler (1993: 2) calls the 'reiterative power of discourse to produce the phenomena that it regulates and constrains'. Recognising a sex and a gender involves both identification, where the discourse of sexual difference enables some identifications and not others, and abjection, where some bodies form the constitutive outside which borders the domain of the subject. The zone of abjection incorporates those who are not subjects, but who provide

> that site of dreadful identification against which – and by virtue of which – the domain of the subject will circumscribe its own claim to autonomy and to life. In this sense, then, the subject is constituted through the force of exclusion and abjection, one which produces a constitutive outside to the subject, an abjected outside, which is, after all, 'inside' the subject as its own founding assumption. (Butler 1993: 3)

This abject being, repudiated as the other which guarantees gendered subjectivity, is created when children de-humanise and decompose the bodies of toys, de-sexing and de-gendering them in the process. An adult memory of this abjectification of a toy's body (Barbie's) has been described by Dea Birkett (1998: 13):

> First, I cut off her long flaxen hair. Then, I pierced her sky-blue eyes, until the needle emerged on the other side of her squishy, putty-coloured head. Her perfect row of pearl-white teeth begged to be blackened with a pencil. Then, once her head was mutilated, I removed it from the stiff column of her neck. Without a face, her

> decapitated frame was barely recognisable as human. It was useless. You couldn't build anything out of it, even if you had several of them. The plastic was too cold to cuddle. It couldn't even stand up on its own. I began to twist each overlong leg out from its socket. Then I discarded the bits of the body into the bin.

Barbie becomes abject, no longer the representation of a body. This is the opposite of the role conventionally occupied by Barbie and Action Man, which are conventionally recognised as models of adult gendered bodies, and are more often played with in fantasy scenarios which model the activities of functioning subjects, making them available for identificatory relationships and gender identities. But the recognition of toys' bodies as sexed and gendered bodies relies both on the 'positive' ability of toys to symbolise, and on their 'negative' ability to become abject, for each of these roles is necessary to the system of symbolisation. Toy figures with adult bodies represent completed adult gendered bodies for children and thus engage their anxiety about their own future bodies and selves. This anxiety is not only about what the 'final' form of their adult bodily self will be, but also how they will manage the transition from the present about-to-be-lost self to the future one. Projective desires and anxieties can be attached and displaced on to the doll, producing the toy's body as an other with which to identify, and producing the child's body as already other to itself.

Identification is not only an imitative activity involving one subject and another, but also the process by which an ego first emerges. In Lacan's well-known account of the 'mirror stage', the ego is first a bodily projection, an imaginary morphology. As a projection, the body is not only a source from which projection issues, but is also a thing in the world which is estranged from the subject, and thus substitutable with the bodies of Action Man or Barbie. The possibilities for identification with Action Man and Barbie are suggested and reinforced by the multiple texts produced by their manufacturers which surround the toys, and picture them in fantasy or play scenarios. Both Action Man and Barbie feature in eponymous monthly comics containing picture stories which supply outlines for play, and both toys have websites created by their manufacturers and have featured in television series. The anxieties which experts on play have about this scripting of the uses of toys by their manufacturers derive from two contrasting views of children. Children are regarded as incomplete, irrational and disposed to disordered behaviour, so that intervention is required in order to push play in a legitimised direction, towards adulthood. On the other hand, children are also regarded as uncorrupted, innocent and authentic, so that they need to be protected from the adult world. This representation of the child is a sign of loss and nostalgia, a potential and an origin which is always already lost and thus desired (Lesnik-Oberstein 1998). The hard and completed bodies of adult-shaped toys like Barbie and Action Man represent a recognition of the child's body as always-already lost, and always-already in the process of assimilation into an adult body and an adult world. This is evident in the kinds of discourse provided for the talking versions of Action Man and Barbie. Talking Barbie says, for example: 'Cool! Let's play our favourite music with Midge tonight!', 'Oh dear, what shall I wear to dinner', and 'Help me fix my hair'. Talking Action Man has a contrasting selection of phrases relating to military action, like 'Enemy approaching – range 2000'. At Christmas 1993 the Barbie Liberation Organisation exchanged the voiceboxes of Barbie and GI Joe dolls, in order to foreground the gender politics involved in the attribution of these discourses to the bodies of the toys, and the containment of their bodies in gendered narrative scenarios.

But since children are not yet adult, and thus other to the adult world of gendered identities, there is considerable space for them to adopt subject-positions other to those which the toys, associated texts and social expectations encode. A child may react in unexpected ways to the identities represented by Barbie and Action Man, or devise alternative or oppositional play forms and narratives. Since the child sometimes experiences itself as other (bad rather than good, messy rather than tidy, aggressive rather than ascetic), the range of options in using toys as representatives of self or other is very wide. Barbie and Acton Man are small, inanimate, breakable and dumb, and they take part in fantasies through the agency of the child. Action Man can be played with in the context of 'feminine' caring play, just as Barbie could take a role in a warlike play scenario. Toys are in the power of the children who play with them, whether as masculine or feminine figures in play narratives, and/or as objects of the child's sadistic (conventionally masculine) or nurturing (conventionally feminine) impulses. Toys borrow from, and attain meaning through, the gender identities of adult culture, and thus also inherit the contradictions, resistances and alternatives inherent in them.

Children's knowledge about, and desire for, brands like Action Man and Barbie is part of their socialisation into consumer culture, and thus a sign of the adulthood which Ellen Seiter calls 'a system of meaningful social categories embedded in commodities and sets of commodities'

(1993: 205). The social categories signalled by differences between the bodies of toys include gender, age-group and race. Early Barbies had pale colouring and a slightly oriental appearance, but by the fourth Barbie in the late 1960s a warmer flesh tone had been introduced, and Barbies resembled contemporary images of blue-eyed blonde American beauty, though Mattel has provided Barbie with friends of different races. While it would be mistaken to simply decry Barbie's whiteness (since this assumes that identification with the child's like is simply based on mimesis and imitation) it is important to consider the globalisation of normative representations of the white gendered body across diverse cultures and markets. Barbie, for example, has never been manufactured in the United States. There are two Barbie factories in Guangdong Province, China, employing about 11 000 women. Much of the production of all toys takes place in China (Fleming 1996: 110–12), from where toys are transferred to Hong Kong and exported to Western markets. Sixty per cent of Hong Kong's annual toy exports (worth more than $3 billion) come from Chinese producers, and this trade accounts for about 80 per cent of the world's toy business (excluding computer games). Barbie sales in 1997 topped $1.2 billion, when around ninety different dolls were produced by Mattel. So while Barbie now has friends who are black or Hispanic, all of their bodies are representations designed in the United States, made in China, and exported worldwide. The economics of the toy industry in its current form lead towards this form of global multinational capitalism: the world toy market is worth £45 billion, but industry growth is hard to sustain because of crazes which destabilise trade. Mattel and Hasbro are the largest toy companies, with a combined 30 per cent share of the annual $13 billion American market and 25 per cent of the £1.5 billion British market. In 1996, Mattel-Fisher Price launched a $5.2 billion hostile takeover bid for Hasbro (owners of Action Man), in order to create a massive and stable global corporation (Cope 1996). The domination of the market by a large number of interrelated products made by a small number of producers is a response to anxieties about the sustainability of growth, the unpredictability of demand and the difficulty of maintaining brands. The normative bodies of Action Man and Barbie are combined with short-lived and numerous costume and accessory designs, in order to sustain long-lived brands with rapid turnover of new brand extensions and spin-off products.

It is the physical bodies of Action Man and Barbie which are the most complex and expensive aspects of the toys. The meaning of gender difference in toy figures cannot be read off from their physical characteristics, but there are gendered modes of use which are prepared for in their design. Judy Attfield (1996: 85) has discussed the history and significance of the articulated joints of Barbie and Action Man in these terms, to show 'how the cliché of "feminine" as passive and "masculine" as active is literally embodied in the design of the toys'. Barbie originally had joints only where her head, arms and legs join her body, and this is still the case with cheaper models. Action Man has twenty moveable joints, at the wrist and ankles as well as at limb junctions, and he also has twisting biceps which enable his arms to be moved in ways impossible for the human body. The implication of Attfield's analysis of joints is that the functioning of toys' bodies determine the play scenarios which can be engaged in, and thus their relation to gender identities. Play in this context is an anticipation and modelling of social life in the adult world: Action Man with his mobile body, equipped with guns and swords, would support the construction of masculinity as active (see Bignell 1996), while Barbie would restrict play activity to the framing of display postures, collecting, nurturing or crafting, for instance, reflecting a division of roles for adult men and women.

However, Action Man is a doll, and his desirability as a totem of masculinity depends on a rigid separation from the feminine characteristics represented in dolls for girls. As an adventure hero, he is always represented either alone or in the company of other male figures. The *Action Man Bumper 1996 Annual* reports (p. 4) that one of his friends is 'Natalie – also known as Action Woman – they work together, but she is not his girlfriend'. A dangerous slippage from excessive manliness to effeminacy to homosexuality is displaced on to Action Man's opponent, the evil Dr X, who functions as his negative mirror-image, for Dr X is a repository of femininity in an Action Man world without women, and with an unstable notion of masculinity. When Daniel Gifford (aged ten) wrote to ask Dr X in *Action Man* comic (no. 5, Nov. 1995, p. 25), 'Do you like girls, yes or no?', he replied, 'Some of my best friends are girls. We like to swop clothes and help each other with our hair.' Play involving haircare is one of the key features of Barbie's feminine world, and features, along with making simple foods and jewellery, in *Barbie* comic. But bodily adornment and fetishism are not absent from Action Man figures. For example, the Action Man Operation T. I. G. E. R. figure is supplied with decals which can be used as temporary tattoos on the toy's body or on the child's body. There is a code of bodily adornment and narcissistic behaviour in the Action Man world, and this code stigmatises some activities as feminine while other quite similar activities are positively valued as masculine.

Having a gender identity requires learning a code and appearing to others as though one conforms to it. As Graham Dawson has argued, children project onto toys like Action Man, which become symbolic representatives of themselves. But when the child becomes Action Man, he can subsist in this identity only if other children (or adults) will accept him in this role; in play,

> identities are imagined through projection directed at omnipotently controlled, purely symbolic objects, these social imaginings position real others, inviting approval and affirmation and running the risk of refusal and negation. At stake here is the winning and withholding of social recognition: 'who I can imagine myself to be' becomes inseparable from 'who they will recognise me as'. (Dawson 1994: 261)

Toys of all kinds prepare the child to be a participant in discourses of the body and gender, but the ambiguities and contradictions of these discourses are also at play in the culture of toys, and the notion of role and performance is one way in which Action Man and Barbie, as well as children themselves, can destabilise their apparent certainties. Freud said in his lecture on 'Femininity': 'When you meet a human being, the first distinction you make is "male or female?" and you are accustomed to make this distinction with unhesitating certainty' (Freud 1933: 146). The certainty of this distinction in toys covers over a doubt about the ease of making it. It is not the biological body of the doll which is usually seen, and even so the bodies of Action Man and Barbie are not marked by the presence or absence of penises, since there is no penis in either. Instead it is the secondary signs of clothing or hair which are read, and not as disguises or problems in relation to the body beneath, but as evidence which substitutes for the invisibility of the distinguishing penis. Action Man's and Barbie's clothes are in many different styles, are made to be looked at, and are exchangeable between many different fantasy scenarios. Putting on and off identities through clothes is what is expected of women, and what is expected of Barbie, but it is also Action Man's condition.

Both Action Man and Barbie 'masquerade' by taking on clothes which depend on a presumed psychic identity as either masculine-active-warlike or feminine-passive-domestic. For it cannot be their incomplete biology which determines their gender role, but instead cultural identities which code their bodies (as much as their clothes) as masculine or feminine. Since the dolls are both castrated, and both inactive objects, each could be regarded as female and feminine, and the question of the indeterminacy of gender occurs in the context of a universal emasculation and therefore feminisation in bodily terms. Action Man and Barbie might express or disguise their apparent sex and gender by taking on the dress of one or the other sex. They open up the possibility of the relativity of gender, since outward appearance may express or disguise a body underneath, and their play roles (as solder or fashion model, for example) may also either contradict their bodies and their clothes, or match them. Barbie and Action Man, despite the efforts of their producers to enforce them, have the potential to demonstrate the precariousness of the symbolisations of sex and gender, and the multiple ways in which these symbolisations can be consciously and unconsciously undermined. Returning to the methodological issues outlined at the start of this essay, it is far from true that Barbie and Action Man can be dismissed as obviously and crudely emblematic of contrasting sexed and gendered bodies. The multiple determinations of their sex and gender sometimes coalesce in an apparent enforcement of identity, but neither are these determinations always additive in their effect, and nor are their effects themselves simply determinable in the conflicted experience of play. The significance of the study of toys, then, lies in its relationship to the study of the body in culture in general. While recent work on the body has emphasised the continual renegotiation of sexed and gendered identity in adult culture, the study of toys points to a continuity between the states of adulthood and childhood in this respect. Child and adult are contrastive and mutually defining modes of being, though their definitions and determinations have always been a subject of debate, often in relation to distinctions between the bodies of the child and of the adult. Determinations of sex and gender, in adults, in children and in toys, have both a significant specificity but also share the theoretical and methodological terrain of the body. For each, the body is a material and discursive object whose own materialities and meanings are perpetually displaced, dispersed and deconstructed by competing determinations.

Works cited

Attfield 1996 Judy Attfield, 'Barbie and Action Man: Adult Toys for Girls and Boys, 1959–93', in Pat Kirkham (ed.), *The Gendered Object* (Manchester: Manchester University Press), 80–9

Bazalgette and Buckingham 1995 Cary Bazalgette and David Buckingham (eds), *In Front of the Children: Screen Entertainment and Young Audiences* (London: BFI)

Bignell 1996 Jonathan Bignell, 'The Meanings of War Toys and War Games', in Ian Stewart and Susan Carruthers (eds), *War Culture and the Media: Representations of the Military in 20th Century Britain* (Trowbridge: Flicks Books), 165–84

Bignell 2000a Jonathan Bignell, '"Get Ready For Action!": Reading Action Man Toys', in Dudley Jones and Tony Watkins (eds), *'A Necessary Fantasy?': the Heroic Figure in Children's Popular Culture* (New York: Garland Press), 231–50

Bignell 2000b Jonathan Bignell, *Postmodern Media Culture* (Edinburgh: Edinburgh University Press)

Birkett 1998 Dea Birkett, 'I'm Barbie, Buy Me', *The Guardian*, Weekend section, 28 November, 13–19

Butler 1993 Judith Butler, *Bodies that Matter: On the Discursive Limits of Sex* (London: Routledge)

Cope 1996 Nigel Cope, 'Barbie Eyes Up Action Man in Toytown Battle', *The Independent*, 26 January, 6

Dawson 1989 Graham Dawson, 'War Toys', in Gary Day (ed.), *Readings in Popular Culture: Trivial Pursuits?* (Basingstoke: Macmillan), 98–111

Dawson 1994 Graham Dawson, *Soldier Heroes: British Adventure, Empire and the Imagining of Masculinities* (London: Routledge)

Fleming 1996 Dan Fleming, *Powerplay: Toys as Popular Culture* (Manchester: Manchester University Press)

Freud 1933 Sigmund Freud, 'Die Weiblichkeit', translated by James Strachey as 'Femininity', in Sigmund Freud, *New Introductory Lectures on Psychoanalysis*, ed. James Strachey (Harmondsworth: Penguin, edn of 1991)

Goldstein 1994 Jeffrey Goldstein (ed.), *Toys, Play and Child Development* (Cambridge: Cambridge University Press)

Kline 1993 Stephen Kline, *Out of the Garden: Toys and Children's Culture in the Age of TV Marketing* (London: Verso)

Lesnik-Oberstein 1998 Karín Lesnik-Oberstein, 'Childhood and Textuality: Culture, History, Literature', in Karín Lesnik-Oberstein (ed.), *Children in Culture: Approaches to Childhood* (Basingstoke: Macmillan), 1–28

Miedzian 1992 Myriam Miedzian, *Boys Will Be Boys* (London: Virago)

Seiter 1993 Ellen Seiter, *Sold Separately: Parents and Children in Consumer Culture* (New Brunswick: Rutgers University Press)

3
The Ideology of the Genderless Sporting Body: Reflections on the Czech State-Socialist Concept of Physical Culture

Libora Oates-Indruchová[1]

Much Western theory still operates with the Cartesian concept of binaries when discussing body and mind. The surviving body/mind dualism is often noted in contemporary studies of the body on the one hand, and sports and physical education on the other (Tinning 1990: 22; Frank 1991; Riordan 1991: 11; Turner 1991). In his overview of the theory of the body, Bryan S. Turner shows that this way of thinking even extends to the disappearance or submergence of the body in mainstream theory with the exception of anthropology (Turner 1991: 12–18). He refers to Adorno and Horkheimer's work *Dialectic of the Enlightenment* (1944) to point out the negative overtones of the body in contemporary culture: 'Adorno and Horkheimer go on to argue that Christianity and capitalism have joined forces to declare that work is virtuous, but the body is flesh and the source of evil' (15). This will ring a familiar bell to feminist critics: in traditional thinking women are the flesh, the body is associated with female characteristics and the mind with male.[2] I would like to propose that if it were possible to promote a unity rather than a split between the body and the mind, a framework for a useful theory of the body could be created, in which the male/female binary would lose its significance. Such a theory would also be beneficial to research with a gender perspective. It would open up the possibility of studying the relationship of women and men to their bodies without the hierarchy implied in standard gender studies approaches. These approaches work with the prevailing social and cultural assumption of the lesser value of the female/feminine in relation to the male/masculine, or show how the assumption operates. Further, feminist and gender theory could then be rid of the binaristic thinking within itself, that is, of the kind of an approach which sees the body entirely as a social construction providing a basis for creating the hierarchy of gender. Such an approach suppresses and does not take into consideration the physical reality and the functions of the body. For example, Susan Bordo (1993) writes against the 'ideology of dieting' and presents a convincing argument about how advertising, with alarming consistency, attempts to instil in women a guilty feeling towards eating. However, she introduces her argument with what could be read as an equally disturbing nostalgia for large female bodies:

> Many cultures, clearly, have revered expansiveness in women's bodies and appetites. Some still do. But in the 1980s and 1990s an increasingly universal equation of slenderness with beauty and success has rendered the competing claims of cultural diversity even feebler. (Bordo 1993: 102)

The disturbing element in a statement like this is that there is no qualification to consider the physiological effects of excessive weight. The body, in this argument, is a mere social construct, which does not have a system of functions with effects in themselves.

In this essay, I would like to explore the possibility of an approach to the theory of the body with a non-normative criterion of sex distinction. As a case study of such an approach, I will use the concept and theory of 'physical culture' researched and taught in degree programmes in physical education in the Czech Republic since the late 1970s. Due to the constraints of a single article, I will restrict myself to the analysis of the concept as presented in key textbooks for this type of degree programme: *Teorie tělesné kultury* (Theory of physical culture; Šprynar 1983), *Dějiny tělesné výchovy I: od nejstarších dob do roku 1848* (History of physical education I: from the earliest times to 1848; Krátký 1974) and *Dějiny tělesné výchovy II: od roku 1848 do současnosti* (History of physical education II: from 1848 to the present; Kössl et al. 1986). First, I will try to place the physical-cultural approach within the logic and ideology of Czech state socialism. Then I will define the concept of physical culture itself since it is a concept virtually unknown to Western theory.[3] Finally, I will look into two concrete claims which the textbooks of physical culture made in order to produce a model of the body free from the hierarchy between male and female, in which the body thus becomes genderless in the sense of having no markers of femininity and masculinity. These claims were: the unity of body and mind promoted, particularly, by the textbooks of the history of physical education (Krátký 1974; Kössl et al. 1986), and the claim of physical activities having aesthetic values emphasised, primarily, in the textbook of the theory of physical culture (Šprynar 1983).

My effort to use a concept developed under the oppressive ideology of state socialism can easily be seen as quixotic, because the devastating effects of the regime on most social sciences and humanities were so vast and so notorious that it may seem outrageous to propose that there might have been anything productive in it. It is well-known that state socialism subjected research efforts to the singular purpose of its totalising ideology, separating them from the developments of Western critical theory and imposing restrictions or bans on 'politically unreliable' researchers. Yet I will play the devil's advocate and make the heretical proposition that since a large amount of research was produced in a number of academic fields, of which physical culture was a very active one due to the state interest in its development, it is not necessary to write off all that work as mere ideological ballast. I believe that, in this case, the authors of the textbooks at which I am looking did not only strive to serve the ideology of state socialism, but that they also pursued original research advancing our knowledge of society and its mechanisms. Therefore, I will try to sift through the heavily ideologised theories and concepts and explore whether it is possible to find somewhere underneath the ideological purposes and meanings a model which could be useful for contemporary theory of the body.

As with any inter-cultural research, it is important to clarify the possible points of misinterpretation when working with a piece of research conducted under state socialism and relating it to Western scholarly perceptions. First of all, it is necessary to understand that state-socialist ideology created its own system of binaries and hierarchy of group interests. In *The Unbearable Lightness of Being* Milan Kundera sums it up mockingly in his rendition of the theory of socialist art:

> Soviet society had made such progress that the basic conflict was no longer between good and evil but between good and better. So shit (that is, whatever is essentially unacceptable) could exist only 'on the other side' (in America, for instance), and only from there, from the outside, as something alien (a spy, for instance), could it penetrate the world of 'good and better'. (Kundera 1984: 245–6)

The Cold War propaganda created by both sides of the divided world about who stands on the 'good' side and who on the 'evil' side is, of course, common knowledge and this is not the place to dwell on it. Kundera's quotation, however, reveals a system of internal dichotomies in the ideological rhetoric of state socialism derived from the political opposition between the Western world and the Soviet world. Kundera's analysis of what he calls 'totalitarian kitsch', which extends to any rule of a single political agenda, also explains why the dichotomies are ideologically essential: 'In the realm of totalitarian kitsch all answers are given in advance and preclude any questions. It follows, then, that the true opponent of totalitarian kitsch is the person who asks questions' (247).

These two quotations from a work of fiction illustrate well the reality of state-socialist ideology: everything had to be divided into the simple categories of good and bad, following the doctrines of Marxism-Leninism. The 'good' was synonymous with Soviet, socialist, working class and collectivism, while the realm of the 'bad' included America (or simply the West), capitalist, bourgeois and individualism, to mention just a few categories. Perhaps nowhere else were these categories expressed more explicitly than in the educational environment, such as in textbooks, for the obvious reason that education was the foremost ideological tool of the state. In the language of textbooks of physical culture, the dichotomies had to be clearly presented. For example, if whatever concerning 'the working class' was 'good', everything concerning some other group had to be 'bad'. The interests of the working class were the highest value, therefore, by implication, interests of other groups, like women, were inferior in the hierarchy of group interests and had to be either placed in the category of 'bourgeois'/ 'bad', assimilated into the 'working-class' interests, or eliminated (that is, deleted from discussion) as 'essentially unacceptable', as Kundera puts it.

It is not necessary to explain the oppressiveness of such ideology. However, its implementation in textbooks – and perhaps also in a larger societal context – produced another effect than attempting to brainwash the student population into black-and-white thinking. It allowed a certain 're-grouping' of binaries: the categories which, in another system of thought/ideology may be each other's opposites, did not make sense as antagonists in the state-socialist ideology. They could become more flexible in their relation and maybe even cease to create a mutual tension. Within the categories listed above, it would be difficult to oppose male and female, or body and mind, as 'good' and 'bad', as one having a higher value and the other lower. These terms did not fit into the neat binaries of state-socialist ideology – in other words, their opposition was not politically important. On the contrary, given the working-class struggle as the highest goal, the unity and equality of some concepts – like male/female, body/mind – was politically desirable to preclude the dissipation of purpose and power, which would occur if various groups struggled for various conflicting interests.

This consideration of the binaries in state socialism was necessary in order to explain some of the qualifications and adjustments which have to be made in studying theories produced under that political system. I have still left out one very important set of qualifications and that is the problematic relationship between state socialism and patriarchy. While I will return to this problem at the end of this essay, at this point I will simply mention that although state socialism proclaimed the equality of men and women, it appeared practically overnight within a fairly patriarchal society. Patriarchal discourse, then, functioned during the period of state socialism as what Raymond Williams theorised as *the residual* which, 'by definition, has been effectively formed in the past, but it is still active in the cultural process, not only and often not at all as an element of the past, but as an effective element of the present' (Williams 1977: 122). For the present discussion, it means that whatever gender-neutral theory may have been produced, it was still created and applied in an environment with some patriarchal prejudices and relations in place.

The term *physical culture* was used also in other state-socialist countries (*fizicheskaia kultura, fizkultura* in the Soviet Union, *Körperkultur* in GDR). The textbook *The Theory of Physical Culture* (Šprynar 1983), written for students of the Faculty of Physical Education and Sports, defines the activities included in physical culture as 'a process of human appropriation of the world, as a process of cultivating humanness' (Šprynar 1983: 49).[4] Physical culture (or 'body' culture, as the literal translation of the Czech phrase would go) consists of three components: physical education, sports and active leisure pursuits. The aim of sport is to achieve the highest performance, while that of leisure activity is to provide relaxation or relief from stress. The focus of physical education is to learn about the values of physical culture and to develop one's character through physical activity.[5] For a Western reader, physical activities may perhaps associate with competitive sport or again competitive games in school physical education. The referential system of physical culture may become clearer, if we think, for example, of non-competitive gymnastics or swimming instead. Physical culture is far from limited to these two activities, I am suggesting them merely for convenience. Nevertheless, it is true that the curricula of the degree programmes for which the textbooks were written included many more hours for each of gymnastics, swimming and athletics than for any single game.

It is important to emphasise that the textbooks presented an *abstract ideal* of what physical culture is and this is how I am treating it in my argument. As a part of culture, the values of the ideal were expected to be shared equally by those actively involved in a physical activity and those viewing the performers. The values would then be expected to carry over to the components of physical culture: to physical education, sport and leisure pursuits. My argument is that, providing we bear in mind the constraints of state-socialist ideology explained above, it is possible to accept the ideal of physical culture without irony, although the political language through which the ideal is constructed often begs an ironical attitude from the reader (we will see examples throughout this essay). It is in the application of the ideal in the practice of the three concrete components that difficulties arise if we consider it in terms of *feminist/gender* theory of the body. The problems stem from the fact that whether we are concerned with physical education, sports or leisure activities, these are all practised in the environment of a hierarchical relation between the masculine and the feminine.

In the presented ideal of physical culture, however, the idea of the masculine and the feminine cannot exist: there is no gender in the sense used in contemporary feminist/gender theory, that is in the sense of culturally constructed values ascribed to the two sexes. Physical culture, indeed, works only with 'male' and 'female' and the differences between them are recorded as mere biological facts without any social or cultural value attached to them. The statement from Šprynar (1983) about 'cultivating humanness' quoted above thus needs to be taken literally: it speaks about the human race as a homogeneous entity with regard to the value of its members.

In the degree programmes of physical education, the theory of physical culture had roughly three groups of research fields which together developed what I would call its 'scientific content'. These were history, 'body' sciences like anatomy and physiology, and 'mathematical' sciences like anthropometry and biomechanics. From the perspective of the body and feminist/gender theory the methods and/or premises of the three groups have a number of features which together create the ideal of the *internal body*, as opposed to the preoccupation with the outward body appearance. I say internal, because the leading features of the body are never ideal shapes, but ideal *functions*.[6] Thus, history revolves around the premise of the philosophical tradition of the body/mind unity; anatomy and physiology work with a kind of 'one-sex' body – not in the sense presented by Thomas Laqueur (1990) as existing in pre-Enlightenment medical texts according to which the genitals are the same in the female as in the male only turned inside, but in the sense that the emphasis is placed on the sameness of body functions,[7] and anthropometry and biomechanics develop models of the correct execution of movement on the basis of the forces and angles which together put the body in the optimal position for achieving the best performance (Čelikovský et al. 1979, Karas et al. 1983). In this last case, body is again examined from the 'inside', that is, it is the position of its body parts (literally, the bones and the joints) which is seen as crucial in thinking about the body.

In the rest of this essay, I will look more closely at history, namely at the claim of the body/mind unity underlying the account of the history of physical education in two textbooks: *History of Physical Education I: from the Earliest Times to 1848* (Krátký 1974) and *History of Physical Education II: from 1848 to the Present* (Kössl et al. 1986). As I will show below, body/mind unity is important for the whole concept of physical culture, because it provides a philosophical basis for its overemphasised ultimate goal of harmony, which claimed aesthetic qualities for physical activities. Of course, historicising this unity was also important from the point of view of the Marxist interpretation of the world. Wojciech Lipoński sees the role of history in the system of physical culture thus:

> Sports history was to discuss the emergence of sport in a class society and the role of physical activities among workers in their attempts to elevate their social position and the sporting forms of their class struggle against social and political injustice. (Lipoński 1996: 1)

In this view, it was important to establish that workers who were involved in both class struggle and physical/sporting activities were doing so with a higher purpose, that their physical exercises related to their characters, their minds. This point implies what is meant by 'mind' in the argument about body and mind: it is that which concerns mental processes in terms of 'intellectual and emotional capacities' as opposed to 'neural processes'. James Riordan argues that the treatment of body and mind as a unified and interdependent system derives from Marx, Engels and Lenin: 'Marx and Engels rejected the dualist philosophy and emphasised that not only was there an intimate relationship existing between matter and mind, but that the former largely determined the latter' (Riordan 1991: 20). While any of the texts used in the educational process under state socialism, to which I refer in this essay, were certainly written from a conscious Marxist-Leninist perspective, the idea of the unity of the body and mind does not appear for the first time in Engels. As we will see below, Krátký (1974) painstakingly creates the tradition of this mode of thinking by tracing it back to primitive proto-Communist societies,[8] in which, he argues, people already consciously practised physical education:

> Physical education served fitness and health, increased the productivity and defence of labour.[9] It was conducted in the unity of theory and practice, the physical and the psychological. Wanting to see the prevalence of the physical at this developmental stage means introducing a crude, one-sided approach. (Krátký 1974: 42)

The analysis in this text can be criticised for a number of flaws, both methodological and factual, but, for our purposes, its importance does not lie in its accuracy of observation, but in enabling us to look at what argumentation was used to create a particular ideology of physical culture which provided no space for gender markers. According to Krátký, women became disadvantaged with the development of ancient civilisations with a slave mode of production, in which the unity of work and defence of the workplace was disrupted, and a privileged military class – consisting only of selected men – was created (54–5). The tradition of the body/mind unity then continues through references to the concept in Plato, Plutarch and Aristotle, with the admonition that 'on the issue of the equality of women with men also in physical education, Plato was more progressive than his clever critic Aristotle' (92). The philosophical tradition further includes Comenius, Locke, Rousseau and Bolzano. Both the textbooks of the history of physical education (Krátký 1974; Kössl et al. 1986) and also the textbook of the theory of physical culture (Šprynar 1983) emphasise Juvenal's phrase *mens sana in corpore sano* (a sound mind in a sound body)[10] echoed by Comenius. The history textbooks outline the history of physical education as an unbroken sequence of European physical educational systems striving for the unity of body and mind: the German, Danish, Swiss, English, Swedish, French and finally Czech systems of physical education. The account does not work with binaries, but emphasises the interrelatedness of body and mind: exercising the body is a means of accessing and improving the spirit. It is symptomatic that the 'Foreword' to *History of Physical Education II* (Kössl et al. 1986) covering the more recent, and therefore more politically sensitive period of history, defines the content of the textbook as

> [T]he history of world and Czechoslovak physical culture from the revolutionary year 1848 to the present, that is, of a period whose understanding is a pre-condition to the correct [*sic*] interpretation of our time. (Kössl et al. 1986: 5)

The ideological premise and the legitimising effects of the authorities of world philosophy laid down by Krátký (1974) are necessary to define physical education as an important part of culture, and also to claim allegiance to physical educational traditions which existed long before the establishment of the Soviet system of physical culture. The argument carried through the volume is, by definition, incoherent, if only because of the obvious difficulty of reconciling the Soviet emphasis on asserting the superiority of the state-socialist system through competitive sports with the Czech tradition of non-competitive, and often anti-sport, physical activity motivated by nineteenth-century revivalist ideals of national sovereignty, which I will discuss below. For our argument, however, the essential point is the central role of the founder of the influential physical educational organisation, Sokol, and of the Czech physical educational system, Miroslav Tyrš (1832–84), in the historical perspective taken by Kössl et al. (1986) and carried over also to other textbooks of physical education of the time. Tyrš, a doctor of philosophy and a professor of art history at the Czech University in Prague, is presented as almost the ideal of a thinker rooting his work in the unity of the body and mind. His views on the goals of Sokol are presented as political: 'According to Tyrš, Sokol was to be an "unbreachable dam" against all enemies of the nation' (25). For him, physical education had political, philosophical and aesthetic values, as is documented in his theoretical approach to the physical educational movement and the definition of its functions in society (see Fig. 3.1). Kössl et al. (1986) also emphasise Tyrš's support for the equality of men and women in physical education by exercising with both sexes and initiating the foundation of the first women's physical educational association in Prague in 1869.[11] Tyrš's ideas on the inclusion of women in physical activities are perhaps connected to the political goals of the Czech National Revival for self-determination of the small nation within the Austro-Hungarian Empire: it was necessary to mobilise all nation members, and therefore, women had to be included.[12]

Tyrš is also the author of the Czech gymnastic terminology which has been used to the present day. This only confirms his strong influence on

Czech ideas on the role of physical exercise. The emphasis on naming and creating orderly systems, which then provided a basis for aesthetic appreciation, helped to create a strong tradition of non-competitive activities. Non-competitiveness became a feature also of working-class physical educational organisations, although clubs whose members practised competitive sports existed as well. In order to understand the Czech state-socialist concept of physical culture, however, it is important to bear in mind that despite the high political competitiveness of state-socialist sport,[13] the non-competitive component was always strongly present. During the period of state socialism, the non-competitiveness of practising physical activities has to be understood in the logic of the ideology. The state supposedly represented all citizens, whose well-being was in its care. The ultimate goals of the society were to build first socialism and then communism. In this logic, all citizens had to be fit and healthy to achieve those goals. Therefore, an individual's body was not his or her own, but s/he had to take care of it in the public interest: an individual was in the service of society. It follows that the only appropriate competition was really with the capitalist West. In all other cases, an individual's physical activity was to be motivated by solidarity and co-operation. Even competition with oneself was not emphasised, because that was not the final goal.

Instead of the focus on competition, physical culture placed emphasis on aesthetics, while the connection of physical activity – particularly, sports – with aesthetics has traditionally been a contested territory in Western culture. For the purposes of this essay, I propose to think about the aesthetics of the body practising physical activity in the following terms:

> to see something *as* an aesthetic object is to see it and attend to it *as* an object worthy of observation and attention in and for itself, for its own sake, in its own right, quite apart from any instrumental use or practical purpose to which it may be put, or from any consequence that it may have – whether religious, economic, or moral. (Aspin 1974: 129; original emphasis)

To explain this approach to a Western reader who may be used to associating aesthetics with art only, I will add the claims about the aesthetic values of sport made by Carlisle: expressive and evocative elements, intellectual beauty, drama and unity (Carlisle 1974: 25–7). By unity he understands a quality 'which is not based solely on the drama, but on the movement qualities, the skilled performance, and the intellectual aspects, too' (27).

The approach to physical culture in the state-socialist Czech Republic created a structure of thinking about the body in which it was seen as an aesthetic object in the sense of the harmony of its functions, the Greek *kalokaghatia*.[14] Here it might seem dangerously close to the Nazi ideology of the body, which also turned to ancient history. However, the state-socialist aesthetic ideal had to be created in dissociation from any tradition which was placed on the 'bad' side. Needless to say Nazism was seen as the worst possible tradition. The simplest way of dealing with an unacceptable concept was not to mention it at all. In the case of Nazism this would not work, because the general ideological rhetoric used the defeat of Nazism in the Second World War as a landmark in the development of Czech society towards the adoption of Marxist-Leninist principles. Thus, Kössl et al. (1986) treat the history of physical education in the states with fascist governments in the prewar period at some length. Nevertheless, they place emphasis on the abuse of physical education by the Nazis through the educational system and youth organisations, but they do not once allude to the aesthetic ideals of the body. Their account starts with the following paragraph:

> In the period of the overall crisis of capitalism, the most reactionary groups of the bourgeoisie attempted to stop the revolutionary process by installing openly fascist regimes in power in several European countries. After these seized power, they tried to fascisise all public life, education, science and culture by installing totalitarian regimes, which persecuted all members of progressive and democratic forces. Physical education, sport and extra-curricular education of children and youth played an exceptionally important role in their intentions. (Kössl et al. 1986: 123)

Framed in the vocabulary of the 'bad' group and thus delivering clearly the 'value' of the historical development described after that introduction, Kössl et al. dissociated the Nazi ideology and concept of physical exercise from the traditions on which they built the Czech model of physical culture. The goal declared by the official system of Czech physical culture was 'the harmonious all-round development of the individual' (this translation from Riordan 1991: 24). It was presumed that this harmony was carried over to the spirit: body and mind had to be in balance. In other words, a body with a 'crooked character' does not fulfil the idea of harmony.[15] Šprynar (1983) treats harmony as a commonly understood value which does not require further explanation.

From his treatment and from what was already said about state-socialist ideology and physical culture, harmony seems to refer to an internal balance of body and mind. This means the equal development of the physical and mental capacities of an individual, which is directed towards the overall social goals of building socialism and communism.

Thus, the traditionally studied aspects of the body – sexuality and outward appearance – were no longer its key aspects. In this theoretical framework, the body, aesthetic and physical pleasure all centred on the functionality of bodily parts and systems, with the goal of 'the development of health, fitness for labour and defence, of an all-round development of a human individual in the spirit of Communism' (Šprynar 1983: 24). Since body and mind were closely related, not only did the whole system of physical culture carry a meaning, but whenever any non-competitive or even competitive performances were considered, they had to contain a message, a narrative beyond a mere set of exercises. This would be a requirement for any physical activity in which performance could not be measured empirically, such as routines in gymnastics or floor gymnastics, but much more in non-competitive public performances, of which the best examples were the Spartakiads festivals (see Figs 3.2 and 3.3). This name was given to mass public physical performances by Jiří František Chaloupecký (1890–1922), a key figure in the development of working-class physical education in the first years after the First World War, to suggest a connection between the contemporary working-class and the uprising of the Roman gladiator Spartacus. They began in 1921 and were revived by the state administration of physical culture in 1955.[16] According to Šprynar:

> The connection of the cultural traditions of the past with the new traditions of the present made the Spartakiads a unique school of preservation and cultivation of national traditions, committed ideas, and good taste in the name of life, happiness and beauty. And thus the new tradition of Spartakiads [...] further develops the progressive traditions of connecting physical culture with aesthetic culture. (Šprynar 1983: 33)

This is, of course, a very general and ideologically informed statement. Nevertheless, if we look at any documentary films about the Spartakiads, we will be able to discern clearly certain communicative patterns in the performances: each of them would be telling a story or expressing an idea. None of the textbooks I have analysed talks specifically about a concrete narrative in any of the post-war

Spartakiads beyond a general ideological message about the defence and achievements of socialism, but Šprynar refers specifically to the men's routine at the Sokol performance in 1938, which 'expressed the determination to protect the country against fascism' (Šprynar 1983: 33). Thus the communicative potential and function of physical education was emphasised, which brings physical education close to art in the sense that there was an idea to be conveyed by the performers to the audience, and shared both among the performers and with the audience. This corresponds to a large degree with the theory of *the communicative body* suggested by Arthur W. Frank in his discussion of the types of bodies in theory. He maintains that the communicative body is the most productive way of thinking about bodies. He focuses on

> [t]he aesthetic practices of dance and performance and the caring practices of medicine. The essential quality of the communicative body is that it is a body *in process* of creating itself. Theory cannot describe such a body, nor can it prescribe it. The task is rather to bring together fragments of its emergence. [...] [The communicative body] produces itself not as a surface mirroring all around it, but as an expressiveness recreating *a* world of which it is a part. (Frank 1991: 79–80; my emphasis)

I propose that the sum of the thinking about the body in the system of physical culture, as discussed above, can provide a theoretical framework for the emergence of the communicative body, because it is not divorced from the whole concept of the mental/spiritual. The politicisation of sports and physical education under state socialism can even significantly enhance the communicative potential of the body – although within the constraints of the ideology – because that way the body is specifically given the task of recreating *the* 'world of which it is a part' (as opposed to *a* world, but that is, perhaps, the case with any ideology). By definition, a male and a female body have an equal role in this task, although the two sexes may not always recreate the part of their world in the same way.

The approach to the body and mind used in physical culture may be useful for feminist/gender theory. By not having the concept of gender, but only the concept of sex, it allows us to think about women's bodies without the burden of having to match up to or negate the male standard. Gender, in this framework, is not the leading characteristic of the body. It is replaced by the functions which the body, whether male or female, is capable of performing – which makes gender irrelevant to the aesthetic value of physical activities (whether from the perspective of the performer or of the audience). The value is in the beauty contained in the harmony of well-executed bodily movements and of the synthesis of the physical and the spiritual. In the words of Šprynar, the important aspect of physical culture lies, among others, in

> [T]he aesthetic values created by the connection of exercise or contest with music, song, the unique beauty of mass performances and the experience of expression in dance. [...] It is desirable that the process of physical culture become a source of pleasant atmosphere, happiness, friendship and genuine comradely relations (Šprynar 1983: 73)

In this quotation, there is space for the state-socialist ideology ('comradely relations' refer to the ideal of workers making their bodies fit for building socialism), but by virtue of the logic of a different binary system described in the introduction, there is no space for creating the categories of femininity and masculinity. A more precise formulation would be that there is no space for *continuing* these categories, since they existed before state socialism and continued to exist in various degrees in it outside the theoretical model of physical culture.

This last point brings me to the complications of the concept of physical culture: merging the theory with practice and applying a model without the hierarchies of gender in an environment, in which these hierarchies still operate. A detailed discussion of this is beyond the scope of this essay; however, I would like to make at least few points in this direction, calling on the authority of my own experience within the institutions of Czech physical culture.

I was a member of an athletic club in my teens and a student of physical education in the first half of my twenties. No matter how hard I try, I cannot think of a single incidence of somebody from among the authorities in these environments, that is, coaches and educators, ever displaying any gender discriminatory attitudes or making comments to that effect. I was always free to think about and 'live' my body according to the ideal described above, in whose favour I have been arguing. There certainly were sex specific differences in the activities – in sports, particularly – in which women and men were involved, but these were determined by the fact that rules of such and such a sport required them. For example, as an athlete, I could not compete in triple-jump (an example of *sex* discrimination), because some authority in the international association who wrote the rules did not consider it a suitable event for women. My coaches or peers in the club, nevertheless, did not find anything wrong with me and other women practising it (an example of *gender* perception within a group influenced by the concept of physical culture).

Problems with retaining this gender-free attitude arose only when I left the institutional environment – whether in the literal sense of going to another place or in thinking about myself from another perspective. Another place could have been a simple crossing of the line between the university class and the living quarters. Only students of physical education lived in our halls of residence. Yet the women there were subjected to perpetual scrutiny by their male colleagues for the degree of femininity they, as sportswomen, retained. A number of these men (but not all of them) refused to consider a female student of physical education as their prospective partner. I myself refused to follow the recommendation of my (male) coach to specialise in heptathlon, because that involved shot putting. Shot putters were traditionally heavy muscular women and even heptathlonists had a stronger build than female athletes in other events. I did not want to look like them because having so much muscle was unfeminine. These examples show how the traditional *residual* patriarchal values affected even those who were involved in a project which was supposed to have overcome such binaries.

The feminine/masculine division extended beyond the subjective perceptions and personal relations. The practice in the institutions of physical culture also differed from the theoretical ideal which practically created a body without the markers of gender. Frank refers to Lynne Hanna's book *Dance, Sex and Gender* (1988), documenting that although dance may be a space in which a body can become communicative regardless of its sex, the institutional power is male (Frank 1991: 81–2). Similarly, in the whole of my own involvement with physical education and sports in the Czech Republic, I have met only a few women as chairpersons of sports clubs and local physical educational associations, and almost none in the higher institutional echelons. The executive power in the *practice* of physical culture thus runs counter to the ideal: it remains male-dominated, the markers of gender with respect to power are in place according to the traditional division.

The theory of physical culture in the Czech state-socialist system might well be a useful framework for a theory of the body and for a theory with a feminist/gender perspective by making it possible to study the body without the hierarchical implications of the feminine and the masculine. The different system of binaries defined by the ideology of state-socialism necessitated, among other things, such a theory of the body which would reflect the ideological division. Under the special conditions, in which the male/female dualism was not ideologically acceptable, the binary 'loosened up'. With it, the related binary of mind/body also lost its oppositional force. Crudely speaking, the socialist = good/capitalist = bad dualism, enabled all four terms – female, male, body and mind – to reside on the 'good' side. The examples that I have looked at show that this new point of departure resulted in a different approach to the body: first, the emphasis was placed on the 'internal' body and its functionality, rather than on its external appearance and/or sex; second, the sporting body was treated as an aesthetic object and, therefore, clearly belonging to the realm of the mind; and finally, the latter point was further amplified by the emphasis on the development of the mind/spirit through the practice of bodily performance. Saying all this, however, the limitations of the applicability of the theory also have to be considered: although the theory dispensed with the binaries of gender, it was still applied in an environment with residual patriarchal norms. This significantly restricted the 'target audience' and 'target context' of this theoretical approach. Nevertheless, the state-socialist physical culture shows that under certain conditions, a productive approach to the body and, by extension, to males and females, is possible.

Notes

1 I would like to thank Naomi Segal for her stimulating comments on the earlier drafts of this essay. This study was written with the support of a Fellowship from Collegium Budapest/Institute for Advanced Study.

2 Perhaps the first feminist study on the subject was carried out by Simone de Beauvoir, *Le deuxième sexe* (Paris: Gallimard, 1949).

3 I use 'Western', here and in the rest of this essay, to designate Western European and North American thought, as distinct from Central/East European state-socialist thought.

4 From this point, all translations from Czech texts are my own.

5 In physical culture, the phrase 'physical activity' refers to bodily movements which are not an inseparable part of work, such as manual labour, but which are conducted for the purpose of the movements themselves and which are perceived as having a value in themselves.

6 It follows that categories like age, race or type of physical activity are again all equal in the ideal, because each body and each activity can have its own 'correct' functions. This concept, together with the fact that it is rooted in

Marxism-Leninism, certainly gives rise to prescriptiveness of a particular kind. Thus, the concept of physical culture rejects any profit-motivated physical activity as contradicting the moral and aesthetic values of its ideal. The practice of physical culture can then take the idea of aesthetics further and have various prescriptions concerning, for example, an acceptable attire for each particular activity.

7 The textbooks to which I am referring are Fleischmann and Linc (1964), Seliger et al. (1977) and Seliger et al. (1983). They do mention physiological differences between the male and the female body, such as lower average blood volume in one heart contraction in women, but they are not consistent in listing them all and they again only record the differences without attaching a value to them.

8 This terminology, of course, comes from the traditional Marxist-Leninist periodisation of history according to the mode of production and ownership of the means of production into primitive proto-communist, slave-owning, feudal, capitalist, socialist, and communist societies. Czech state-socialist textbooks in any field had to work within the framework of this periodisation, since that was the official doctrine.

9 Both the words 'productivity' and 'defence' of labour have to be understood again within the rhetoric of Czech state socialism: only increased productivity of labour could bring the socialist countries (the 'good' countries) ahead of the capitalist countries (the 'bad' ones) and, because the propaganda emphasised the constant threat to the products of labour of the working classes from the 'bad' capitalist countries, the defence of labour was an important and frequently stressed value. 'Defence purposes' were in the 'good' group of categories in the binaristic system, while 'militaristic purposes' belonged solely to the 'bad' side. Proto-communist societies were non-exploitative and therefore 'good', which means that the vocabulary from the 'good' group was used about them.

10 Decimus Junius Juvenalis (AD 55–60–127?). See *The New Encyclopaedia Britannica*, vol. 6 (Chicago, 15th edn, 1991) p. 667.

11 Tělocvičný spolek paní a dívek pražských [An association for physical exercise of the ladies and maidens of Prague] headed by Klemeňa Hanušová, a former student of Tyrš's.

12 The nineteenth century was also the period of a strong women's movement among Czech intellectual women, but I will not discuss its role in this essay, because it is not referred to in any of the textbooks I am analysing. Therefore, it is not a part of the concept of physical culture as constructed in the recent past.

13 I have not discussed this point at length, because the politicisation of physical education and sports in the Eastern bloc is well-known and well-documented. For an extensive discussion of the Soviet system of sport, see Riordan 1991.

14 'Ancient Greeks wanted to be good and beautiful physically and spiritually. They promoted the ideal of kalokaghatia (Gr. kalos – beautiful, kai-a, agathos – good). The Greek connection of beauty and health is well expressed in mythology: Apollo is the father of Aesculap, the god of health and medicine. The symbols of Apollo, a bow with an arrow or a lyre, represent the harmony of physical and spiritual education' (Krátký 1974: 86; original emphasis).

15 An objection can be raised that the reverse of this example, that is, a noble spirit cannot be found in a crippled body, has strong discriminatory overtones against disabled people. However, such an assumption works with a particular idea of a perfect body and body shape, while physical culture – as I pointed out earlier – is not so much concerned with external appearance as it is with the internal harmony of the body and mind. Krátký (1974) makes this point clear when criticising the practice of killing weak and sick babies in ancient Sparta: '[The Spartans] overestimated hereditary attributes and physical appearance, while underestimating the power of education and environment' (87).

16 Spartakiads were far from the first performances of this kind in the Czech Republic. Sokol (falcon) organised their first festival as early as 1882 and continued with breaks during wartime until 1948.

Works cited

Aspin 1974 D. N. Aspin, 'Sport and the Concept of "The Aesthetic"', in H. T. A. Whiting and D. W. Masterson (eds), *Readings in the Aesthetics of Sport* (London: Lepus)

Beauvoir 1949 Simone de Beauvoir, *Le deuxième sexe* (Paris: Gallimard)

Bordo 1993 Susan Bordo, *Unbearable Weight* (Berkeley: University of California Press)

Carlisle 1974 R. Carlisle, 'Physical Education and Aesthetics', in H. T. A. Whiting and D. W. Masterson (eds), *Readings in the Aesthetics of Sport* (London: Lepus)

Čelikovský et al. 1979 S. Čelikovský et al., *Antropomotorika pro studující tělesnou výchovu* [Anthropometry for students of PE] (Praha: SPN)

Fleischmann and Linc 1964 J. Fleischmann and R. Linc, *Anatomie člověka* [Anatomy of humans], vols I and II (Praha: SPN, edn of 1981 – vol. I and 1979 – vol. II)

Frank 1991 A. W. Frank, 'For Sociology of the Body: an Analytical Overview', in M. Featherstone, M. Hepworth and B. S. Turner (eds), *The Body: Social Process and Cultural Theory* (London: Sage)

Karas et al. 1983 V. Karas, P. Sušanka and S. Otáhal, *Základy biomechaniky tělesných cvičení* [Elementary biomechanics of physical exercise] (Praha: Katedra antropomotoriky, biomechaniky a anatomie, Fakulta tělesné výchovy a sportu, Universita Karlova)

Kössl et al. 1986 J. Kössl, F. Krátký and J. Marek, *Dějiny tělesné výchovy II: od roku 1848 do současnosti* [History of physical education II: from 1848 to the present] (Praha: Olympia)

Krátký 1974 F. Krátký, *Dějiny tělesné výchovy I: od nejstarších dob do roku 1848* [History of physical education I: from the earliest times to 1848] (Praha: Olympia)

Kundera 1984 M. Kundera, *The Unbearable Lightness of Being*, translated by M. H. Heim (London and Boston: Faber and Faber, edn of 1985)

Laqueur 1990 T. Laqueur, *Making Sex: Body and Gender from the Greeks to Freud* (Cambridge, MA and London: Harvard University Press)

Lipoński 1996 W. Lipoński, 'Still an Unknown European Tradition: Polish Sport in the European Cultural Heritage', *The International Journal of the History of Sport*, 13, 2 (August 1996), 1–41

Martin 1987 Emily Martin, *The Woman in the Body: a Cultural Analysis of Reproduction* (Buckingham: Open University Press, edn of 1989)

Morava 1992 J. Morava, 'Tyršova smrt v Tyrolích' [The death of Tyrš in Tyrolia] *Tvar*, 1992, 16, 6–7

The New Encyclopaedia Britannica, vol. 6 (Chicago, 15th edn of 1991)

Riordan 1991 J. Riordan, *Sport, Politics and Communism* (Manchester and New York: Manchester University Press)

Seliger et al. 1977 V. Seliger et al., *Fyziologie tělesných cvičení* [Physiology of physical exercise] (Praha: Universita Karlova)

Seliger et al. 1983 V. Seliger, R. Vinařický and Z. Trefný, *Fyziologie člověka pro fakulty tělesné výchovy a sportu* [Human physiology for students of the faculty of PE and sports] (Praha: SPN)

Šprynar 1983 Z. Šprynar, *Teorie tělesné kultury* [Theory of physical culture] (Praha: Katedra teorie tělesné kultury, Fakulta tělesné výchovy a sportu, Universita Karlova)

Tinning 1990 R. Tinning, *Ideology and Physical Education: Opening Pandora's Box* (Geelong, Victoria: Deaking University Press)

Turner 1991 Bryan S. Turner, 'Recent Developments in the Theory of the Body', in M. Featherstone, M. Hepworth and B. S. Turner (eds), *The Body: Social Process and Cultural Theory* (London: Sage)

Williams 1977 Raymond Williams, *Marxism and Literature* (Oxford and New York: Oxford University Press)

4

'Lying beneath me she is only a shape': *American Psycho* and the Representation of Madness

Ann Scott[1]

> I pick up this morning's *Wall Street Journal* and scan the front page – all of it one ink-stained senseless typeset blur. 'I think I was hallucinating while watching it. I don't know. I can't be sure. I don't remember,' I murmur [...] She just stands there, waiting for instructions.
>
> (Ellis 1991: 64)

> The Street hadn't changed. It was the same mixture as before. The mute, the catatonic, the schizoid, the paranoiac. And Johnny Barrett.
>
> (Avallone 1963: 99)

Bret Easton Ellis's *American Psycho*, the story of Patrick Bateman, a Wall Street trader who is a serial killer at night and is never caught, is conventionally taken as a darkly evocative satire on 1980s greed and consumerism. Much less has been written about the representation of madness in the novel: the hypnotic narrative shifts between the idea of culture as a site of insanity, and a narrator who sees himself as able to 'ward off total madness' only rarely, and for whom all frontiers become 'detachable'. Following recent clinical and cultural studies debates on trauma and memory (see, for example, Target 1998, Caruth 1995), I want to suggest that, alongside the satire, the novel's additional layer of reference, sometimes implicit, sometimes explicit, portrays indeterminacy as a state in which psychic interiority bears little relationship to the structures of an external world, be they those of law enforcement, the role of the name in conferring identity, or the normal relationships of sexuality, pleasure and the body. It is this uncertainty, this shifting set of possibilities, which gives the novel its haunting power and its ability to draw the reader in to its fictional world.

This lack of congruence between inner and outer states, and the bleaching of affect that permeates the novel, is suggestive of extreme psychic disturbance in the narrator. It is the textual display of such incongruities that in my view brings the reader close to feeling he or she is losing their mind (usually termed 'finding the book simultaneously disgusting and impossible to put down'). I am therefore suggesting that it is also worth juxtaposing the novel with readings of clinical madness, especially cinematic ones of an earlier period which straddle actuality and fiction, in order to bring out its dizzying instability more clearly.[2] The linkage is not arbitrary. In using cinematic conventions to track the narrator's intensifying disturbance, *American Psycho* calls to mind a group of works that include the fiction *Shock Corridor* (1963) and the documentary *Titicut Follies* (1967). Both films posed large questions about American culture via a consideration of madness in its 'proper' place – the asylum; *American Psycho* inverts that frame while borrowing from it, to pose questions about the madness of culture by considering business in its 'proper' place. I am suggesting that although *American Psycho* is set on Wall Street, the novel's structure and tempo paradoxically invite comparison with films set in traditional American psychiatric spaces, and that it is these unconscious resonances, and not just the overt depictions of killings, actual or hallucinated, which make the novel so frightening. In that sense the novel's cultural forebear is not, as one might think, Hitchcock's *Psycho*, despite the implicit acknowledgement, in Ellis's hero's name, to Norman Bates.

To develop this argument I will first address the confusion of place, person and setting in the novel, and the relationship with readers that is set up by this confusion; then comment on the breakdown of language and insistent use of cinematic imagery in Bateman's narrative; and, lastly, consider the imagery of American culture in two films about madness.

As is well known, *American Psycho* tells the story of a Wall Street trader whose killings may or may not take place in the mind.[3] The novel is written in the first person, and almost entirely in the present tense, although the action in the novel appears to span (roughly) two years. We gather that Bateman's family owns either the company he works in, or most of Wall Street, or some combination, but we never find out; we gather that his mother is in an institution, but it isn't clear where, or of what sort. Bateman appears in some passages to be a political liberal, in others a racist republican. And so it goes. The novel is famously plotless, cross-cutting in documentary style between a range of settings – chiefly bars, clubs, restaurants, Wall Street and its neighbouring streets, midtown, and Bateman's apartment on the Upper

West Side. The unstable relationship of space and shape, place and mind, is the terrain of the novel; 'Lying beneath me she is only a shape', which I have used as my title, depicts the loss of bodily form, in Bateman's mind, of his 'other'.

In fact questions about the setting, and about the body, are posed in the novel's first sentence, in which the word 'blood' appears within the phrase 'blood red lettering'.[4] 'Blood' speaks of the body, 'blood red' of a text; an uncertain movement between the inside and outside of the body is already in play. As a switchword, 'blood' establishes an immediate point of exchange, an association between the properties of the body and of marks on a building, here Wall Street graffiti, dissolving the boundary between the body and its material surroundings. This instability of interiority frames the representation of the city itself, and of its culture, so that the experience of reading the novel can be one of total, yet compelling confusion, with repetition upon repetition of toneless uncertainty: it is sometimes day, sometimes night; Bateman is 'somewhere downtown, though I don't know where'; a taxi driver's accent could be New Jersey or Mediterranean; more surreally, creatures that are part-bird, part-rodent are sighted in Harlem making their way to midtown; main courses in fashionable restaurants look identical, though they are made of different foods; living people (Tom Cruise, Donald Trump) alternate with other fictional characters (Gordon Gekko from Oliver Stone's *Wall Street*, a character from a Jay McInerney novel).

The confusion of place and setting is enhanced in a confusion of person, framing all aspects of Bateman's existence as a fictional character, and of his co-workers on Wall Street and their girlfriends. Characters misrecognise each other continually (as they do in the mental hospital in *Shock Corridor*), mistaking one trader for another, and routinely greeting each other by different names, as in the following extract, which I am reproducing as typical of the whole book (with the exception of the violent scenes):

> After someone who I think is Hamilton Conway mistakes me for someone named Ted Owen and asks if I can get him into Petty's tonight – I tell him, 'I'll see what I can do', then turn what's left of my attention to Jean, who sits across from me in the near-empty dining room of Arcadia – after he leaves, only five of the restaurant's tables have people at them. I've ordered a J&B on the rocks. Jean's sipping a glass of white wine and talking about how what she really wants to do is 'get into merchant banking' and

> I'm thinking: Dare to dream. Someone else, Frederick Dibble, stops by and congratulates me on the Larson account and then has the nerve to say, 'Talk to you later, Saul'. But I'm in a daze, millions of miles away, and Jean doesn't notice; she's talking about a new novel she's been reading by some young author – its cover, I've seen, slathered with neon; its subject, lofty suffering. Accidentally I think she's talking about something else and I find myself saying, without really looking over at her, 'You need a tough skin to survive in this city'. (262)

At the heart of the confusion is the uncertainty over the killings. As I have said, Bateman is never caught, an absence of resolution, a narrative ambiguity which the author (presumably deliberately) sustains throughout the novel, though many clues are planted: 'Even after I tell the table, "Listen, guys, my life is a living hell", they utterly ignore me' (347). Plays on words create cross-currents of punning and slippage:

> 'You know, guys, it's not beyond my capacity to drive a lead pipe repeatedly into a girl's vagina,' I tell Van Patten and McDermott, then add, after a silence I mistake for shock, finally on their parts an acute perception of my cruelty, 'but compassionately.' 'We all know about *your* lead pipe, Bateman', McDermott says. 'Stop bragging'. (325)

And just as it is the ability of the pun to introduce ambiguity, doubling of meaning, which allows Bateman's apparent violence to go unnoticed, so the indefiniteness of the name also allows a constant sliding of identity. In one of the most moving and telling moments of the novel, Bateman 'decide[s] to make public what has been, until now, my private dementia' by confessing his killings to a colleague's answering machine, only to find that the culture defeats him by mistaking him for another trader. Unsurprisingly, that question of accountability preoccupies Bateman ('Will I ever do time?') and it has preoccupied critics and readers for years. It goes on being rehearsed in an on-line readers' debate over whether Bateman, a fictional character in the first place, 'actually' committed any of his crimes, or whether they are hallucinations (see Amazon.com 1996–2001). The following are representative examples of the 820-odd nerdish yet sincere comments by readers on Amazon's website.[5] In a mirroring of the novel's hypnotic quality, they endlessly rehearse the same range of thoughts:

> Did Bateman ever kill anyone, or was the entire novel a fiction of his imagination? If it was real, was the world as oblivious as he believed? ('Plenty to think about', 9 September 1998)

> You go crazy screaming at the book, 'Why doesn't anyone figure out what he's doing!!!' But I guess that is Bret's point, nobody cares. ('Intense, foul, anxiety-inducing reading; loved it!', 1 July 1998)

> I hated the non-ending, but with so many real crimes being unsolved I guess it was realistic. ('Bad reaction', 28 June 1998)

But it is the actual geography of New York which leads one website commentator to scepticism:

> Too many readers of this book have not recognized what an unreliable narrator Bateman is [...] New Yorkers will recognize the paths that he takes on foot and in cabs are NOT POSSIBLE. [....] If you cannot believe him about his clothes, why would you buy a ludicrous story about his killing his ex with an axe? ('Brilliant', 22 August 1997)

Well, why would you? The novel's representation of the body and body-parts is indeed disturbingly resonant of the breakdown and eruption of language well documented in psychotic states, in which any relationship to external reality is fractured. *American Psycho* can be seen as a novel of excess, of repetition and perseveration, in which the urban framework which begins the novel gradually slips to one side and organs are sliced away, existing on the page as part-objects.[6] Words then start to function like part-objects, providing disruption rather than closure (see Scott 1998). Punctuation and the absence of punctuation convey the increasing destabilization of the narrator's voice, as in the following example, from fairly late in the novel, of a chapter ending in an unstopped sentence:

> In my locker in the locker room at Xclusive [*Bateman's health club*] lie three vaginas I recently sliced out of various women I've attacked in the past week. Two are washed off, one isn't. There's a barrette clipped to one of them, a blue ribbon from Hermès tied around my favorite (370)

Here a sliced-out part of a body – normally regarded as a cavity, a space – changes into an object and is treated like hair (the barrette); becomes a gift (the ribbon). We are in fact in the realm of Freud's distinction between thing and word presentation in psychosis, in which the signifier is separated from the signified (see also Tesone 1996), and words are separated from their conventional meanings. As I have suggested, the realm that the novel gestures towards moves somewhat closer to that of clinical insanity than is made explicit in the text itself, in which business insanity is the primary trope.

At the same time, Bateman's picture of himself as part of a movie threads through the novel. Significantly, as the beat of violence (actual or imagined) steps up, and as his insanity intensifies – albeit his own awareness of that intensification fluctuates – the cinematic references become more defensively insistent. Bateman films his killings: 'this is my reality. Everything outside it is like some movie I once saw'; guns flash like in a movie; he moves 'in jump cut', 'as if this film had speeded up'. As I have suggested, in using cinematic conventions to track the narrator's intensifying disturbance, the novel calls to mind a group of works that posed large questions about American culture via a consideration of madness in its 'proper' place – the asylum; *American Psycho* reverses that frame while borrowing from it. Wall Street becomes, by implication, America's asylum.

And where have we met the confusion of name? Or the loss of identity? Or the preoccupation with murder, and unsolved murder at that? In the asylum in *Shock Corridor*, and more specifically in the 'corridor' known as the Street (ironically, the area of the hospital where patients 'who behave' are permitted to congregate). So I want to suggest a cultural background to the symbolic space that Wall Street represents in the novel. The mental hospital's role is to contain illness by creating demarcations and languages for private and public space (see, above all, Stanton and Schwartz 1954, and Goffman 1961), to re-educate the disturbed, to preserve the public domain (at the simplest level) for secondary process thought. Of course, these demarcations and languages are always at risk of breaking down, and leak out into the wider culture. Thus the unannounced 'other' of *American Psycho* – as should perhaps be inferred from the second word of the title – is the mental hospital, in a powerful return of the culturally repressed.[7] After all, the characters in *American Psycho* are doing not just cocaine, but also Parnate (a strong anti-depressant), Valium (an addictive anti-anxiety drug), Lithium (which also appears as a sorbet), Halcion (a mild hypnotic), Xanax (an anti-anxiety drug), Elavil (an anti-depressant), clonopin, Sominex, Dalmane (a hypnotic), Xanax half-hourly, and at one point 'anything'. Affect is thereby muted and distorted.[8]

To situate this 'unannounced other' a little more closely, we need to remember the feel of Sam Fuller's *Shock Corridor*. As has been observed, *Shock Corridor* is 'a film about the crazy that is crazy. It is a film made with a delirious obliviousness to the conventional need for coherence and believability' (Server 1994: 88).[9] Unlike the story of our trader-at-large, it recounts the experiences of a reporter, Johnny Barrett, who goes *into* a state mental hospital, as a patient, to try and solve a crime (and win the Pulitzer Prize in the process). Yet the film's representation of the group – that is, of the culture of an in-patient community – bears surprising similarities to the representation of Wall Street's traders in *American Psycho*: 'They each were grey, indistinct, part of a common mass' (Avallone 1963: 36). Moreover Barrett rapidly becomes enmeshed in an uncertainty of identity, a confusion of naming in the face of death: 'Maybe I'm looking at the killer right now, he thought. The faces of the men told him nothing [...] Individually each man had admitted the crime and then accused each other. One of them had even claimed he was Sloan [*the patient who was killed*]. Then they had all sworn that Sloan never existed' (36), an uncanny echo of Bateman's failure to succeed in a confession since his name signifies nothing, leads nowhere.

And in this environment of indeterminacy and disturbance, where the names given to spatial relationships in the hospital are nevertheless intended to replicate those of the outside world ('the corridor', 'the wall', 'the outside', 'the exit'), identity and memory are as elusive and uncertain as they are in *American Psycho*: 'Boden gave me the name of the killer. He named the killer and I can't remember that name!' (121). In one respect only does the 'real' prevail in the asylum: when Barrett does eventually identify the patient's killer, he has become so deranged himself that his capacity for certainty all but deserts him: '"I'm telling you I remember. Call my paper. Call Swanee. Tell him I know. I know the killer. It's Dr Cristo. No – it's Cathy. No, I killed Sloan. Yes, that's it. I killed Sloan!"' (122). And while Barrett is now to be kept 'under restraint until further orders' (122), it is Bateman who slips away unnoticed. But whereas *Shock Corridor* depicts the life of an 'official' space of madness, a low-status institution sequestered from the mainstream of culture, *American Psycho* represents Wall Street as an 'unofficial' space of madness, high-status in the wider culture but governed by similar misrecognitions, misreadings, mad wordplays, and undetected criminality.

Let us move on to the idea of *American Psycho* as a novel about criminality in the style of a documentary. The novel plays with the ambiguous relationship between hallucination and actuality, since Ellis has spoken frequently of how he researched the violence. 'Nearly all of it is based on very thorough research that I did on serial killers and sex criminals. It's very real and it was very disturbing to write' (quoted in Kmetyk 1991: 32). Ellis 'combed FBI archive material for details of serial killers and their victims and then pretty much cut-and-pasted these murders into his already completed book' (Amoore 1998: n.p.).[10] As one of the American critics observed, when the novel was first published, 'Ellis' plot line is, of course, true to criminal statistics [*on men's violence towards women*], and to our intuitive sense that terrible physical violence is all too often perpetrated by men on women' (Iyer 1991: 94). The seriousness of the issue is echoed in readers' responses, and it is striking that readers are indeed troubled and agitated about it. Again, the following website comments (Amazon.com 1996–2001) are representative:

> The story walks a fine line between fiction and true crime. It is told in such a nonchalant way that the horror creeps up on you. ('Crazy. Genius', 11 November 1998)

> Patrick himself has no remorse for killing anyone at all ... has lost every ounce of his humanity, which in itself is a comment on the money laden lifestyle of the mid 80s yuppie. ('Insightful, original and disgusting', 30 July 1998)

> I just recently was working in the 'Diamond District' of Manhattan on Fifth Avenue and I saw so many Batemans that could easily fall through the cracks. ('Brilliantly chaotic', 15 July 1998)

To stay with actuality for a moment, let us recall that about a year after *American Psycho* was published, a documentary film about criminal insanity was unbanned in the United States; similarities in the two representations are worth exploring. For over twenty years, exhibition of Frederick Wiseman's *Titicut Follies* (1967), a documentary about a Massachusetts prison-hospital, had been restricted by order of the Masachussetts courts (Anderson and Benson 1991: ix). *American Psycho* was also the subject of controversy before publication (on grounds of indecency), was in fact banned in Australia initially, and was considered for prosecution in the UK (which would have made it the first novel to be prosecuted for obscenity since Hubert Selby's *Last Exit to Brooklyn*, had the prosecution gone ahead). Both *Titicut Follies* and

American Psycho were seen as posing difficult questions about the limits of representability, in the public domain, of extreme human behaviour.

But *American Psycho* presents all readers with an additional dilemma. It is situated *as* a novel, yet its author, as we have seen, speaks freely of the actuality in its violence: 'Nearly all of it is based on very thorough research [...] It's very real and was very disturbing to write'. It is also very disturbing to read. While working on the novel I encountered personally or heard of several people – usually men, gay and straight – who could not even bear to have the book in their homes, so powerful was the sense of spatial contamination by it, a response echoed in many Amazon customer comments. Perhaps as readers we can tolerate it only as the uncertainty of a 'reality dream' or 'reality fiction' – to invoke Wiseman's term for the paradox of documentary editing: the cutting that would 'give the film an imaginative and poetic quality [...] like putting together a reality dream' (quoted in Anderson and Benson 1991: 38). And there are indeed formal parallels between the novel and the documentary which resonate in the mind, partly as 'reality', partly as a 'dream' sequence which defies belief. Speech has curiously similar qualities, whether between inmates or between traders. Just as Wall Street's traders fail to meet in speech, so do the inmates at MCI-Bridgewater. The inmates do not talk to one another, or if they do they respond affectlessly and incongruously to questions ('How come your room's messed up?' 'I mind my own business'). Perhaps most interestingly, however, the narrative structure of *American Psycho* bears an uncanny resemblance to that of its documentary predecessor, equivalent to the spatial parallels between Wall Street and the Street in *Shock Corridor*. Just as *Titicut Follies* moves from the front to the back wards, with 'progressively more helpless occupants' (Anderson and Benson 1991: 42) – interspersing these scenes with cameos from the hospital revue that gives the film its name, so *American Psycho* constructs an equivalent deterioration of mind for its central protagonist, interspersed with guys, meals, clubs, an urban round of entertainment.

Significantly, the very last image in *Titicut Follies* is of a 'young inmate-performer in stage makeup and costume, smiling and clapping; we are left with the suggestion that he will waste his life in Bridgewater' (48). Forming part of the last scene of the documentary, in which the Follies revue is ending ('So long, time to go', with cheering), it anticipates the last scene of *American Psycho,* where 'all the guys are cheering in a friendly way [...] I think it's me who says I have to return some videotapes ...yup! This is what it means to be Patrick at the end of the century'. The last sentence of *American Psycho* ('This is not an exit'), so often remarked on as a sign that Bateman's apparent liberty is impermanent, that the culture will conceal him only for so long ('so long, time to go'?), returns us to the clapping young inmate of Bridgewater. He *is* incarcerated and he may, or may not, be Bateman's cultural precursor.

To conclude. Of *American Psycho* Ellis has said 'To me it was experimental fiction', and at the end of the (actual) century Ellis gets the last word. We are back in fiction in *Glamorama*, Ellis's most recent novel, whose theme is celebrity. Patrick Bateman appears once, in an obvious acknowledgement of this fictional character's celebrity, alongside the other celebrities (living people) attending the opening of a club which begins the novel (Ellis 1999: 38). Eight years later, in real time, he has not been caught – at least within the ambiguous framework of fiction. Little has changed; he has 'weird stains' on his Armani lapels. But perhaps we are better able to understand the power of the novel which introduced him to us, by linking it with other readings of the mad culture within which Ellis believes a Bateman is produced; the body of the hero as a synecdoche for the body of American culture.

These 'weird stains' both suggest and obscure. They remain uncertain in the mind of the other, are then disavowed. I am reminded of the stunning depiction of cultural disorder which kickstarts *American Psycho*, in the words of one of Bateman's business associates, perusing the day's newspaper in a cab off Wall Street and reading aloud to Bateman:

> 'In one issue – in one issue – let's see here [...] strangled models, babies thrown from tenement rooftops, kids killed in the subway, a Communist rally, Mafia boss wiped out, Nazis' – he flips through the pages excitedly – 'baseball players with AIDS, more Mafia shit, gridlock, the homeless, various maniacs, faggots dropping like flies in the streets, surrogate mothers, the cancellation of a soap opera, kids who broke into a zoo and tortured and burned various animals alive, more Nazis [...] and the joke is, the punch line is, it's all in this city – nowhere else, just here, it sucks, whoa wait, more Nazis, gridlock, gridlock, baby-sellers, black-market babies, AIDS babies, baby junkies, building collapses on baby, maniac baby, gridlock, bridge collapses – ' [...] Then asks without looking over, 'Why aren't you wearing the worsted navy blue blazer with the gray pants?' (4)

Here it is a remark about correctness in fashion – that is, about the culture and its concern with the icon – which first signals the disavowals and affective incongruence that run throughout the novel, and which invites the reader to consider what insanity is in play, and where that insanity belongs. Is it the mind? Corporate culture? An institution? An asylum? Or, properly, a prison? It is part of the achievement of *American Psycho* that the location of that insanity remains indeterminate, lingering in the mind as a dream, if not as a nightmare.

Acknowledgements

I am grateful to Peter Straus and Becky Senior of Macmillan Ltd for giving me access to their publicity and reviews file on *American Psycho*. Thanks also to the editors of *Indeterminate Bodies* for their comments, the discussion of a draft of this paper at the Writers' Workshop at The University of Reading, March 1999, and especially to Naomi Segal for her unstinting interest in this project alongside her concerns about the novel.

Notes

1 This article was revised for publication six weeks before 11 September 2001. Because many of the Lower Manhattan streets mentioned in *American Psycho* border the World Trade Center site, any reading of the novel now is inflected by this all-too-determinate – and determinant – event. As the 'brat-pack' novelist Jay McInerney noted, in a sober, unadorned account of the terrorist attack, 'I have a felling that everything will be "before" and "after" now' (McInerney 2001). The very title of his *Guardian* feature, 'Brightness Falls', echoes McInerney's novel of the same name and, by playing with the fiction/non-fiction divide, brings us back to the impact of the event.

2 My approach to *American Psycho* and its affective impact on the reader is influenced by Evelyne Keitel's work on the psychotic text (Keitel 1989), rather than the more usual concern with the fictional serial killer as exemplar of American cultural anxiety (cf., for example, Simpson 2000). My approach to *American Psycho* and cinematic narrative is influenced by Mandy Merck's reading of Andrea Dworkin's *Intercourse* alongside the film *Fatal Attraction* (Merck 1993), and Melanie Klein's *Notes on Citizen Kane* (Klein with Introduction by Mulvey 1998).

3 The extreme sexual violence in the book led Ellis's initial publisher, Simon and Schuster, to cancel his contract at the last moment, and the book was published by Random House in 1991, generating a furore on both indecency and feminist grounds. The author received death threats and was in hiding for a time. Ten years later, the book has achieved 'contemporary classic' status and a film of it has been made (Harron, dir. 2000). It is outside the scope of this chapter to explore the relationship between the novel and the screen adaptation, but suffice to note that Harron's well-received adaptation paradoxically made *watchable* a book that is almost literally impossible to *read* (see especially Blake Morrison's review of the film: 'there's something – pain, terror, disgust, authenti-

cally raw emotion – missing from its core' (Morrison 2000)). See also Peter Bradshaw's capsule review: 'Mary Harron has transformed Bret Easton Ellis's showy, explicit novel into a stylish and unexpectedly witty piece of cinema' (Bradshaw 2000); and, finally, Ellis's own comments about the commodification of *American Psycho* (Ellis 2000).

4 'ABANDON ALL HOPE YE WHO ENTER HERE is scrawled in blood red lettering on the side of the Chemical Bank near the corner of Eleventh and First ...' (opening sentence of *American Psycho*: 3)

5 At the time of final revision of this article (July 2001).

6 Bion (1959: 102) represents the part-object relationship as 'not with the anatomical structures only but with function [...] with feeding, poisoning, living, hating' (cited in Hinshelwood 1991 ['Part-objects'], 378).

7 Cf. also Richards 1999, for a discussion of the traditional segregation of mental disorder.

8 See Shader 1986 for an account of psychotropic medication at the time the novel was written.

9 As Sam Fuller has said, regarding his intentions for *Shock Corridor*: 'I thought I could represent some things about the country, how it was like an insane asylum' (Server 1994: 45). Martin Scorsese has observed, of the film: 'Every form of American insanity was represented [...] The metaphor was clear. America was on its way to becoming an insane asylum' (Scorsese 1995). See also Malcolm 1999.

10 Sonny Mehta, president of Knopf, who published *American Psycho* in the USA, for example, called him 'a significant writer writing in a documentary manner about a particular segment of American society... [The book] does reflect something about our times' (quoted in Kmetyk 1991: 32).

Works cited

Amazon.com 1996-2001 Customer comments on Bret Easton Ellis, *American Psycho (*http://www.amazon. com)

Amoore 1998 T. Amoore, 'The most hated man in America' (*The Express*, 9 July)

Anderson and Benson 1991 C. Anderson and T. Benson, *Documentary Dilemmas: Frederick Wiseman's Titicut Follies* (Carbondale, Il: Southern Illinois University Press)

Avallone 1963 M. Avallone, *Shock Corridor* [novelization of Sam Fuller's screenplay] (New York: Belmont Books)

Bion 1959 W. Bion, 'Attacks on Linking', *International Journal of Psycho-Analysis*, 40: 308–15

Bradshaw 2000 P. Bradshaw, 'Top 10 Films' (*The Guardian*, 21 April), G2, 15

Caruth 1995 C. Caruth (ed.), *Explorations in Memory* (Baltimore, MD and London: Johns Hopkins University Press)

Ellis 1991 Bret Easton Ellis, *American Psycho: a Novel* (New York: Vintage, London: Picador)

Ellis 1999 Bret Easton Ellis, *Glamorama* (New York: Knopf. London: Picador)

Ellis 2000 Bret Easton Ellis, 'American Psychos, Fur and Violence are OK Now', in *Harper's Bazaar* (February), extracted in *The Editor* (*The Guardian*, 3 March), 20

Goffman 1961 E. Goffman, *Asylums: Essays on the Social Situation of Mental Patients and Other Inmates* (New York: Bantam)

Hinshelwood 1991 R. D. Hinshelwood, *A Dictionary of Kleinian Thought*, 2nd edn (London: Free Association Books)

Hoban 1990 P. Hoban, '"Psycho"drama' (*New York*, 17 December), 33–7

Iyer 1991 P. Iyer, 'Are Men Really So Bad?' (*Time*, 22 April), 94

Keitel 1989 E. Keitel, *Reading Psychosis: Readers, Texts and Psychoanalysis* (Oxford: Blackwell)

Klein with Introduction by Mulvey 1998 Melanie Klein [n.d.] with Introduction by Laura Mulvey, 'Notes on *Citizen Kane*', in Lyndsey Stonebridge and John Phillips (eds), *Reading Melanie Klein* (London: Routledge)

Kmetyk 1991 T. Kmetyk, 'When Killing is too Ghastly for Words' (*The Guardian*, 15 January), 32

Malcolm 1999 Derek Malcolm '"He's got this crazy idea..." A Century of Films. Derek Malcolm's 100 Greatest Movies. This Week, number 25: *Shock Corridor*' (*The Guardian*, 8 July)

McInerney 2001 Jay McInerney, 'Brightness Falls' (*The Guardian,* 15 September)

Merck 1993 Mandy Merck, 'The Fatal Attraction of *Intercourse*', in *Perversions: Deviant Readings* (London: Virago)

Morrison 2000 B. Morrison, 'What Once Seemed so Controversial is Now Stylish, but Not Very Scary', review of Mary Harron's *American Psycho* (*The Independent on Sunday*, 23 April), Culture: 3

Richards 1999 B. Richards, 'Authority and Popularity in Britain 2000: a Psychosocial Analysis': unpublished Inaugural Lecture, University of East London Department of Human Relations, March

Scorsese 1995 M. Scorsese, 'A Personal Journey with Martin Scorsese Through American Movies' (Channel 4 TV, 4 June).

Scott 1998 A. Scott, 'Language as a Skin', keynote paper presented at 'Trauma and Memory in Cross-Cultural Perspective' conference, Sydney. Revised version in Jill Bennett and Rosanne Kennedy (eds), *World Memory* (Basingstoke: Palgrave, forthcoming)

Server 1994 L. Server, *Sam Fuller: Life is a Battleground. A Critical Study, with Interviews, a Filmography and a Bibliography* (Jeffers, NC: McFarland)

Shader 1986 R. I. Shader (ed.), *Manual of Psychiatric Therapeutics*, 16th printing (Boston: Little Brown)

Simpson 2000 Philip L. Simpson, *Psycho Paths: Tracking the Serial Killer through Contemporary American Film and Fiction* (Illinois: Southern Illinois University Press)

Stanton and Schwartz 1954 A. Stanton and M. Schwartz, *The Mental Hospital: a Study of Institutional Participation in Psychiatric Illness and Treatment* (New York: Basic)

Target 1998 M. Target, 'Book Review Essay: the Recovered Memory Controversy', *International Journal of Psycho-Analysis*, 79 (5): 1015ff.

Tesone 1996 J. Tesone, 'Multi-lingualism, Word Presentations, Thing Presentations and Psychic Reality', *International Journal of Psycho-Analysis*, 77, 871–81

5
Determined Indeterminacy in the Work of Lari Pittman

Roger Cook[1]

> There is a particularly lovely/ugly fish that swims the western coastal waters. It is the Californian grouper. As a fish, it privileges practice over theory. The supposed inimitability of gender is contested by its own complete periodic transformation. Specimen at the San Francisco Aquarium, coincidentally close in age to myself, is in its third sex change. Female to male to female again. Such polymorphousness, possible in the oceans, is absolutely threatening on land – most pointedly in the land of art.

This was said by the Los Angeleno painter Lari Pittman in a live panel at the School of Visual Arts, New York on the evening of 26 March 1996. And he continued in a similar vein:

> Name it, play it, refine it, and stick to it. Suffice it to say that this is the forty-something mantra for identity. My ongoing ambivalence to this litany is its uncanny mimicry of the linearity of modernism.
>
> Having being born in Los Angeles in 1952, spending my formative youth in South America, and coming of age as an artist in southern California, heavy investment in any polemic arising from the friction of oppositional dynamics remains baffling if not simply puritan. Journalistic criticism from coast to coast offers only binary bipolar reactions. (http://adaweb.walkerart.org/context/events/strange_days/pittman.html)

As a racially mixed gay artist, Lari Pittman has a highly developed sensitivity to the dominant social and cultural imperatives he experienced in the American art world from his student days in southern

California. Like most innovative and original artists working within the tradition of the avant-garde, his whole artistic struggle can be seen as a struggle against determination by social and cultural imperatives. One of those imperatives has been *heteropolar sex/gender dimorphism.*

Anthropologists of sexuality, like Gilbert Herdt, are among those who have rapidly become aware of the inadequacy (the binary reductionism) of these terms to describe the complexity and variety of human sexual experience and its practices and pleasures. Herdt writes:

> By *sexual dimorphism* is typically meant a phylogenetically inherited structure of two types of human and sexual nature, male and female, present in all human groups [...] much of the historical and anthropological literature suggests that this emphasis on dimorphism reveals a deeper stress on 'reproduction' as a paradigm of science and society. The reproductive paradigm remains prominent today in studies that go far beyond evolutionary thinking, to such an extent that I will refer to this as a 'principle of sexual dimorphism', since it is represented as if it were a uniform law of nature like gravity. That is, it is believed canonical that, everywhere and at all times, sex and/or gender exist for reproduction of individuals and species. In short, reproduction, as suggested in the critiques formulated by feminist and gay and lesbian scholars for a generation, has been the 'real object' of normative science, both in biology and social science, for much of the past century. (Herdt 1994: 25–6)

And in an earlier text he writes:

> We must resist the strong tendency in Western culture to dualize [...]: notice how easily our discourse converts subjects into objects in the Western tradition, as when same-sex practices of any kind, playful or committed, are labeled 'homosexuality'. By comparison, the form of same-sex desire in old China did not nominalize the subject or objectify the practice in the same way. The ancient Chinese spoke of what persons 'do' or 'enjoy' rather than what they 'are' as essentialized objects. (Herdt 1993: xii)

It is precisely this that Lari Pittman protests. Doubtless Pittman's statement will seem exaggerated to many in the art world to this day. It is still difficult for those embedded in the binary reductionism of the heteropolar gender dimorphic norms to really appreciate how it feels to be positioned outside this naturalized 'cultural ontology':

> By cultural ontology I mean the sense in which reality is phenomenologically formed by active participation – 'lived experience' – that defines the kind of world it is; the categories of meaning that are formative of that world; and the kinds of persons who inhabit it. Such ontologies are critical in the effort to define the same-sex eroticism distinctive of a particular people. (Herdt 1993: xii)

This desire to be free of social categorization and cultural determination is essential to the history of the avant-garde and is common to both advanced art and sexual liberation.

As Pierre Bourdieu has shown in *The Rules of Art*, from the end of the nineteenth century 'avant-garde' artists sought freedom from social determination. This can be seen as one of the prime motivations for making art: the utopian wish to be able to become self-determined: to be a *self-created* creator. Bourdieu quotes Flaubert from a letter of 1886:

> That is why I love Art. There, at least, everything is freedom, in this world of fictions. There, one is satisfied, does everything, is both a king and his subject, active and passive, victim and priest. (Bourdieu 1992: 26)

As Bourdieu indicates, art 'abolishes the determinations, constraints and limits which are constitutive of social existence' for 'to exist socially means to occupy a determined position in the social structure and to bear the marks of it' (27). An iconographic image of the freedom from determination in art has been that of the saltimbanques, the street acrobats, beloved of Picasso and Rilke. They make their appearance in Pittman's major series of paintings, ONCE A NOUN, NOW A VERB, trapezing through the space of the city of LA (Fig. 5.1).

The first determination that avant-garde 'apostles of freedom' struggle against is that of economic necessity: a studio must be rented, materials purchased and work made. In Pittman's case, on leaving art college he felt unable to fit into the determinations of the art and art educational field, which – it may be difficult to realize from our present-day perspective – were, at this time, normatively and oppressively straight, and in which, not unnaturally, as a gay man, he did not feel at ease. Instead he earned his living working in the interior decoration trade, a *commercial* trade, pejoratively associated with homosexuality, and traditionally looked down on by the *fine art* tradition. Pittman has been happy to bring these craft skills into the realm of fine art. In fact, as we know, the traffic between skills from the 'large-scale field of cultural production' (graphics, advertising, decoration etc.) and the 'restricted field' has been highly productive in the history of modern art and culture.

There are also the sociogenetic determinations, within the inherited language of art itself. As Matisse said: 'A talented artist cannot do just as he likes [...] We are not the masters of what we produce. It is imposed on us' (Flam 1973: 74), echoing Flaubert's: 'One does not write what one wants' (Bourdieu 1996: 3). Matisse and Flaubert refer to the socio-cultural imperatives of their respective times. If one wants to write or paint what one wants, then one must work through the artistic determinations of the day to transform and 'negate' them. A talented artist enters the field at a particular temporal and geographical moment, and as George Kubler wrote many years ago, is fortunate if he or she is able to make a 'good' entrance:

> 'Good' or 'bad' entrances are more than matters of position in the sequence. They also depend upon the union of temperamental endowments with specific positions. Every position is keyed, as it were, to the action of a certain range of temperaments. When a specific temperament interlocks with a favorable position, the fortunate individual can extract from the situation a wealth of previously unimagined consequences. This achievement may be denied to other persons, as well as to the same person at a different time. Thus every birth can be imagined as set into play on two wheels of fortune, one governing the allotment of its temperament, and the other ruling its entrance into a sequence. (Kubler 1962: 7)

By virtue of the union of his specific temperament, that of a feminized gay-Latino man, with a specific geographically located moment in the historical sequence of the history of painting in North America, Lari Pittman has been able to 'extract from the situation a wealth of previously unimagined consequences' and overcome the hegemonic social determinations in the socio-cultural field which would have constrained him. He has found that relative autonomy and freedom from necessity (economic and social) which has enabled him to invent his own particular visual language: to intervene in history and effect a transformation, which will have immense repercussions in the field. He has successfully challenged a number of *doxas* in this field.

Pittman took up painting at a moment when it was being seriously challenged by other avant-garde practices in the field of contemporary art in the 1970s. As he has said: 'it was clearly a moment when there was not much evidence of painting practices, but for me it became an elected practice'. In fact he was a graduate student at a very particular moment, in a very particular place, southern California, where there was a radical shift in the field; to this day he teaches alongside some of the artists who brought about this radical shift. He is a professor at UCLA, where he teaches art alongside Paul McCarthy, Chris Burden, Mike Kelley and Charles Ray, artists who have made considerable contributions to the development of contemporary art, not in relation to painting, but to the 'expanded field' of sculpture and installation art.

Pittman stands in a unique position, in contributing something fundamental to the understanding of the development of painting, at a very particular juncture in the history of twentieth-century art. He has been making paintings or as he now prefers to call them 'painted objects' or 'tableaux' since the 1970s, the period when these so-called 'postmodernist' forms of art practice – performance, conceptual, video and installation art – were initiated. These forms challenged the dual hegemonic determinations of sculptural and painterly practice that had previously reigned in the international art world. Pittman was a graduate student at Cal Arts, a famous school in the 1970s for the propagation of these diversified forms of art practice. This was also the school in which the issue of gender in the practice of art first made a strong appearance with the initiative of the 1972–5 Feminist Art Program, run by Judy Chicago and Miriam Shapiro. Shapiro initiated what became known as the 'Pattern and Decoration Movement' (Broude and Garrard 1994: 208–25). It celebrated pattern and decoration as essentially feminine and understood their pejorative connotations in the history of modernism as a heterosexist male exclusion. Whilst Pittman did not participate in the Feminist Art Program because he was male, he was nevertheless very aware of these issues and enjoyed discussing them with women artists at Cal Arts, many of whom remain to this day his friends. From them he learned that there was an alternative history of painting represented by neglected women artists, like Frida Kahlo, Florine Stettheimer and Leonora Carrington. As an artist who happened to be gay he was interested in addressing these exclusions relating to gender. In fact, he was in a somewhat embarrassing position, since this was the time of a historically necessary gender essentialism on the part of feminists, from which he felt excluded. On the other hand, as he has said, he was immensely invested in the issues of pattern and decoration through the 'lens of his sexuality' (Cook 1998). Furthermore, he had never been attracted to some of the more muscular heterosexual art practices around conceptualism and performance art (as practiced by Vito Acconci and Chris Burden); on the contrary he had always espoused the relatively feminized craft-based practice of painting. Like the women, he was and remains positively invested in painting *as craft*, something pejoratively associated in American culture with the domestic and the feminine. In fact as Christopher Knight pointed out in his catalogue essay for Lari Pittman's first major British show: in 1977, Ann Douglas in her important book *The Feminization of American Culture* traces the history of how, in the wake of the civil war and the industrial revolution, the arts in America, through what she describes as clerical disestablishment and feminine disestablishment, became increasingly associated with the domestic and the feminine. So, as Knight writes:

> By the turn of the century identification of the arts with feminine feeling was complete. (To compensate, male artists tended toward a hyper-masculinized expression.) In the popular subconscious the identification has remained in force ever since.
>
> That is, it has remained subconscious until now. Pittman's paintings shove it into the foreground [...] for the past five years he has been unpacking painting's engendered baggage more joyfully, more wickedly, more beautifully than any other artist you can name.
>
> He has restored American painting to the cultural significance it had lost by the 1970s, with the demise of modernism. These are paintings that make some people happy and some people anxious and other people both – and who could ask for more from art? (Bayley 1998: unpaginated)

Pittman continued to paint at a time when amongst the dominant elite more radical and apparently 'avant-garde' photo-conceptual and performance-based practices were in favour: the practice of painting was frowned upon as not only conservative but also highly feminized, and therefore degraded. Awkwardly, he persisted in perversely painting highly crafted decorative works. The earlier works were more invested in forms of decorative abstraction than the later overtly representational work, the allusions to sexuality implicit rather than explicit, for example the little painting on paper *Headhunter* (1982) which exudes a camp theatricality (Fig. 5.2).

It was in 1985 that Pittman's work took on a new insistence. On 3 July, 1985, Pittman suprised a night-time intruder in his home and was shot twice in the abdomen, his intestine punctured in over one hundred places. He was hospitalized for over five weeks and required extensive surgery. Toward the end of that time, his older brother Oscar died unexpectedly of a burst aorta. Rocked by these events and profoundly weak from his injuries, he only returned to work at the encouragement and insistence of his partner, Roy Dowell.

This struggle finally led in 1992–4 to his making what may prove to be one of the masterworks of the latter half of the twentieth- century as far as painting is concerned: UNTITLED # 1 (A DECORATED CHRONOLOGY OF INSISTENCE AND RESIGNATION) 1992 (Fig. 5.3). This is a work which I believe will go down in history, in terms of its subject, its formal complexity and the originality and skill that went into its fabrication, as comparable (I believe, without exaggeration) with the great public works of Picasso, Miró, Léger or Jackson Pollock. Its subject is the highly ambitious one of the 'cycle of life'. It has a traditional narrative structure consisting of four 'moments' painted on four mahogany panels. In the first 'moment' an indeterminately gendered figure appears, a figure with both male and female attributes. In the first panel the figure says 'HEY!' to gain attention and initiate something. Then, in the second panel, there's a response: it's 'F.Y', either 'for you' (if the response is positive) or 'fuck you' (if the response is negative). Then, in the third panel, it is 'S.O.S' (Save Our Souls), panic in the face of death represented by the painted noose and fear of death represented by loss of control of the bowels. And then, in the fourth panel, before the panic is resolved, death 'R.I.P.' (Rest In Peace). Then there is a hinted repeat of the cycle again with the 'HEY' signs appearing again in the bottom of the picture. But the artist has said that none of this is meant as morbid: 'That is why it's a "decorated" chronology [...] though it's a discussion of death, it's an ebullient, highly decorated one.' This painting participates in the topsy-turvy world of the carnivalesque as described by Mikhail Bakhtin (Bakhtin 1965). Pittman has drawn attention to the Latin American love of simultaneity and hybridity in his work: remembering how at Christmas his Latin American grandmother would be simultaneously joyful and tearful when she declared how happy she was that all the family were together and how sad she was that they would soon be parted! This 'bittersweet' simultaneity of tears and laughter and pleasure and pain is fundamental to the work and to its Bakhtinian counter-hegemonic chronotopes of the carnivalesque. Pittman works in series and in the 'Like You' series that followed that of the 'Decorated Chronologies' campy comedic, sexually polymorphous hermaphroditic pixies appeared (Fig. 5.4). Pittman has said: 'I completely understand what my sexuality is but I don't have a clue as to what my gender is and never have' (Brown 1996: 74), and in the public interview I conducted with him in Manchester (Cook 1998) he said:

> Latino culture is patriarchal and very macho, but outsiders don't understand that within that rubric there's actually tremendous elasticity for male identity. So in other words the idea of the queen, the prissy male, the dandy and so forth, actually are allowed and accorded position and status. That aspect of my culture allowed and emphasized a predisposition.

Pittman's paintings are sometimes thought to be kitsch, but in the same interview he made an important distinction between his evaluation of camp and that of kitsch:

> Kitsch is a problematic term. I would rather use camp. Kitsch is used sloppily. Camp and kitsch are very precise. Kitsch is when you elicit pleasure based on slumming it, a gaze related to class structure. Camp is where the language of the paintings is invested [...] So the negotiation is: 'I know that you know that I know that you know that I know that you know' – that becomes a primary moment. Whereas kitsch is all about distancing and degradation. I think the language of camp calls for an elasticity and actually taps into the potential polymorphousness of any individual culture.

The paintings are also sometimes thought to wilfully elicit the idea of 'bad taste', a notion the artist challenges. He is fond of quoting from his friend the critic Dave Hickey a statement in his essay on Liberace 'A Rhinestone as Big as the Ritz': 'Bad taste is real taste; and good taste is the residue of someone else's privilege' (Hickey 1997). And Pittman says:

> I think it's not that you adamantly privilege bad taste. It's just simply that it is a call to the roots of authenticity. In the sense, that at any given point, bad taste at least signals authenticity, as opposed to borrowed, extrapolated, or inherited taste. But the works themselves are not bad taste. I think the construction of bad taste and the construction of the bad boy in the art world go hand in hand. In other words, the way this work looks is not meant to be transgressive. It's actually meant to be beautiful. It might take from its roots ideas that might be located in culture's bad taste, but it is not ironic, in that it indulges in bad taste so that the audience

> gets all worked up about it. I think that is actually a conservative bad boy manoeuvre. Bad taste has nothing to do with aesthetics for me. What we are talking about is quotidian taste, re-orchestrating it, re-representing it.

Pittman has a very acute understanding of his position in relation to the heterosexual 'bad boy' male artist's investment in dysfunctionality:

> I cannot help but look at representations of dysfunctionality as straight identity work. I can't afford publicly and culturally to indulge in representations of dysfunctionality. The world couldn't care less and would not give it the time of day or centralize it in elite critical discussion. So in the same way that people endlessly talk about gay identity politics, gay identity in work I want to return the conversation and say, let's openly out heterosexuals. Forget about outing homosexuals. I want to out heterosexuality, because actually it isn't outed. And so I have to look at what representations have become privileged both critically and commercially and given my generation, there's an abundance of both critically and commercially privileged representations of dysfunctionality. I just can't leave it at that. I have to say, well, let's start naming it, let's place it, let's give that dysfunctionality a cultural location. Where exactly is it located in culture? And I must say I quickly deduce, that is straight identity. Straight identity can actually, because of its privilege, luxuriate in its dysfunctionality. I don't have that option at all. So that's I think a differentiation with a lot of the kind of representations of my peer group.

In spite of his wondering whether the camp aesthetic may socially prove to be the work's undoing as far as its cultural distribution is concerned, the work is undoubtedly invested with hope, the kind of realistic hope that the utopian philosopher Ernst Bloch spoke of in a 1964 conversation with Theodor Adorno:

> Hope is not confidence. If it could not be disappointed, it would not be hope. That is part of it. Otherwise, it would be cast in a picture. It would let itself be bargained down. It would capitulate and say, that is what I had hoped for. Thus, hope is critical and can be disappointed. However, hope still nails a flag on the mast, even in decline, in that the decline is not accepted, even when this decline is still very strong. Hope is not confidence. Hope is surrounded by

> dangers, and it is the consciousness of danger and at the same time the determined negation of that which continually makes the opposite of the hoped-for object possible.
>
> Possibility is not hurray-patriotism. The opposite is also in the possible. The hindering element is also in the possible. The hindrance is implied in hope aside from the capacity to succeed. But I employ the word 'process,' which has many meanings – chemical, medical, legal, and religious. There would not be any process at all if there were not something that should not be so. In conclusion, I would like to quote a phrase, a very simple one, strangely enough from Oscar Wilde: 'A map of the world that does not include Utopia is not even worth glancing at.' (Bloch 1988: 16–17)

The joyous figure of the campily comedic, indeterminate, polymorphously pleasured hermaphroditic pixie in the work of Lari Pittman is a cultural cipher of such hope for our time. Pittman's paintings problematize the dimorphism of Western patriarchal models of sex and gender, just as his racial hybridity problematizes its models of ethnic identity. Pittman promotes plurality, fluidity and flux.

Whilst preparing this essay, I happened upon an interesting new book on Paul Gauguin entitled *Gauguin's Skirt* by Stephen Eisenman, professor of art history at the Occidental College, Los Angeles. In a chapter entitled 'Sex in Tahiti', Eisenman discusses the by-now-common anthropological understanding of non-dimorphic sex and gender positioning in many non-Western cultures.

> The result of these [...] studies has been to dismantle any universal categories of women and men, and to erect in their place a set of diverse, polymorphous and transient structures of meaning permitting an increased understanding of the specific modalities of patriarchal power and sexual oppression
>
> Once the 'fictitious unity' of sex was undermined, and the tendency to view sex and gender as binaries was disrupted, the historical and ethnographic record began to yield previously unexpected evidence of sexual diversity and creativity from all parts of the globe and all places in time. Homosexuality, lesbianism and transvestism departed from the circumscribed precincts of *psychopathia sexualis* and began to be understood cross-culturally as manifestations of love, relation, work, art and even kin-group solidarity. (Eisenman 1997: 94)

In Tahiti, for example, there are the *mahu*, first described as early as 1787 by James Morrison, a mutineer from HMS *Bounty*:

> [In Tahiti] they have a set of men called *Mahu*. These men are in some respects like the eunuchs in India but are not castrated. They never cohabit with women, but live as they do. They pick their beards out and dress as women, dance and sing with them and are effeminate in their voice. They are generally excellent hands at making and painting cloth, making mats, and every other women's employment. (Eisenman 1997: 104)

Eisenman goes on to suggest the important social function that the Polynesian *mahus* along with their third sex counterparts, the *berdaches* of the American Indian south-west and the *hijras* of India, perform; stating that they are at once valued members of their communities and the butt of numerous jokes. They are like the comic and the fool: 'liminal figures who may be said to mediate, patrol or negotiate relations between different families, adjacent communities, and natives and foreigners'.

Negotiating the relationship between differences is indeed an important cultural role, and one that the campy, comic, bittersweet, love-sexi, utopian and publicly homosexual paintings of Lari Pittman perform only too well. Furthermore this is very much in line with the thinking of recent feminists and queer theorists. In the introduction to their anthology *Sexy Bodies: the Strange Carnalities of Feminism,* Elizabeth Grosz and Elspeth Probyn suggest:

> a quite wild and disconcerting idea: that perhaps sex, and for that matter queer, could function as *verbs* rather than as *nouns* or adjectives. Conjugated, they could be fully conceived as activities and processes, rather than objects or impulses, as movements rather than identities, as lines more than locations, as motions of making rather than as forms of expression. (Grosz and Probyn 1995: x)

Their words betray the influence of the anti-oedipal 'schizoanalysis' of Gilles Deleuze and Félix Guattari (Deleuze and Guattari 1972) who seek to deterritorialize the heteropolar dimorphism, of the oedipalized nuclear family of capitalism which leads to the inequality and domination of women and homosexuals. In an interview with George Stambolian, Guattari says:

> I would say that each time the body is emphasized in a situation – by dancers, by homosexuals, etc. – something breaks with the dominant semiotics that crush these semiotics of the body. In heterosexual relations as well, when a man becomes body, he becomes feminine. In a certain way, a successful heterosexual relation becomes homosexual

> and feminine [...] I would say first that there is only one sexuality, it is neither masculine, nor feminine, nor infantile; it is something that is ultimately flow, body. It seems to me that in true love there is always a moment when the man is no longer a man. This does not mean that he becomes a woman. But because of her alienation woman is relatively closer to the situation of desire. And in a sense, perhaps from the point of view of representation, to accede to desire implies for a man first a position of homosexuality as such and second a feminine becoming. (Stambolian 1979: 58)

One of the positive lessons that both homosexuality and heterosexuality might learn is the ability to engage in more fluid and equal erotic exchanges in which both partners play out active and passive roles. The invasiveness and positive destructiveness of individual selfhood that is inherent in the violent bliss of sexual activity is ideally experienced as a *mutual* one in which both partners feel equally shattered and united in *la petite mort* of orgasm.

Perhaps the time has come for a new critical and realistic assessment of the hope of artists who, like Lari Pittman, continue to believe that art, through enjoyment, has that 'miraculous and needy' ability to help bring about a social transfiguration of the long and painful history of culturally and socially oppressive sex and gender dimorphism in Western culture. Pittman's work demonstrates that 'a high level of artistry is the only lastingly effective form of propaganda' (Indiana 1996: 195) that 'through a systematic decentring of desire [...] will lead to soft subversions and imperceptible revolutions that will eventually change the face of the world' (Guattari: 1996).

Note

1 Lari Pittman (b.1952) is a well-known artist in the field of contemporary art, especially in the United States. In 1996–7 he had major retrospective exhibitions of his paintings at the LA County Museum, Contemporary Arts Museum, Houston, Corcoran Gallery of Art, Washington, and of his drawings at UCLA at the Armand Hammer Museum of Art and Cultural Center, University of California, University Art Museum, University of California, Santa Barbara. In 1998–9 a retrospective exhibition of his paintings was shown at the Spacex Gallery, Exeter, the Cornerhouse, Manchester, the ICA, London and the Centre d'Art Contemporain, Geneva. An exhibition of recent works on paper was shown at the Grassi Gallery, London in 1998. He is represented by Regen Projects, Los Angeles and the Barbara Gladstone Gallery, New York.

Works cited

Bakhtin 1965 M. M. Bakhtin, *Rabelais and his World,* first published Moscow, translated by H. Iswolsky (Cambridge, Mass: MIT Press, 1984)

Bayley 1998 Paul Bayley (ed.) *Lari Pittman* (Manchester: Cornerhouse Publications)

Bloch 1988 'Something's Missing: a Discussion between Ernst Bloch and Theodor W. Adorno on the Contradiction of Utopian Longing', in Ernst Bloch, *The Utopian Function of Art and Literature: Selected Essays,* translated by Jack Zipes and Frank Mecklenburg (Cambridge Massachusetts: MIT Press)

Bourdieu 1992 Pierre Bourdieu, *Les Règles de l'art* (Paris: Seuil), translated as *The Rules of Art* by Susan Emanuel (Cambridge: Polity Press, 1996)

Broude and Garrard1994 Norma Broude and Mary D. Garrard, *The Power of Feminist Art: Emergence, Impact and Triumph of the American Feminist Art Movement* (London: Thames & Hudson)

Brown 1996 Elizabeth A. Brown, *Lari Pittman Drawings* (Seattle and London: University of Washington Press)

Cook 1998 Roger Cook, unpublished interview with Lari Pittman

Deleuze and Guattari 1972 Gilles Deleuze and Félix Guattari, *Anti-Oedipus: Capitalism and Schizophrenia* (Minneapolis: University of Minnesota), trans R. Hurley, M. Seem and H. R. Lane from *L'Anti-Oedipe* (Paris: Minuit)

Eisenman 1997 Stephen F. Eisenman, *Gauguin's Skirt* (London: Thames & Hudson)

Flam 1973 J. D. Flam, *Matisse on Art* (London and New York: Phaidon)

Grosz and Probyn 1995 Elizabeth Grosz and Elspeth Probyn (eds), *Sexy Bodies: the Strange Carnalities of Feminism* (London and New York: Routledge)

Guattari 1996 Félix Guattari, *Soft Subversions* (New York: Semiotext(e))

Herdt 1993 Gilbert Herdt (ed.), *Ritualized Homosexuality in Melanesia* (Berkeley LA and London: Columbia University Press)

Herdt 1994 Gilbert Herdt (ed.), *Third Sex, Third Gender: Beyond Sexual Dimorphism in Culture and Society* (New York: Zone Books)

Hickey 1997 Dave Hickey, *Air Guitar: Essays on Art & Democracy* (Los Angeles: Art Issues Press)

Indiana 1996 Gary Indiana, *Let it Bleed: Essays 1985–1995* (London and New York: Serpent's Tail)

Kubler 1962 George Kubler, *The Shape of Time: Remarks on the History of Things* (Yale: New Haven and London)

Stambolian 1979 Félix Guattari, 'A Liberation of Desire: an Interview with George Stambolian' in George Stambolian and Elaine Marks (eds), *Homosexualities and French Literature: Cultural Contexts/Critical Texts* (Ithaca and London: Cornell University Press)

6

'Then some had rather it were *She* than *I*': Sexing the Textual Body

Naomi Segal

> The literary object has no other substance than the subjectivity of the reader: Raskolnikov's waiting is my waiting, which I lend him; without the reader's impatience he would be nothing but a collection of languishing signs. His hatred for the police magistrate interrogating him is my hatred, stimulated and captured by signs, and as for the magistrate himself, he would not exist without the hatred I feel towards him through Raskolnikov; this hatred animates him, it is his flesh.
>
> (Sartre 1948: 95)

> by a reversal intrinsic to the imaginary object, it is not [Raskolnikov's] actions that provoke my indignation or admiration but my indignation and admiration which give solidity and objectivity to his actions.
>
> (Sartre 1948: 100)

This is what Sartre wrote in 1947 on the subject of bodies and books. Raskolnikov, the magistrate, their actions and the sentiments I feel about or through them all exist only as effects of my assent. Their bodies are the product of my body, becoming 'flesh' only if I animate them, and stimulated by signs which without my 'freedom' (101) would be merely 'languishing' marks on a page. Reading, in this schema, is a 'pact of generosity between author and reader' (105),[1] based not on an abstract concept of liberty but on the 'free gift of [my][2] whole person, with its passions and prejudices, its likes and dislikes, its sexual temperament and scale of values' (100). And if 'a message is ultimately a soul made object' (82) this is because 'we are inside language as we are inside our body' (71). Two bodies, almost certainly absent to each other in time and space but not unaware of each other's crucial virtual existence, collude to produce a third body, the person in the text.

Half a generation later, he describes the books in his grandfather's study:

> Well before I knew how to read, I revered them, those standing stones; upright or leaning, packed close together like bricks on the library shelves or spaced out nobly in avenues of menhirs, I knew that our family's prosperity somehow depended upon them. [...] My grandfather – normally so clumsy that my mother had to button his gloves – would handle these cultural objects with the skill of an officiating priest. [...] Sometimes I drew near to gaze at these boxes that split open like oysters and I would discover the nakedness of their internal organs, livid mildewed leaves, slightly swollen, covered in a tracery of black veins, which drank up ink and smelt of mushrooms. (Sartre 1964: 37)

Here the body re-enters the text, securely ironized by the sixty-year-old autobiographer (whose lifelong aversion to oysters and mushrooms is well documented), as the affect invested in books by a child whose animism depends on his analphabetism. Because he cannot read he reads the patriarch's books as the solid stones on which family fortunes depend, the sacred objects of a writer's graceful mastery which, however, when the child approaches them break open, with a shock, in a primal scene of the discovery of the uncanny – the gate to the mother's inner body.

Both these images will be essential in the discussion that follows. From the point of view of sweet reason, I find Sartre's first representation of the process of reading admirable; but we also need the second representation in order to incorporate what is at stake when we draw near to the body in the library. Affect, fantasy, horror and seduction attend every act of reading, all the more if we accept that to 'be inside' (or to 'have entered') a thing of language is like being inside (or entering) a body. In 1853 Flaubert contrasted the travail of writing two very different books: '*Saint Antoine* did not cost me a quarter of the intellectual tension that *Bovary* demands. It spilled out of me [*C'était un déversoir*]: I had nothing but pleasure in the writing, and the eighteen months I spent in writing its 500 pages were the most deeply voluptuous of my whole life. Consider then, every minute I am having to get under *skins* that are antipathetic to me' (Flaubert 1980: 297). Man and boy, writer and reader, here both treat the text as a woman they hesitate to enter. Any approach to a text is a fantasmatic adventure of the body.

For this reason, however uncomfortable it may make you or me feel, I will use the first-person singular to represent the reader in the rest of this essay. I will look in turn at three first-person narratives whose textual figures raise questions of how we read bodily indeterminacy in a text. The three authors are in ascending order writers whom I know well and in descending order writers with whom I have sexual-political sympathies.[3] In turn their fictions problematise the reading of sex, gender and sexuality.[4] I will suggest, first, that the effort to read any one of these categories involves assumptions about the two others; and second, that the ways in which such indeterminacy works will depend on a number of implied theories of difference.

*

> Some, indeed, will have it, that when you read any thing that is very pleasant; as for example, the burning of the Castle and *Silvia*'s being carried in a swoon out of the House in the arms of *Birague*; her being in the Closet with *Englesac*: It is more pleasant still to have it in the first person, by reason of an application, and a certain interim [*sic*] that the Reader takes in it: But when the case is altered, and that *Silvia* is lockt up in another Closet with the Old Countess, or guarded in the Cloyster, or stript of the Prince of *Salmes* his clothes, as you shall see in the second part. Then, I believe, some had rather it were *She* than *I*. (Mylne 1965: 46)[5]

It is with these words that the translator of a seventeenth-century French memoir justifies the decision to change a first-person narrative into the third person: that the fair reader would prefer the hazards of identification to be kept only for the pleasurable bits. But the concept of identification is an infinitely complicated one. What is actually going on when I read the 'I'of a text?

The first person is not an isolated phenomenon but half of a twin: it always implies a second person. There is a fundamental difference between the third person and the first two persons: while the former refers to a noun recently mentioned in the linguistic space, the latter are defined only by an 'instance of discourse' (Benveniste 1966: 252), referring to a materially localised body uttering the word 'I'or 'you'. A first-person textual character ought to be a contradiction in terms –

there is no body to fix it by – and probably for this very reason, it is instrinsically exciting. If the second person is always accusatory (see Butor 1964: 80–1), the first person is always seductive, the siren-cry of the unhoused phantom demanding a host: 'body me!'

What then can I do with a statement like this: 'He told me that the Imam was saying that I must hold no services in Trabzon, or he would call the police. I said I would hold no services, since I was not, as he could see, a priest' (Macaulay 1956: 115).[6] The speaker is the narrator of Rose Macaulay's (1881–1958) *The Towers of Trebizond*, whom other characters occasionally address by the indeterminate name of Laurie. Laurie goes 'bathing' in waters where local women are not allowed to swim, but I do not know whether this is because s/he is a man or simply not a local woman. In the same way I do not know why s/he cannot possibly be a priest. In order to read these lines I need to know what it is in the visible appearance of this character that makes secularity so obvious. Not knowing how to 'see' the speaker of the text is both a bar and a stimulus to entry into it.

There are a number of ways in which I may try to resolve the issue. 1950s readers would have known what few will nowadays: that Macaulay was, like Laurie, a traveller and writer, had been to Cambridge, and wrote books in which sex-role surprises are by no means exceptional, though never in quite this form. Her novels open with such phrases as 'Johnny was at Balliol and Jane at Somerville [...] Jane had always been just a shade cleverer' (Macaulay 1920: 3–5), or 'Mrs Richard Aubrey, [...] a Cambridge classical don' (Macaulay 1934: 7), and she carefully starts a feminist discussion by inviting her reader to 'consider some of the problems incidental to belonging, *as we nearly all must*, to one of the two sexes commonly found upon this planet' (Macaulay 1926: 95, italics mine). As Jeanette Passty points out, she specialises in refined male and robust female characters, and was very insistent that the blurb and publicity material of all her novels 'must not reveal the sex of the chief figure' (Passty 1988: 143).[7]

But let's assume I discover this text in 2001, and am entirely ignorant of its author, now dropped from the canon. How do I situate Laurie in the following adverbial comment? The benighted Father Chantry-Pigg is describing the shock of Arab missionaries in London at

> 'our bare-headed and bare-armed women in the streets. They said it led to unbridled temptation among men.'

> 'Men must learn to bridle their temptations,' said Aunt Dot, always an optimist. (Macaulay 1956: 21)

Or in the following chain of pairs: '[Love] had submerged Anthony and Cleopatra, and Abelard and Heloïse, and Lancelot and Guinevere, and Paolo and Francesca, and Romeo and Juliet, and Charles Parnell and Faust, and Oscar Wilde and me' (84).

When s/he buys a love-potion from a magician or offers a lift to a man whose wife is slogging along with the bags several yards behind, or takes a dip a mile down the coast from the boys' bathing-place, or on the other hand goes swimming with the male student Xenophon with whom s/he also shares the job of putting up the tent, I want to know if these gestures must be measured from the polar norms of male or female behaviour. And yet as soon as I make my assumptions I observe other possible causes of deviance: the alienation of the traveller, the upper-class dilettante, the non-Muslim or lapsed Anglican... Or again I might pursue a vaguely gendered discourse-theory. But do the characters who exclaim 'my poor Laurie' (100) or 'my dear sweet child' (156) feminise their addressee or themselves?[8] And is the *faux-naïf* tone of Laurie's narrative, with its endless strings – 'The Byzantines [...] had had no dull moments, they had babbled and built and painted and quarrelled and murdered and tortured and prayed and formed heresies and doctrines and creeds and sacramentaries' (118–9) – a sign of native simplicity, feminine ignorance or a parody of theological and historical one-trackmindedness?

All these ways of trying to form a protagonist 'belonging, as we nearly all must, to one of the two sexes' prove to have less to do with sex than with gender. But the key to the undecidability of this text lies in the third possible direction, that of desire. Laurie is in love with a second cousin called Vere. While Laurie rides a camel through testing terrain, Vere luxuriates on a rich friend's yacht. When they rendezvous after a long time apart: 'what I saw [...] was Vere standing at the reception desk and giving a note to the reception clerk, and so we met, and then nothing else seemed to matter' (148). It matters to us. At the instant of recognition, the reader is excluded from the erotics of the first-/second-person encounter, kept out by the impossibility of visualising the two lovers. Usually in fiction we are allowed all the voyeurism we wish, if not by direct representation then by the stimulation of hints and winks. Here there is neither circumlocution nor reification. Eventually – but only after he has been killed in a car crash – the reader learns that the beloved was a man. Laurie, who is partially to blame for the accident, reflects:

> I had come between Vere and his wife for ten years; he had given me his love, mental and physical, and I had taken it; to that extent I was a thief. His wife knew it, but we had never spoken of it; indeed, I barely knew her. We had none of us wanted divorce, because of the children; I liked it better as it was, love and no ties. I suppose I had ruined the wife's life, because she had adored him. Vere always said that he was fonder of her because of me; men are given to saying this. But really she bored him; if she had not bored him, he would not have fallen in love with me. If I had refused to be his lover he would no doubt, sooner or later, have found someone else. (219)

To derive from this whether Laurie is a woman or a man I need to have a narrow assumption of sexual practice which the text does little to encourage. Earlier in the text I have seen the two partners in another presumably sexual couple part and complain about each other; one is eaten by a shark and the other plagiarises his notebooks. These two characters have the unproblematically male names of David and Charles. It is clear that Laurie's and Vere's names are sexually unspecific – but not perhaps clear why. Compare the names of shady Clare Quilty and anagrammatic Vivian Darkbloom that haunt the doubly-named Humbert Humbert desperate to guess which of them might be the man who will steal his beloved. What difference would it make, after all: it is polymorphous perversity that is taking Lolita away from his excessive heterosexuality,[9] and the fizzing names are merely the symptom. This is not what is going on with Laurie and Vere.

Like her exact contemporary Woolf rather than Nabokov who was writing in the same year, Macaulay is interested in creating an androgynous text and corresponding desires in her reader. The cousins are so close that 'when one of us is abroad without the other, we both keep a kind of daily journal and post it once a week' (75). Thus they are united by text and passion, divided by the guilt that splits Laurie off from a comfortably internalised piety. Then Vere dies and the balance ceases: 'when a companionship like ours suddenly ends, it is to lose a limb, or the faculty of sight; one is, quite simply, cut off from life and scattered adrift, lacking the coherence and integration of love' (219). Each one falls away from the other, Vere into the rigor mortis of a suddenly sexed resolution which is *less* than the indeterminacy of desire, and Laurie now torn within and without, half of a double-sexed self now that s/he is no longer half of a double-sexed partnership.

*

> 'You can say everything', he exclaimed, 'but only if you never say "I".'
> (Gide 1996: 1124)

Marcel Proust (1871–1922) is perhaps the extreme example of a writer for whom the body is coextensive with the book. He spent the last part of his life, crippled by asthma and creativity, lying in bed in a cork-lined room, going out occasionally to check facts for his unfinishable text. That text, eight long volumes of dense, sinuous, dazzling prose, is both a fictionalised autobiography and the explanation of why and how the writing could never be started – until, finally, an experience of involuntary memory similar to one described on p. 46 of volume 1 assures the narrator that the past is not gone but can be what we would now call 'accessed' by such a recollection or by art.

Proust's text is bodily in two other ways. First because, for all its intellectual delicacy of expression, it includes elements of physical experience that were still new to serious fiction: wet dreams, a child's masturbation, an adolescent's or young man's orgasm pressed up against the body of a playmate or a sleeping mistress, the pleasure of smelling your chamberpot after eating asparagus, the fellatial joys of a tower of ice-cream. And second because everything (bar one section) is represented through the strictly limited viewpoint of a protagonist who, like a real person, says 'I' and never utters his own name. He is known as 'Marcel' because of a joke in the text and his avowed closeness to the author, but he differs from his model in being none of the things Proust was and felt ashamed of: he is not a snob or Jewish or homosexual. Instead these characteristics are spread out among the other characters, by the end so insistently that scarcely anyone is not revealed to be secretly, usually abjectly perverse.

André Gide (1869–1951) knew Proust and disliked him for his frivolity, effeminacy, brilliance and Jewishness.[10] For a cluster of connected reasons he rejected *Du Côté de chez Swann* when it was submitted to Gallimard and of course regretted it afterwards. In May 1921, he

> Spent an hour with Proust yesterday evening. For the last four days he has sent a cab every evening to pick me up but it has missed me each time... Yesterday, since I had told him I did not think I'd be

> free, he was getting ready to go out to see someone. He told me he had not got up for a long time. Though it was stifling in the bedroom where he received me, he was shivering; he had just left a much warmer room in which he had been dripping with sweat; he complained that his life is just one long death-agony and though he had begun, the moment I arrived, to talk to me about uranism [male homosexuality], he interrupted himself to ask if I could give him a few ideas about the teaching of the New Testament, on which someone or other had told him I speak particularly well. He is hoping to find some support or consolation for his pain, which he described to me at great length as appalling. He is fat, or rather puffy; he reminds me of Jean Lorrain. I had brought him *Corydon* and he promised me he would not talk to anyone about it; and as I was telling him briefly about my autobiography,
>
> 'You can say everything', he exclaimed, 'but only if you never say "I".' That would not do for me.
>
> Far from denying or hiding his uranism, he displays it; I might even say, he shows it off. He says he has never loved women other than spiritually and has never known love except with men. His conversation, endlessly criss-crossed with subordinate clauses, runs on in no logical order [*court sans suite*]. He tells me he is convinced Baudelaire was a uranist. 'The way he talks about Lesbos, even the need to talk of it, would be proof enough' – and as I protest:
>
> 'Well if he was it must have been almost without knowing it; you can't believe he ever actually acted on it...'
>
> 'Whatever do you mean!', he cries, 'I am convinced of it; how can you doubt he acted on it? *Baudelaire*?'
>
> Judging by the tone of his voice, he felt that my doubt was an insult to Baudelaire. But I do believe he may be right, and that uranists are indeed quite a bit more common than I thought at first. In any case I had no idea Proust was so exclusively so. (Gide 1996: 1124–5)

A week or two later Proust summons Gide again; despite his scepticism the latter finds him genuinely ill, maniacally running an anxious hand over his nose:

> On this occasion, again, we talked of little else but uranism. He said he regretted the 'indecisiveness' that had made him fill out the heterosexual parts of his book by transposing all his most graceful, tender and charming homosexual memories into the 'shade of young

> girls in flower', with the result that nothing was left for *Sodome et Gomorrhe* but grotesque and abject aspects. But he seemed very upset when I said it seemed as though he was deliberately stigmatising uranism. He protested; and I came to realise that what we find ignoble, ridiculous or disgusting does not appear so repulsive to him.
>
> When I asked him if he is never going to present this Eros in a youthful or beautiful guise, he replied that first of all what attracts him is almost never beauty, which he thinks has little to do with desire – and that, as far as youth is concerned, this is the aspect that is easiest to transpose (that lends itself best to transposition). (1126–7)

The transposition in *A l'Ombre des jeunes filles en fleurs* is most obvious in the 'little band' of girls glimpsed at the seaside resort of Balbec. Dressed in sports clothes, wheeling cycles or wielding golf-clubs as they stride down the beach 'like a luminous comet' (Proust 1954a: 791), shouldering through the crowd and even jumping over an elderly man who happens to be sitting in their path, graceful in their bodies and slangy in their speech, displaying to the world a 'bold, frivolous, hard' (790) character that combines irresistibly with a cluster of different kinds of beauty, they fascinate 'Marcel' as a multiple unity he long resists individuating. But eventually he meets Albertine Simonet at the studio of the painter Elstir and from then on, she becomes the object of his obsession.

Indeterminacy attends this decision in two ways, then: a focused passion grows arbitrarily out of a string of possible choices, and the beloved follows the mysterious Freudian trajectory by which 'a woman develops out of a child with a bisexual disposition' (Freud 1933: 149). Thus when I am so astonished to see young women of around 1900 jumping over little old men on a beach, because the image runs counter to all my expectations of gender-behaviour in pre-World-War-One Europe, that I tell myself they 'must really' be boys, what I am actually surprised at is seeing the focus of an ostensibly heterosexual desire start out as androgynous as this.

The figure of Albertine appears in three quite distinct stages. The first ends when 'Marcel', alone with her in a hotel room, tries to kiss her and is violently rebuffed. He loses interest and they lose touch. A few years later, she comes to visit him in Paris, taller now, calm and lady-like, nicely spoken; they see each other regularly but are just good friends – until one day the third stage is instigated. 'Marcel' watches her waltzing with her friend Andrée and his companion Dr Cottard points out how closely their breasts are touching. 'I can't see very well, but you can be sure they are in ecstasy [*au comble de la jouissance*]. People do not realise that that's the place where women feel most pleasure' (Proust 1954b: 796). At this the young man begins to experience a generalised jealousy which will from now on fuel and direct his desire. He feels calm only when accompanying Albertine everywhere – a demand which she obligingly (inexplicably) concedes to – passing her off as his cousin, monitoring her every word, watching her especially in the company of his best friend Saint-Loup. In a typically Proustian zigzag between pain and boredom he begins to tire of the strain until one day she inadvertantly reveals that she once lived with a woman he knows to be a lesbian. From this point begins the incarceration of Albertine by 'Marcel' and 'Marcel' by his obsession that will end only in her escape, accidental death, and his even deeper submersion in an impossible wish to know.

What does 'Marcel' want to know about Albertine which first instigates, then rekindles and finally disincarnates desire in such a way that both the presence and the absence of the beloved's living body are somehow irrelevant to its power? During the period of her 'imprisonment' he leans towards her once to kiss her cheek and it fades into a grotesque and dizzying close-up; or he describes how, daunted by the implied betrayal of her very consciousness, he can only reach orgasm beside her when she is asleep. In both scenes the human is dissolved into geological or vegetal matter, the body disappeared from a desire so excessively focused that it has no object. What he wants, essentially, is to know what it is like to be inside her skin, so far inside that she desires not him but another woman. Only in that way can he feel the meltdown of her indifference as searingly equivalent to his own need.

Now if, knowing that Proust never desired women and with the minimal biographical information to pin down the *grand amour* in the figure of his married chauffeur/secretary Alfred Agostinelli,[11] I try to understand the dynamics of this transposition, I find something more complex than Gide and perhaps Proust himself seem to have suspected. When the biographical structure *homosexual man desires bisexual man who desires women* is transposed in fiction into *heterosexual man desires bisexual woman who desires women*, an equivalent logic of frustration and jealousy is turned into a different logic of identification. If 'Marcel' cannot epistemologically enter into Albertine's desire, and is thus eternally tormented by it, it is because he cannot imagine himself in that scene as her object, just as Proust does not figure as object in Agostinelli's desire when he focuses on his wife. But the epistemological screw is turned a point further. Proust, a man, has a body like Agostinelli's to desire with, and so shares his subject position. 'Marcel', a man, desires the same sex that Albertine does but not, he declares, in the same way. What fantasy scenario has Proust created for himself? Excluded as possible object, he is forced inside as the subject whose soul wants what its body is not and whose soul is what its body cannot want. This is the essence of the inversion theory.

The inversion theory was introduced in the late nineteenth century by Karl Heinrich Ulrichs and others as an explanation of the newly identified category of homosexual. Summed up in the Latin phrase *anima muliebris virili corpore inclusa* ('a woman's soul enclosed in a man's body'), it was accepted by Proust and rejected by Gide, as their discussions show. When Proust's super-virile Charlus is unaware that he is being watched, his desire for another man makes him show forth 'as a woman' (P2, p. 604), one of the 'accursed race doomed to falsehood and perjury' (Proust 1954b: 615) whose bodily exterior conflicts with their 'inner' self. The transposition of Proust's boys into girls must be understood in the light of this disturbing logic.

*

> He speaks of my book again, praising it with just a touch of reticence. At last the carriage stops. He says goodbye, is about to get out, then suddenly says:
>
> 'Listen, my dear, you must promise me something. The *Nourritures terrestres* is good... very good... But, dear, promise me: don't ever write "I" any more...'
>
> And, as I did not seem to understand fully, he repeated: 'In art, don't you know, there is no such thing as the first person'. (Gide 1910: 46)

This conversation took place soon after Oscar Wilde came out of prison in June 1897.[12] Gide went on to write several more books in the first person but never in the lyrical tone to which his friend took exception. Instead his first-person texts are studies in irony, using the '*je*' to indict an unreliable narrator of sins the author is correspondingly cleared of. On one occasion he describes this as 'the acme of objectivity', on another as the botanical experiment of transplanting a 'dormant eye' to see how it will grow uprooted from the parent plant.[13] Neither can, of course, be true, as Gide knew perfectly well. On the contrary, however multiple the reference-points, the first person brings together implied author and implied reader in a waltzing (whirling) embrace.

In 1919, the same year as *A l'Ombre des jeunes filles en fleurs*, Gide published *La Symphonie pastorale*, the diary account of the education of a blind girl by a pastor who falls in love with her. Betraying his children, his wife and his religious sincerity as he gradually 'brings out' a lovely intelligent creature from what at first seemed a lump of inert matter, he is punished when Gertrude recovers her sight, realises it was his son she loved all along (this son has meanwhile decided to become a Catholic priest) and then commits suicide. The main burden of the irony seems to be directed at the pastor's spiritual blindness, the fault being implicitly shared among his unadmitted sensuality, a confusion between different meanings of the word 'love' and the Protestant religion's susceptibility to such misreadings. Less explicitly, the disaster is shown to be the result of a well-meaning educator falsifying the imperfect state of the world to a pupil unable to test out his descriptions. From the point that the pastor – he is never named – admits that Gertrude, 'whom I brought out of her darkness only for adoration and love' (Gide 1958: 877), is in reality more avid for knowledge: '"I don't care about being happy. I want to know"' (921) – his conscious/unconscious project is doomed.

Gide began writing this fiction, for which he had carried round the idea for twenty-five years, when he was in love for the first time. Hitherto his unconsummated devotion to his cousin-wife Madeleine was balanced by his desire for young boys in such a way that love and sex were distinctively directed and gendered. This polar structure is not quite as simple as it seems since he insists that his same-sex desire is predicated on difference: 'there are some people who fall in love with what resembles them; others with what is different. I am among the latter' (Gide 2001: 283). But devotion and desire had never been directed at the same object. Then he became involved with a seventeen-year-old family friend, Marc Allégret, and in June 1918 he took Marc to England for the summer, leaving Madeleine alone in Normandy. While he was away she saved herself from suicide by burning her 'most precious possession' (Gide 1996: 1075), the collection of his letters to her from childhood on, a holocaust for which he never forgave her.

La Symphonie pastorale was written on either side of this crisis, the first 'notebook' before the trip to England, the second after the discovery of the burnt letters. The guilt, bitterness and self-justification of adultery first happy then angry are visible in both sections. Most critics simply identify the pastor with Gide and Gertrude with Marc Allégret.

This is not unjustified: in his Journal of 1917 and 1918, alongside exclamations of delight and fulfiment, he notes: 'I wonder sometimes if what I love in all this is not so much the music as the study of the piano, and if perhaps what drives me is the need to create something perfect' (1038). This makes him Pygmalion (as he said elsewhere)[14] and Marc the product of a creative education as coloured by desire as the pastor's. The pastor is, after all, as well as an educator and lover, a careful and even mendacious writer.[15] Others have pointed out (with rather less psychological justification) that Gertrude might be modelled on Élisabeth Van Rysselberghe (1890–1980), a feminist and former lover of Rupert Brooke,[16] with whom Gide had a daughter in 1923. More challengingly, sex transposition takes a different turn in the suggestion, sketched in a number of earlier critics and central in a recent article by Scott Sprenger, that Gide's essential identification is with Gertrude.[17] Such a move would allow him, Sprenger argues, to present a narcissistic motive in the pastor and also to give an adequately flexible incarnation to his own. It would be Jacques who would then incarnate Marc Allégret, and a homoerotic motive would obtain the 'involuntary approval' of the most heterosexually blinkered reader who longs for the love-triangle to have the happy ending that Gide conventionally denies it.

It has, I hope, been obvious in the whole of my argument that this kind of reading is not simply the salacious searching-out of *clefs* in fictions but rather a way of seeing how desire uses fiction to reposition itself in different ways. However matheme-atical psychoanalysis grows, the concept of identification is rooted in plausibly physical likenesses: the older male writer in love with an attractive adolescent ought by its reasoning to be superimposed upon his fictional analogue. But a reading like Sprenger's exposes the impossibility of stopping the parallels there, and encourages the next logical step. In Proust, after all, the whole fictional geography and its population – 'the flowers in our garden or in M. Swann's estate, and the waterlilies of the Vivonne, and the good folk of the village and their little houses and the church and all of Combray and the land around it' (Proust 1954a: 47–8) – springs out of a cup of tea into which a cake has been dunked and slowly tasted. If we are looking for Gide in his fiction, we must see the whole text as his desiring body.

Irony is that use of 'I' which displaces responsibility. The more unreliable the word of Michel, Jérôme or the pastor, as I noted earlier, the clearer is Gide's conscience. Joyce speaks of the author as 'the God of the creation, [that] remains within or behind or beyond or above his [*sic*] handiwork, invisible, refined out of existence, indifferent, paring his fingernails' (Joyce 1916: 219) and Flaubert before him as 'like God in the universe: present everywhere and visible nowhere' (Flaubert 1980: 204). Authors become implied authors, that is, divinities, by ironising their characters, and never more sweetly and completely than by ironising first-person narrators who seem on the face of it very like them. In the gratification and then the defeat of the pastor both by the logic of a conventionally tragic tale and by the beady-eyed scorn of the intelligent reader, Gide gets the pleasure of having his cake (the pun on madeleine is difficult to resist) and eating it. Meanwhile he can pretend the indifference of wisdom which is the implied author's privilege.

Indeed the plot and characters of *La Symphonie pastorale* endorse this. They too live and die by a dream of parthenogenesis. Long before the pastor has 'sinned' by his amorous interest in his pupil he has already used her to imagine giving birth to a child without the mediation of a woman and to a world to keep that child in which has no taint of flawed material reality. It is when Gertrude becomes able to see the 'real' world that she chooses to die rather than live in its embrace, and at the same moment Jacques enters a monastery in reaction against the impossibility of reifying the idea of fatherhood adequately in his body; through celibacy he will become a 'spiritual father' instead. Each one of these creatures, against rather than with the others, tries to produce a dematerial universe conceived on the model of fiction. They are banned from the everyday world which in Gide is always the 'hateful' universe of family life. As they perish, legitimate authorship lives.

If, then, Macaulay conjures up an experience of androgynous desire by an androgynous protagonist creating an androgynous reading, and Proust forces the reader to follow through the logic of perversely imagining the gender spirals of jealousy, Gide is somewhere else. The image of transplanting a 'shoot' of his personality, or of 'slicing into [his] very flesh' to make characters always coexists with the idea that a 'true writer' creates fictional figures that he [*sic*] can watch and listen to.[18] They must both emerge from him [fantasy: her] and depart from him into another kind of life. The pleasure of the act of authorship for Gide is represented in a centrifugal gesture by which he makes himself into that God-like thing, a subject of no sex, no gender and above all no desire.

This would be consistent with his real-life sexual practice. As we read in his own and his friends' accounts, Gide was repelled by penetrative sex, whether heterosexual or homosexual, and his own pleasure, 'taken face to face, reciprocally and without violence' (Gide 2001: 312) was, at its most blissful, a gesture of hand on flesh. At its most anxious, however, it followed a hydraulic logic whereby he could feel no peace until his body was entirely 'emptied out' by six or eight orgasms, produced alongside (not necesssarily 'with' or 'by') one or two consecutive partners but always completed by himself.[19] The ideal state seems to be one not so much of ecstasy as of stasis, the final balance of undesire, the isolated body as empty vessel, pure skin.

This is, essentially, an image of anorexia, and surprising as it may seem, I would suggest it is the best way of understanding the pleasure described by Flaubert in the writing of *La Tentation de Saint Antoine*: a ceaseless outpouring leading to – what? The ending of *La Symphonie pastorale* suggests the bleak answer. Here, with Gertrude drowned in waters hitherto hypostasised as snow, ice or tears,[20] the pastor ends up with a 'heart more arid than the desert' (Gide 1958: 930). What remains of creativity has all evaporated back into the authorial heavens from which it came, leaving the deistic illusion of a seemingly empty sky.

*

> 'What can Love be then?' I said. 'A mortal?' 'Far from it.' 'Well, what?'
>
> 'As in my previous examples, he is half-way between mortal and immortal.'
>
> 'What sort of being is he then, Diotima?'
>
> 'He is a great spirit, Socrates; everything that is of the nature of a spirit is half-god and half-man'. (Plato 1951: 81)

A little earlier in the *Symposium*, Plato's Aristophanes describes the origin of sexual desire in a similarly double image. Like the unhoused phantom of the first-person character in fiction, individual human beings are half of an original whole which once had two faces, four arms, four legs and two sets of genitals; split down the middle by the wrath of the gods, each of these half-creatures now spends its time searching for its other half. Before the great divide there were three sexes – females, males and hermaphrodites – and thus there are three kinds of desire:

> Those men who are halves of a being of the common sex, which was called, as I have told you, hermaphrodite, are lovers of women,

> and most adulterers come from this class, as also do women who are mad about men and sexually promiscuous. Women who are halves of a female whole direct their affections towards women and pay little attention to men; Lesbians belong in this category. But those who are halves of a male whole pursue males, and being slices, so to speak, of the male, love men throughout their boyhood and take pleasure in physical contact with men. Such boys and men are the best of their generation, because they are the most manly. (62)

This fancy attracts the modern imagination above all for its unexpected turns. Those people most focused in their heterosexuality were once part of the wildest double-figure, the hermaphrodite. This would accord with Rose Macaulay's image of a loving completion that must be androgynous. The lesbian who 'pays little attention to men' appears both in Proust's 'Marcel' and in his image of Baudelaire, signifying an inversion theory in which desire is inseparable from jealousy and loss. For Gide, a dedicated sexual platonist, the ideal subject and object of pederastic love are more virile rather than less, and 'the best of their generation', to the precise extent that they have chased out of themselves by centrifugal force the femininity which, in the person of Diotima, haunts even Socrates's plot.

Notes

Unless otherwise stated, translations are my own with reference given to the original text, and all italics are the author's. Page numbers given in brackets refer to the last-cited text.

1 Sartre likens this pact, tellingly, to that of the inheritance between uncle and nephew in the matriarchate, the art-work resembling the mother who transmits titles and powers without herself possessing them (103).
2 I have used 'my' here to render the gender-indeterminate French possessive '*sa*'.
3 On the problems of a feminist reading of Gide, see Segal 1998a.
4 *Pace* the important recent disputations in each and all of these categories, I shall be distinguishing them as follows: *sex* is a question of biological or genetic assignment (female/male), *gender* is a question of behaviours conventionally and arbitrarily assigned to either sex (feminine/masculine), and *sexuality* is a question of habitually desiring a same-sex or other-sex partner (homosexual/heterosexual).
5 The anonymous translator into English of Part I of the *Mémoires de Henriette-Sylvie de Molière* (original and translation 1672), quoted in Mylne 1965.
6 I would like to thank Joan Whitehead for bringing *The Towers of Trebizond* to my attention about fifteen years ago in Cambridge.

7 Mark Bonham Carter, original editor of *The Towers*, quoted Passty 1988. Passty takes the view that Laurie's sex is revealed as female at the end of the text when 'she has slain her male self' (144); Crawford 1995, 148ff., takes 'her' as a woman throughout.
8 The speakers are both women.
9 Vladimir Nabokov, *Lolita* (1955). On the question of the strong implicit contrast between Quilty and Humbert as straight and crooked pedophiles, see Bell 1993, 158–9: 'to desire someone younger than oneself, with less access to power than oneself, is certainly not an abnormal desire. It is the predominant construction of masculine desire in the contemporary form of heterosexuality. If, therefore, one wishes to question the division of adult and child sexuality, one must also stress both the 'normality' of paedophilia and its gendered aspect.'
10 See Segal 1998b: 293–5. Other arguments about Gide in this article can be found referenced and amplified in that book and in Segal 2001.
11 See Haas 1971: 257–76.
12 For the dating see Ellmann 1988: 507.
13 Both remarks refer to the first of his ironic *récits*, *L'Immoraliste*. See Masson 1994: 231 and Gide 1936: 616.
14 See Pierre-Quint 1952: 391.
15 See the brilliant discussion in O'Keefe 1996: 162–224.
16 A curious analogy with Rose Macaulay, who also loved Brooke and seems to have elicited even less reciprocation. Élisabeth was Marc Allégret's lover for several years but the child Gide hoped they would have together miscarried.
17 See Sprenger 2001, in Segal 2001: 203–18.
18 For the image of the plant see note 13 above and also Gide 1927: 70. The other two references are to Gide 1927: 73 and 75–6.
19 See Martin du Gard 1993: 232–3.
20 See Goulet 1972: 27–55.

Works cited

Bell 1993 Vikki Bell, *Interrogating Incest* (London and New York: Routledge)

Benveniste 1966 Émile Benveniste, *Problèmes de linguistique générale*, vol. 1 (Paris: Gallimard)

Butor 1964 Michel Butor, *Essais sur le roman* (Paris: Gallimard)

Crawford 1995 Alice Crawford, *Paradise Pursued* (London and Toronto: Associated University Presses)

Ellmann 1988 Richard Ellmann, *Oscar Wilde* (Harmondsworth: Penguin)

Flaubert 1980 Gustave Flaubert, *Correspondance II*, ed. J. Bruneau (Paris: Gallimard)

Freud 1933 Sigmund Freud, 'Die Weiblichkeit', translated as 'Femininity', by James Strachey, *The Pelican Freud Library*, 15 vols (Harmondsworth: Penguin), vol. 2, 1973

Gide 1910 André Gide, *Oscar Wilde* (Paris: Mercure de France, edn of 1989)

Gide 1927 André Gide, *Journal des Faux-monnayeurs* (Paris: Gallimard)

Gide 1936 André Gide, *Œuvres complètes*, 15 vols, ed. Louis-Martin Chauffier, vol. 11 (Paris: NRF)

Gide 1958 André Gide, *Romans. Récits. Œuvres lyriques*, ed. Yvonne Davet and Jean-Jacques Thierry (Paris: Gallimard)

Gide 1996 André Gide, *Journal 1887–1925*, ed. Éric Marty (Paris: Gallimard)

Gide 2001 André Gide, *Souvenirs et voyages*, ed. Pierre Masson *et al*. (Paris: Gallimard)

Goulet 1972 Alain Goulet, 'La figuration du procès littéraire dans l'écriture de *La Symphonie pastorale*', in *La Revue des Lettres modernes*, vol. 331–5, 27–55

Huas 1971 Jeanine Huas, *Les Femmes chez Proust* (Paris: Hachette)

Joyce 1916 James Joyce, *A Portrait of the Artist as a Young Man* (London: Jonathan Cape, edn of 1964)

Macaulay 1920 Rose Macaulay, *Potterism* (London: Collins)

Macaulay 1926 Rose Macaulay, *A Casual Commentary* (Leipzig: Tauchnitz)

Macaulay 1934 Rose Macaulay, *Going Abroad* (London: John Lehmann, edn of 1948)

Macaulay 1956 Rose Macaulay, *The Towers of Trebizond* (London: Futura, edn of 1981)

Martin du Gard 1993 Roger Martin du Gard, *Journal*, vol. 2, ed. Claude Sicard (Paris: Gallimard)

Masson 1994 Pierre Masson (ed.), *André Gide et Christian Beck Correspondance* (Geneva: Droz)

Mylne 1965 Vivienne Mylne, *The Eighteenth-century French Novel* (Manchester: Manchester University Press)

O'Keefe 1996 Charles O'Keefe, *Void and Voice* (Chapel Hill: University of North Carolina)

Passty 1988 Jeanette Passty, *Eros and Androgyny* (London and Toronto: Associated University Presses)

Pierre-Quint 1952 Léon Pierre-Quint, *André Gide, l'homme, sa vie, son œuvre* (Paris: Stock)

Plato 1951 Plato, *The Symposium*, tr. Walter Hamilton (Harmondsworth: Penguin)

Proust 1954a Marcel Proust, *A la Recherche du temps perdu*, 3 vols, ed. Pierre Clarac and André Ferré (Paris: Gallimard), vol. 1

Proust 1954b Marcel Proust, *A la Recherche du temps perdu*, 3 vols, ed. Pierre Clarac and André Ferré (Paris: Gallimard), vol. 2

Sartre 1948 Jean-Paul Sartre, *Situations II* [*Qu'est-ce que la littérature*] (Paris: Gallimard)

Sartre 1964 Jean-Paul Sartre, *Les Mots* (Paris: Gallimard)

Segal 1998a Naomi Segal, 'André Gide and the Niece's Seduction', in Mandy Merck, Naomi Segal and Elizabeth Wright (eds), *Coming Out of Feminism?* (Oxford: Blackwell)

Segal 1998b Naomi Segal, *André Gide: Pederasty and Pedagogy* (Oxford: Oxford University Press)

Segal 2001 Naomi Segal (ed.), *Le Désir à l'œuvre: André Gide à Cambridge 1918, 1998* (Amsterdam and Atlanta: Rodopi)

Sprenger 2001 Scott Sprenger, 'Gide, Narcisse et la question de la psychobiographie', in Naomi Segal (ed.), *Le Désir à l'œuvre: André Gide à Cambridge 1918, 1998* (Amsterdam and Atlanta: Rodopi)

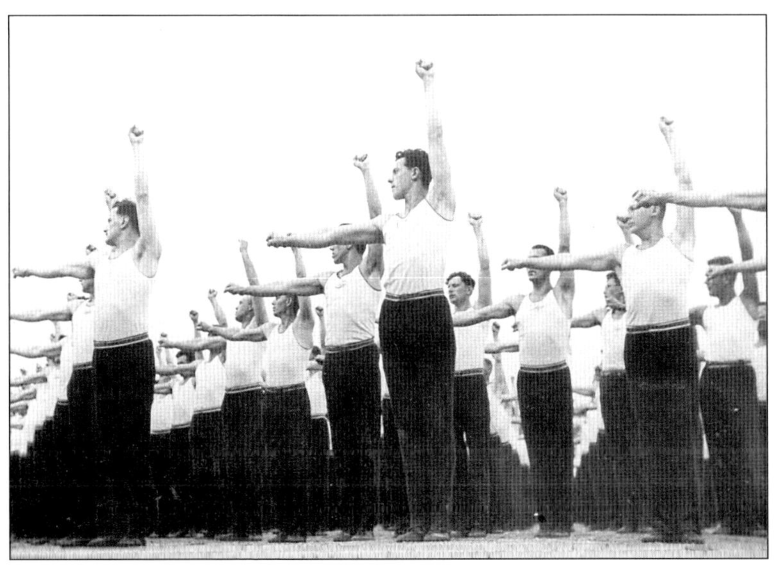

3.1. *Oath to the Republic.* Men's routine, 10th Sokol Festival, Prague, June–July 1938.

3.2. *No Obstacle Prevents the Task from Being Fulfilled.* From the Svazarm Day. 1st Spartakiáda, Prague, July 1955.

3.3. Routine for Working-Class Youth. 6th Czechoslovak Spartakiáda, Prague, June 1985.

5.1. Lari Pittman, *Once a Noun, Now a Verb #2,* 1997.

5.2. Lari Pittman, *Headhunter*, 1982.

5.3. Lari Pittman, *Untitled #1: A Decorated Chronology of Insistence and Resignation*, 1992.

5.4. Lari Pittman, *Like You, Hoping and Wanting But Not Liking,* 1995.

8.1. *Salmacis and Hermaphroditus, Surrounded by Other Ovidian Metamorphoses.*

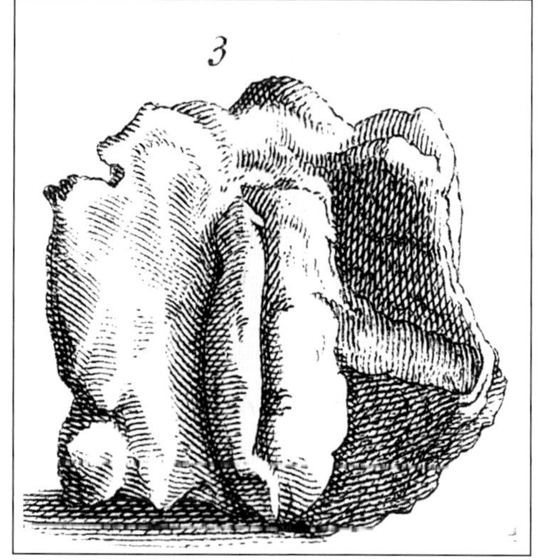

8.2. Histerolithos: Nature's Design for a Human Hermaphrodite.

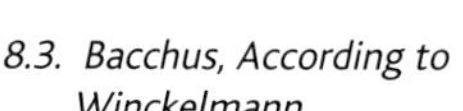

8.3. Bacchus, According to Winckelmann.

8.4. Antique Hermaphrodite.

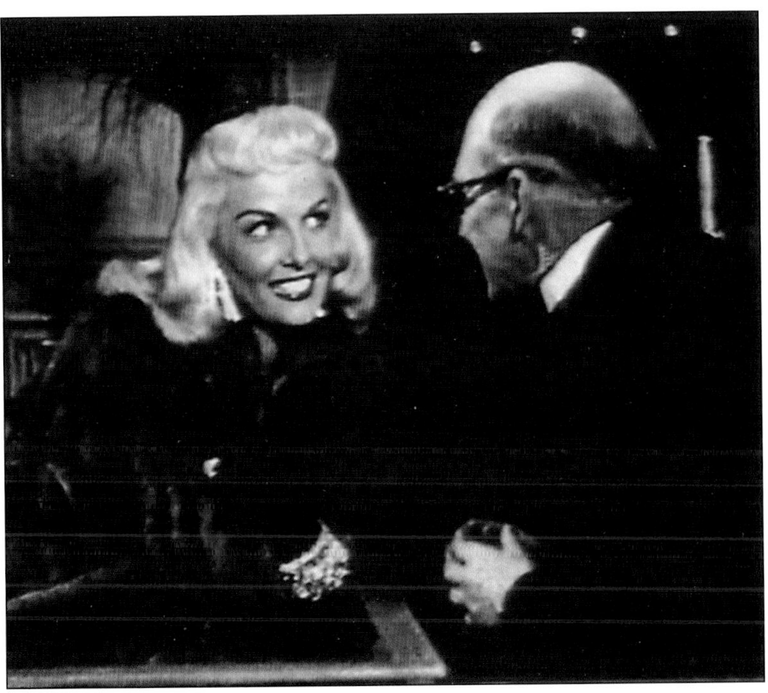

10.1. Dorothy (Jane Russell) posing as Lorelei Lee (Marilyn Monroe) in *Gentlemen Prefer Blondes*, directed by Howard Hawks, 1953.

11.1. Kathryn Hunter as the Skriker in *The Skriker*, by Caryl Churchill, 1994.

11.2. From the left, Mary (Maggy Sherif), Melville (Darren Lee), Elizabeth (Suzie Fowler) in *Mary Stuart* by Friedrich Schiller, directed by Lib Taylor, 1995.

11.3. From the left, Mary (Maggy Sherif), Elizabeth (Suzie Fowler) in *Mary Stuart* by Friedrich Schiller, directed by Lib Taylor, 1995.

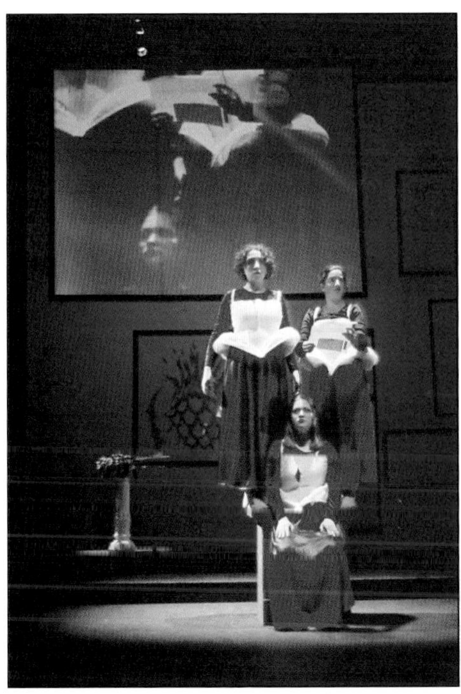

11.4. Jenny Coan, Rosie Hughes and Anna Scott as the Elizabeths in *The cutting up of Mary S*, devised and directed by Lib Taylor, 1997.

11.5. Michelle Addy, Jennie Francis and Cathinka Skotvedt Sundling as the Marys in *The cutting up of Mary S*, devised and directed by Lib Taylor, 1997.

13.1. Pieter Bruegel, *The Parable of the Blind*, 1568.

13.2. Pieter Bruegel, *The Parable of the Blind* (detail), 1568.

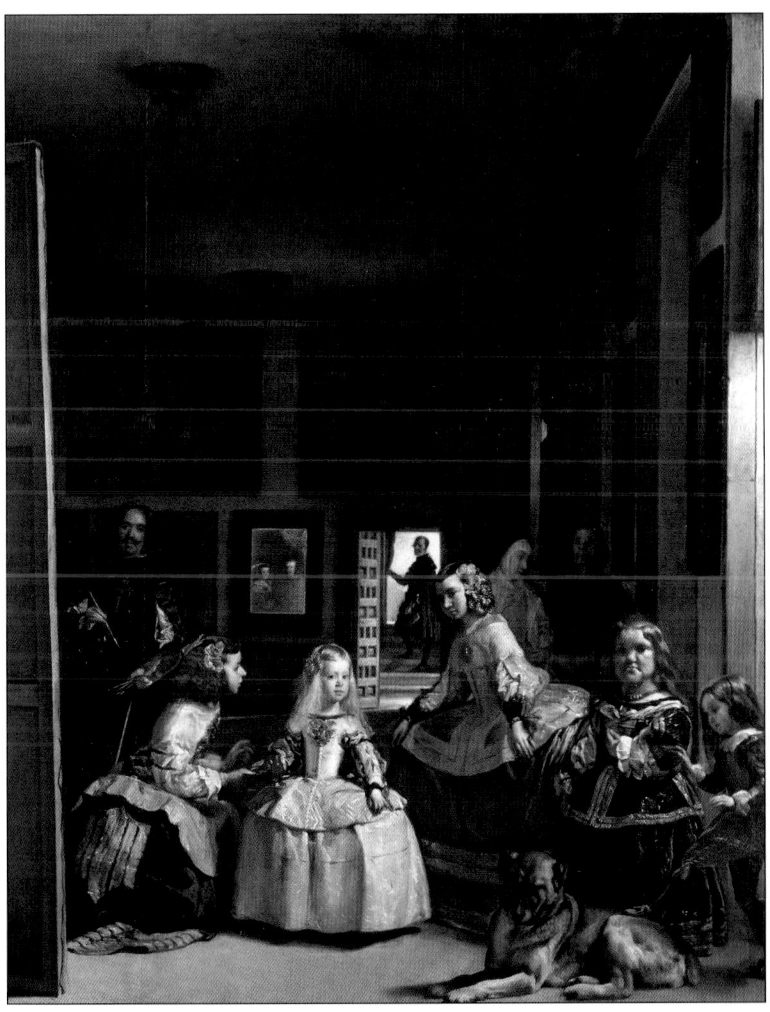

13.3. Diego Velázquez, *Las Meninas*, *c.* 1656.

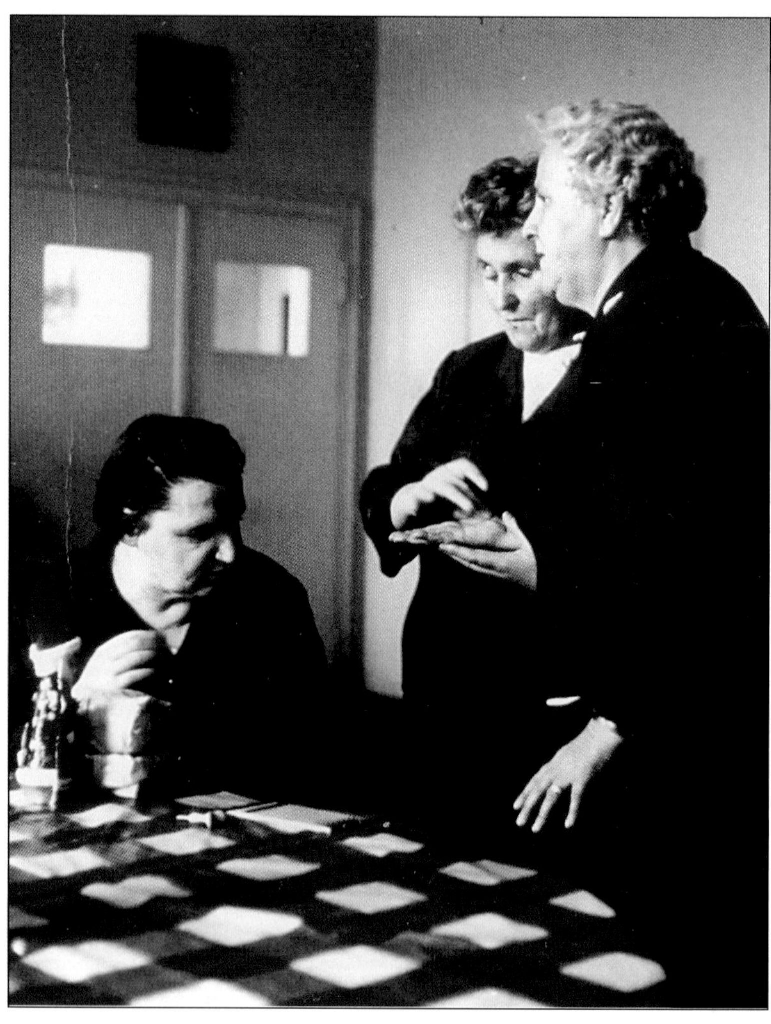

13.4. Else Fährer (*left*) and Fini Straubunger (*right*) in *Land des Schweigens und der Dunkelheit*, directed and produced by Werner Herzog, 1971.

13.5. Blind passenger (Béatrice Dalle), left, and cab driver (Isaach De Bankolé), right, in *Night on Earth*, directed by Jim Jarmusch, 1991.

14.1. Election poster of the Hungarian Democratic Forum (MDF), 1990.

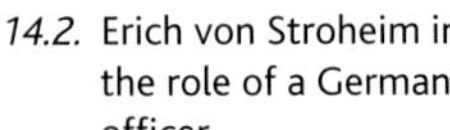

14.2. Erich von Stroheim in the role of a German officer.

14.3. Election poster of the Federation of Young Democrats (FIDESZ), 1990.

14.4. A caricature from the front page of *The Hungarian Economics Weekly* (HVG), May 1998.

14.5. An American postcard caricaturing Ronald and Nancy Reagan.

15.1. Waiting, choreographed and directed by Lea Anderson, 1994.

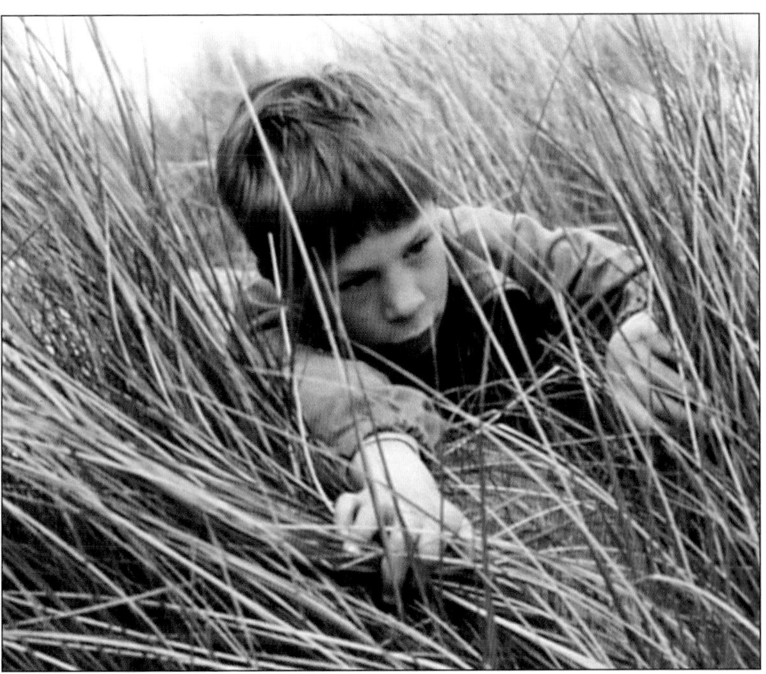

15.2. boy, choreographed by Rosemary Lee, directed by Peter Anderson, 1996.

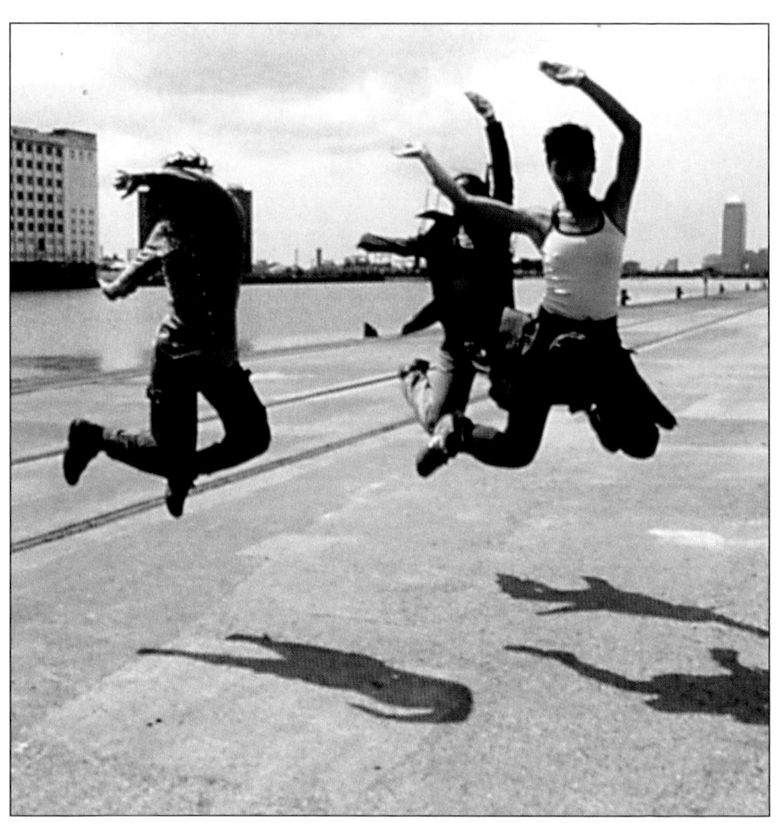

15.3. *Horseplay*, choreographed and directed by Alison Murray, 1996.

7

Not from Adam's Rib: the Origins of Transgender Surgery in Weimar Culture

Sander L. Gilman

The history of transsexual surgery is embedded in the history of the legacy of World War One and the shattering of a clearly defined sense of the masculine. Decades after the end of the war, Ernest Hemingway (1899–1961) remembers having observed the French veterans, 'les gueules cassées' (the broken faces), with their

> *Croix de Guerre* ribbons in their lapels and others also had the yellow and green of the *Médaille militaire*, and I watched how well they were overcoming the handicap of the loss of limbs, and saw the quality of their artificial eyes and the degree of skill with which their faces had been reconstructed. There was always an almost iridescent shiny cast about the considerably reconstructed face, rather like that of a well-packed ski run, and we respected these clients. (Hemingway 1964: 1977; see also Brain 1993)

These were clearly reconstructed faces as Harold Delf Gillies noted twenty years after the war: 'the old gibe of the French that "before" the patient was horrible, and "afterwards" ridiculous held only too true' (Gillies 1935: 2). Yet when Hemingway imagined the wounded soldier after the 'war to end all wars' it was certainly not with a missing face. In *A Farewell to Arms* (1929), his autobiographical novel of the Great War, his protagonist suffers a wounded knee, which makes him all the more a figure of erotic attachment in the fiction. In Frank Borzage's 1932 film of the novel, Gary Cooper's Lt Frederick Henry is certainly not unattractive. Jake Barnes, in his *The Sun Also Rises* (1926), like Clifford Chatterley in D. H. Lawrence's *Lady Chatterley's Lover* (1928), is impotent or castrated because of war wounds. Their faces are unmarred, though their bodies are no longer those of 'real' men.[1] They remain erotic figures in the altered state of their masculinity. Heroes remain erotic figures; men without faces are not imagined as erotic objects. The popularity of the deformed Lon Chaney in the 1925 film of the *Phantom of the Opera* rested to no little degree on this theme.

The visibility of the war wounded was understood as socially parallel to that of the racially visible. Weimar Germany had an intense concern with images of the war wounded. It is fascinating that the spectrum of unacceptable appearances ran the gamut from the war wounded to the racially unacceptable – because of their visibility.

In the 1920s Martin Gumpert (1897–1955), a Jewish reconstructive surgeon and well-known writer, proposed the creation of a public clinic for aesthetic surgery in Berlin (Reinhold 1989: 305–20). Gumpert advocated the creation of a publicly funded centre for 'Entstellungsfürsorge' (care of the mutilated) as part of the social network in the capital which already included clinics for occupational medicine, sport, marriage counselling, the war wounded and children (Gumpert 1939: 211). After much argument in the city council, the Berlin authorities authorised a department of 'social cosmetics' at the Institute for Dermatology at the University of Berlin (206). Gumpert's public institute for 'Entstellungsfürsorge' (a term which applies far more to horrific wounds than to anxiety about a too large or too small nose) reflects the contradictory meaning of being visible in modern Europe. Gumpert's institute was created as a parallel structure to the public clinic for the war wounded, so there was clearly a need for a different centre for aesthetic surgery in the Weimar Republic. Such a clinic did not deal with the mutilated former soldier, but with 'normal' members of Weimar society set apart from the new state by their appearance.

The parallel question of gender was also raised in Gumpert's clinic. For one important category for the acknowledgement of one's successful 'passing' was the erotic. Was one seen as a member of the desirable class and did that class silently acquiesce to one's membership in it? The erotic came to be racialised in the course of the nineteenth and early twentieth centuries because the erotic was linked to healthy reproduction and to productive attraction (cornerstones of the pronatalist movement). In a world in which sexuality and the erotic were no more stable than the ability to read race on the shape of the (new) nose, a new role of aesthetic surgery was to enhance the individual's erotic potential, even to enable one successfully to pass as a member of the other sex. Among Gumpert's patients were 'transvestites whose male forehead lines spoiled their pleasure at wearing women's clothes'.

Male transvestites in Weimar Germany were given police photo-identity cards which legally permitted them to 'disguise' themselves as 'women'. Their ability to do so was a reflection of the quality of their appearance and their ability to pass as 'female' (but not as a racially marked female) (212).

Gumpert's comments lead us to the other strand in the Weimar social history of aesthetic surgery, and that is the role that aesthetic surgery played in the Institute for Sexology, founded by Magnus Hirschfeld (1868–1935). One of Hirschfeld's long-time associates at the Institute was Ludwig Lévy-Lenz, whose role at the Institute, according to a contemporary French source, was the 'castration of certain exhibitionists, the improvement of the skin', and 'plastic surgery' (Merlet 1931: 167). He studied aesthetic surgery with Noël in Paris and with Joseph in Berlin (Lévy-Lenz 1954a: 455). In addition to his surgical activities, Lévy-Lenz was a prolific writer on aesthetic surgery and its implications for sexual health in the 1920s (Lévy-Lenz 1954b). Indeed, his was one of the voices which made aesthetic surgery most acceptable among liberal circles in Weimar Berlin.

However, it was not in the realm of reconstituting the racial body in order to make the Jewish psyche 'happy' that Lévy-Lenz worked. He was primarily a gynaecologist who worked with transgendered males to alter their genitalia and create artificial vaginas and labia (Lévy-Lenz 1954b: 454). (These procedures will be more closely examined later.) One of his transgender patients came to him and complained that 'Doctor, now I am a woman, but even when I wear women's clothes people say to me: "Mrs Schulze you have the nose of a man"' (345) 'Passing' means not being seen by others as inappropriately gendered, even in the form of the nose, but again 'Jewishness' is what being marked with a 'male' nose comes to mean in such circumstances. The construction of the feminine meant the elimination of racial typology through surgery. Jewish transsexuals were new women (and later new men); their Jewishness seemed to vanish under the knife. Lévy-Lenz understood his aesthetic surgery as an art form, unlike other forms of surgery (459), but like Gumpert (and many American surgeons of the 1920s) he also saw aesthetic surgery as a form of psychotherapy that should not be limited to the wealthy (455). He argues against those surgeons who think that surgery should only be undertaken when a life is in danger, and noted that many of the procedures they are pleased to do (such as the repair of a club foot, or of a cleft palate) are also aesthetic procedures. He stressed the role that aesthetic surgery played with the war wounded, where scars define the patient, but even more important the role which aesthetic surgery can play in operations which leave no scars (such as rhinoplasty) (456). Such rhinoplasties, Lévy-Lenz noted, were the most common operation that he performed, 'whether snub noses or Semitic noses or wide or long or potato or hanging noses' (461). Turning men into women meant eliminating the source of their featural as well as their sexual difference.

The 'unhappiness' of one's sexual assignment seems to be the result of the capricious lottery of birth producing males who desire to be females and females who desire to be males. In such dilemmas the absolute boundary between the sexes is not only constructed but also reconstructed. Marjorie Garber, who has written the best account of the culture of transsexualism, has argued that the transsexual is utterly invested in the 'age-old boundary between "male" and "female"' and thus stands for a kind of return to gender essentialism. 'Transsexuals [...] are more concerned with maleness and femaleness than persons who are [not] transsexual. They are emphatically not interested in "unisex" or "androgyny" as erotic styles' (Garber 1992: 101, 110; see also Hausman 1995 and Feinberg 1997). For their intent it is central to 'pass' as a member of the 'other' sex, to become essentially male or female.

The history of transsexual surgery can be approached initially through questions about the transformation of identity and the body. Is this reconstructive surgery? Has there been a wrong sexual assignment? Is this a 'man' (or a 'woman') trapped in the body of the other sex? Does being so trapped mean unhappiness? 'The physician is trained to alleviate suffering, and there can be no doubt about the genuine suffering transsexuals experience' (Volkan and Berent 1976: 449). Or as with Klinefelter's syndrome, if you know only the person's chromosomal identity, whether they are XX or XY, does this make sexual assignment or reassignment easier or more difficult? What of true or pseudo-hermaphroditic individuals born with what seem like or even are the primary sexual characteristics of both sexes?

It is of little consequence whether the transformation is on the level of morphological (the shape of the genitalia), hormonal, chromosomal or social definitions of sexuality and gender. The discussions of sexual transformation centre on the question of identity and the role which aesthetic surgery plays in constructing or mimicking sexual identity. Gary Marx, in an insightful essay on 'fraudulent identification', raises the spectre of whether of not impersonation is a quality of modern culture (Marx 1990). Can we in the age of the Internet and aesthetic surgery not simply recreate ourselves, as we desire? Are not these new selves as valid as all other forms of identity? Marx sees 'cosmetics and plastic surgery' as two of the 'resources available that intentionally or unintentionally aid false presentation' (151). Are transsexuals 'merely' surgical cross-dressers? He contrasts two examples. The first is 'the case of the New York model whose face was cut and who had undergone plastic surgery and wears cover-up makeup' (151). She is not creating a fraudulent identity as 'she can be viewed as trying to create what was once hers'. In a sense she seeks a Platonic ideal, the authentic form of whom she 'really' is. He contrasts this with 'a dark-skinned person who uses skin lightener or a person who undergoes plastic surgery to obtain a more Nordic look' (158). As Marx notes 'there can be a tension in the cultural emphasis to be all you can be, make yourself over versus being yourself, accepting your identity' (158). This is the dilemma of transsexual surgery as aesthetic surgery. Aesthetic surgery resolves ambiguities by allowing an individual to 'pass' unspoken as a member of a definable class. The question remains whether they truly belong to that class.

The American psychologist John Money (b.1921), certainly the most outspoken advocate of transgender surgery during the latter half of the twentieth century, imagines a Platonic ideal of sexual and gender identity.

> When you read about a grown man who has become a woman do you wonder if you yourself are a man or a woman? Of course not. You knew that you were a boy, or that you were a girl, long before you learned to read. And unless you are one of the very few exceptions to an all but universal rule, you've never seriously questioned it since. (Money and Tucker 1975: 3)

Money advocates a restoration of the relationship between the inner and outer selves. An asymmetry between them causes unhappiness; the restoration of an ideal symmetry (dimorphism) results in happiness. There is never the possibility of ambiguity. One is either male or female – though sexual preference is not so defined. One can be a man in a woman's body (erotically attracted to either men or women) or a woman in a man's body (erotically attracted to either men or women) (Money and Ehrhardt 1972: 1–23). Surgery is the path to happiness and for Money such surgery is reconstructive along a spectrum running from the resolution of the ambiguous morphology present in foetal deformation to adult transsexual surgery. Surgery becomes the means of restoring order and making the psyche happy through the establishment of a unitary identity.[2]

The establishment of aesthetic surgery at the close of the nineteenth century made transgender surgery conceptually possible.[3] But it was as much the experience as the fantasies of mutilation in World War One, which we discussed earlier, which enabled surgeons to imagine how such surgery could be done. Sexologists such as Magnus Hirschfeld were concerned with the impact of castration as a war wound to the individual's sense of his masculinity. Once it is claimed that the patient's autonomy defines the physician's approach as well as the 'deformity,' then transgender surgery becomes not only feasible but also inevitable. It is the voluntary nature of the medical contract in aesthetic surgery that is central – patients come to the physician and request certain procedures to ameliorate their unhappiness. In both cases the link between mind and body is absolute and defines health and illness. Transgender surgery is aesthetic surgery if it is deemed to operate on the psyche.[4]

C. G. Jung (1875–1961) dismissed transgender surgery as 'merely' aesthetic surgery in 1950 when he condemned transgender surgery as having nothing at all to do with medicine or psychology (as defined by him). 'Any one, even the patient, could give advice that a surgeon be sought for the procedure' (Jung 1995: 375–6). If the patient initiates treatment, defines treatment, and defines the goals of treatment, according to Jung, this is not 'real' medicine. Jung argued that it is as bad as if someone went to a surgeon and persuaded him to amputate a fully functional finger. The only difference is that the functional penis has a symbolic status in society. For Jung any physician who undertakes such a procedure is to be roundly condemned. For Jung there is no possibility that such 'cosmetic procedures' are medicine in any shape or form.

Of course, if you assumed that the transgendered individual is 'simply' being restored to some type of Platonic ideal, Jung's position would be anathema. Some American legal specialists have argued against this assumption that transgender surgery is aesthetic surgery.

> There is a superficial resemblance between a transsexual's bodily gender projects and a cosmetic surgery such as breast augmentation. Perhaps if a woman who pursues breast augmentation is guilty of an abusive simulation, then a man or a woman who chooses to undergo the more radical procedures of sex-reassignment surgery is [also] guilty [...] Instead of regarding sex-reassignment surgery as producing an imitation in the way that cosmetic surgery produces an imitation, one might say that the choice of such surgery stands in the same relation as masturbation to the appropriate use of one's gendered body: to participate in the 'conjugal good'. (Garet 1991–2: 121)

The contrast so advocated is parallel to that suggested by Gary T. Marx, but such distinctions always play a set of 'real' experiences off against the illegitimate desires of those who are defined as merely vain. Other forms of aesthetic surgery produce only simulacra, while transgender surgery produces 'real' bodies. Such arguments assume the parallel between the creation of bodies that are able to 'pass' and 'real' bodies.

The image of a 'Gender Identity Disorder' as a psychiatric diagnostic category is rooted in the model of the restoration of a prelapsarian 'happiness' with the body. In the 1920s, primarily through Magnus Hirschfeld's Institute for Sexual Science in Berlin, a series of surgical interventions were developed by Ludwig Lévy-Lenz, as we discussed earlier, and Felix Abraham (b.1901). They surgically transformed male genitalia into simulacra of the external female genitalia (without, of course, the ability to reproduce) (Abraham 1931: 223–6; see also Lévy-Lenz 1954a, 1954b). The emphasis in such surgery was the creation of the appearance of female genitals, which could be erotically stimulated. Reproduction was never even imagined as a goal, as the transplantation of ovaries for reproductive purposes was (and has) never been part of the conceptual strategy of 'becoming female' in transsexual surgery.

In an earlier paper, Richard Mühsam (1872–?) of the City Hospital in Berlin recounts that as early as 1920 a male patient referred to him by Magnus Hirschfeld requested that he be castrated and that in 1921 he removed the ovaries of a female transvestite at her request (Mühsam 1926).[5] One can add that in the 1920s and 1930s castration was understood as a medical practice, which was a 'form of therapy for neuroses, perversions, sexual crimes, sexual abnormalities, mental disease and even tuberculosis' (Menninger 1934: 183). His contemporaries in this broader context read Mühsam's paper.

In all the cases in which Mühsam undertook the removal of the gonads, there was no claim that the patient was either a pseudo- or an actual hermaphrodite. There had been a long history of the surgical reconstruction of 'ambiguous' genitalia, usually as female genitalia (see the excellent survey in Neugebauer 1904). Given that one out of a thousand births result in such cases, this was already an established part of reconstructive urology. Indeed the transgender patients were all represented as suffering from psychological difficulties rather than physical anomalies.

Mühsam's first patient, a twenty-three-year-old student, had been dismissed from a military school for 'lack of guts'. He served as an officer during World War One, testing his manhood, and came to

Mühsam after the war when he no longer could function. 'He gave up his medical studies [...] spent the day in bed and slept most of the day.' When he was in public he wore a corset, women's stockings, and high-heeled shoes (Mühsam 1926: 452). Mühsam's text makes it evident that it was the patient who desired to be castrated and transformed into a woman. 'The fate of this man sounds like a novel,' Mühsam wrote, 'it shows that the most active fantasy cannot imagine what feelings, wishes, and imaginings one finds with sexual neurotics.' On 21 June 1921 the young man was castrated and on 23 June, for the first time in a long while, asked for a book and resumed his studies. He requested to have an ovary implanted to generate female hormones rather than for reproductive purposes and this was done in March 1921. Following the surgical interventions, he developed breasts and wore women's clothing in private. He also began to sound 'feminine'. His larynx was examined and revealed a 'laryngeal feminine type structure'.

Mühsam could not bring himself to amputate the penis so he created a mock vagina into which the penis was placed, so that it could be sexually stimulated. By August, 1921 the young man returned to the surgeon and requested that he return his penis to a form more functional for intercourse as he had a new woman friend. After this was done he completed his medical studies and emigrated, informing his physician in a letter that: 'My health is well. I am absolutely happy [*zufrieden*] with myself [...] and my work pleases me greatly' (Mühsam 1926: 453). In this case, as with the other cases, he became both 'happy' and, according to Mühsam, a productive member of society. Indeed, Mühsam stresses, the transformation of this young man from a suicidal, sexual neurotic to a productive member of society is one of the major results of the procedure (Mühsam 1921: 156).

None of the patients that Mühsam records was labelled a 'hermaphrodite'. All were 'normal' in terms of their bodily structure and had been referred by Hirschfeld because of their psychological state. Magnus Hirschfeld's fascination with hermaphrodism was rooted in his own conviction that the homosexual was a 'third sex' bearing psychic qualities of the other sexuality (see Hirschfeld 1913 and Neugebauer 1908). The hermaphrodite provided a biological model for people who were both sexes and yet neither. Since physical hermaphrodites were potentially the subject of 'reconstructive' surgery, by analogy sexually troubled/transgendered individuals (psychological hermaphrodites) could also make this claim. But was it reconstructive or was it aesthetic surgery? Was it the restoration of a pre-existing body, which would match the psyche within, or was it the manipulation of the external aspect of the body to make the individual happier?

Similar surgical procedures as those described in detail by Richard Mühsam and Felix Abraham in their clinical papers were also undertaken by a Dr Gohrbandt at the City Hospital in Berlin. They consisted of the removal of the penis and testicles and the creation of an artificial vagina. The cases reported by Abraham were not cases of hermaphrodism but of male transvestites who desired sex changes. The cases are exemplary. The first case, also reported by Richard Mühsam, was of Rudolph, aka Dora R, who had attempted already at the age of six to amputate his penis because of his intense discomfort with his body. He had himself castrated in 1922 and in 1931 his penis was amputated and the procedure for the construction of the vagina was undertaken.

Arno, aka Toni E, was married and after the death of his wife began to dress as a woman. He was 'calm and intelligent' when dressed as a woman; 'nervous and completely non-functional' when dressed as a man. Within two years he was surgically transformed into a woman. Abraham comments that:

> One could object that such operations are 'luxury' operations with only playful character, since those operated on after a certain time again and again return to the surgeon with greater demands. It was not easy to decide to undertake these procedures but the patients were not only not to be talked out of them, but they were also in a state of mind which led one to believe they would have mutilated themselves and would have had life-threatening complications. (Abraham 1931: 224)

Arno/Toni had procedure after procedure to alter the form of the body. Multiple surgery here is not a sign of neurosis or psychosis, as defined by many of the surgeons and psychoanalysts dealing with aesthetic surgery. Such requests are an indicator of the degree of transformation needed by the patient to turn him into as much of a woman as matches his sense of being able to pass. Thus the initial transsexual operations, as with most of the earlier procedures, were modelled on the desires (and potential actions) of the client. They were also seen as cures, not of bodily anomalies, but of psychic unhappiness.

In his discussion of the central cases of aesthetic surgery during his own professional career, the Parisian aesthetic surgeon Jean

Boivin (b.1907) presents the best known case of such sexual reassignment from the 1930s. It is the case of Einar Wegener (d.1931), the first widely publicised case of a male (pseudo-hermaphrodite) to undergo surgical transformation into a female. While Wegener did not leave an autobiography, s/he did turn a diary and letters over to a German journalist whose account reflects the temper of the time concerning this highly publicised case (Hoyer 1932; see also Bullough 1975).

Wegener's account is the first of a long series of autobiographies or ghosted autobiographies of transsexuals, which include (more recently) those of Christine Jorgensen, Caroline Cossey and Jan Morris.[6] The popularity of such texts seems to speak against the silent acceptance of the individual passing into a new cohort. One can imagine that the new cohort is not at all the overt one represented in the autobiography. Rather the new cohort is the world of the transsexual. Not surprisingly, transsexual surgery makes transsexuals rather than 'men' or 'women'. This may well be why transsexuals need the boundary between the male and the female to be absolute. Acceptance into this cadre can indeed be signalled by public self-representation as a 'man' or a 'woman'. The public's fascination with such books, as in the case of Jorgensen and Morris, may well express its anxiety about the fluid nature of sexual boundaries.

In many of the autobiographies of transsexuals, the theme of the restructuring of the body centres about the ability of the surgeon to alter the psyche. Certainly traditional medicine in the 1920s was not seen as a source of solace by Einar Wegener. According to the fictionalised account, Wegener consulted three doctors: 'the first had declared that he had never in all his life performed "beautifying operations"; the second examined exclusively the blind-gut; the third declared [Einar] to be "perfectly mad"' (Hoyer 1932: 19). Here we have three of the most commonly held views of aesthetic surgery: it is 'merely' cosmetic and can have no therapeutic value; unhappiness with the body is a sign of a diseased body; or unhappiness is a sign of insanity. One doctor 'regarded the whole thing as a fixed idea of mine', and exclusively as a 'diseased imagining without any physical foundation [...] and one of them, the new specialist, even hinted I was really homosexual' (19). The clinical psychiatrist sees the desire to change the body as a symptom of dysmorphophobia and the psychoanalytically oriented therapist reads it as a homosexual fixation at an earlier stage of development. These are two of the strategies to cut Wegener's 'madness' in this world. Surgery offered another alternative (110).

Wegener's body, however, began to change without any medical intervention: 'His eyes looked hollow, his skin took on a pallor which was frightening to behold, and he was unable to sleep. His male organs atrophied and his breasts began to develop' (Boivin 1956: 58). Examined by his physician Werner Kreutz (a pseudonym), he is declared to be a true hermaphrodite – having ovaries as well as testicles, but only according to an external, physical examination, which could hardly establish the presence of ovaries (Hoyer 1932: 25). Wegener needs to be seen as a person whose shift of gender is a 'natural' one, resulting from the bisexual nature of his body (which mirrors his psyche). But the seemingly spontaneous transformation of the adult male body into that of a mature female hints at a psychological rather than a physical explanation.

According to Wegener, the physical and psychic pain arose out of the struggle between the masculine and feminine principles for domination. 'I was both man and woman in one body, and [...] the woman in this body was in the process of gaining the upper hand. Upon this assumption I explained the disturbances, both physical and psychic, from which I was suffering to an increasing extent' (100). The end result of this was extreme unhappiness even for his female alter ego: 'Lili [Elbe] appeared; but she had lost all her gaiety. She wept all the time' (103). Unhappiness is the central marker of the illness.

Surgery enables Wegener to begin to achieve some modicum of happiness. After the first operation in Dresden in 1930 he awakes castrated and asks: '"did I make much noise?" "Well, just a little," said one of the nurses with a smile, "and the strange thing was that your voice had completely changed. It was a shrill woman's voice"' (128). His transformation had begun: his passing as a woman was recognised by the women nurses, representing the group into which Wegener desired to enter. Wegener's (now called Lili Elbe's) diary for the time reads:

> In the first months after my operation it was necessary above all to recuperate. When this had happened to some extent, the physical change in me began. My breasts formed, my hips changed and became softer and rounder. And at the same time other forces began to stir in my brain and to choke whatever remnants of [Einar] still remained there. A new emotional life was arising within me. (243)

Lili's new breasts represented the entire transformation, a transformation of the soul as well as the body, as she writes in a letter to her physician 'Werner Kreutz': 'I feel so changed that it seems as if you had operated not upon my body, but upon my brain' (244). Lili Elbe returned to Dresden for a third operation and died there, as Jean Boivin wrote in his account of her experiences, 'obsessed by the idea that the professor whom she adored as if he were God had never regarded her as anything else but a guinea-pig on which to practice his skill' (Boivin 1956: 54). This is missing in the 'official' published account of the life and death of Lili Elbe. There happiness and love conclude the account. Boivin's statement marks not the restoration of happiness but the anxiety of being the subject of an experiment. For the surgeon to treat the patient for his own ends undermines the patient's autonomy, even if the patient instigated the surgery. This ambiguity shadows Lili Elbe's death.

Sexual surgery is the realm of the gynaecological surgeon undertaking procedures which are 'aesthetic' in order to cure the unhappiness of the patient. Wegener makes the argument that he was a true hermaphrodite in order to argue that he truly was a woman trapped in a male's body and that body revealed its female essence by developing breasts. His/her body desired to pass and s/he was unhappy because her psyche could not understand the body's desires. The sexual identity of the psyche is embodied and/or contradicted by the apparent gender of the body. Correct the error of the physical and the unhappiness of the patient will vanish.

The culture of passing is thus closely related to the world of the transsexual. The extraordinary case of N. O. Body caught Magnus Hirschfeld's attention in 1907 (Body 1907; see also Hartmann 1995). Karl M[artha] Baer (1885–1956) was a man who had been designated as a female at birth because of the ambiguity of his genitalia. Raised as a female, s/he found himself developing in ways that were at odds with her/his gender assignment. S/he recounts her/his growing confusion and intense unhappiness in her/his autobiography, published pseudonymously under the name N. O. Body and accompanied with an afterword by Hirschfeld. His/her confusion is exacerbated with the break of her/his voice (58) which convinced the teenager that s/he was sick, indeed that s/he had developed tuberculosis. His/her schoolmates (in their all-girls school) were developing their 'slim, virginal lines' while Baer remained flat-chested. The girls showed each other their breasts and revelled in the changes of their bodies. (70) This made the author question her/his own female identity: 'What was I? Boy or girl? If I was a girl, why didn't my breasts develop?' (79). Even more than the absence of menstruation, the lack of development of her/his breasts signalled not belonging to the cohort to which s/he had been assigned.

Once s/he is sexually reassigned as a man (which is undertaken with a court order which alters her/his birth certificate) his body is allowed to develop as a man. S/he does gymnastics and becomes 'stronger and broader' (154). No trace of a woman's body remains except for the mark of the corset. Hirschfeld's lesson from N. O. Body's account is that 'the sex of a human being rests much more in his/her soul than in his/her body, or to express myself in a more medical manner, more in the brain than in the genitals' (163–4). Happiness is, according to this model, when the soul and the body are in alignment.

Baer's reassignment does not necessitate any surgical procedure. His ambiguous genitalia were actually male and, while his education as a 'girl' later caused some difficulties to his life as a man, the absence of breasts was the 'true' sign of his sexual identity. In Imperial Germany 'real' men don't have breasts. However, Baer's narrative contains a double passing. He published it pseudononymously and successfully disguised all aspects of his identity, including the fact that he was Jewish. In the narrative he represents this 'exotic' background as 'French'. Indeed, this effacement of Baer's Jewish identity is noticeable only where he stresses the difference of his own body. He praises his body as having a 'fine body shape, long, small feet, and a long, oval face' (10). Quite the antithesis of the anti-Semitic image of the Jew at the turn of the century with his squat body form, misshapen feet and face marked with the curse of 'nostrility'. To pass in the autobiography, an account of an unintended, unconscious passing as a woman, means to become aware that one is too visible, especially as a Jew.

The absence of breasts established the 'true' identity of N. O. Body. This absence signalled that Baer was not passing as a woman, that he was 'really' a man. Yet the question of whether a Jewish male was a 'real' man was one of the most contested aspects of the 'Jewish Problem'. Baer's genitalia would not have been circumcised as he was categorised as a female. Did this make him more of a man even with ambiguous genitalia? The question of passing as anything but a Jew does not arise, for here gender seems to dominate the discourse of race until one examines the idealized body which the male author of the autobiography describes as his own. Baer becomes a senior figure in the Berlin Jewish community in the Weimar period and was able to emigrate in 1938 to Palestine where he died.

The male-to-female sexual surgery of Einar Wegener and the female-to-male transformation of Karl Baer, of course, focuses on the transformation (surgical or otherwise) of the genitalia as the sign which makes the psyche happy. Happiness is the possibility of the escape from imposed, fixed gender identity – and this is the promise of Weimar culture. The rigid notion of masculinity, which dominated German culture before the war, was shattered in 1919. The surgical skills developed on the battlefield were in place and the very notion of reconstructing the genitalia became imaginable by the 1920s. The world of Weimar culture saw the ability to transform the body to make the psyche happy as desirable. And thus transsexual surgery results.

Notes

1 The problem of the damaged body does not vanish in Hemingway's corpus; see McLellan 1992.
2 See the discussion throughout Money and Musaph (eds) 1977, for example on pp. 171, 487, 1295, 1309.
3 This argument about autonomy is made in outlining the legal and ethical question concerning the relationship between aesthetic surgery and transgender surgery in Quadri 1980 and Rouge *et al.* 1990.
4 Thus in the fifth volume of McDowell 1977, 796–7, there is a rubric for transgender surgery.
5 The patient accounts in this paper are more extensive, and include the follow-up to the earlier case reported in his earlier paper on the treatment of 'homosexuality' through castration: Mühsam 1921. See also Sonnenburg and Mühsam 1903 and Bullough 1987.
6 See Wade 1963, Lopes 1969, Jorgensen 1967, Simmons 1970, Buick 1971, Morgan 1973, Morris 1974, Conn 1974, Martino 1977, Fallowell 1982, Hodgkinson 1989, Stirling 1989, Sullivan 1990, Cossey 1991, Rutherford 1993, Spry 1997.

Works cited

Abraham 1931 Felix Abraham, 'Genitalumwandlung an zwei männlichen Transvestiten', *Zeitschrift für Sexualwissenschaft und Sexualpolitik*, 28, 223–6

Body 1907 N. O. Body, *Aus eines Mannes Mädchenjahren* (reprint of 1993, Berlin: Hentrich, with an afterword by Hermann Simon)

Boivin 1956 Jean Boivin, *Mes Opérations esthétiques* (Paris: Gallimard), translated by Eileen Bigland as *Beauty's Scalpel* (London: Jarrolds, 1958)

Brain 1993 D. J. Brain, 'Facial Surgery During World War I', *Facial Plastic Surgery*, 9, 157–64

Buick 1971 Barbara Buick, *L'Étiquette* (Paris: La jeune Parque)

Bullough 1975 Vern L. Bullough, 'Transsexualism in History', *Archives of Sexual Behavior*, 4, 561–71

Bullough 1987 Vern L. Bullough, 'A Nineteenth-century Transsexual', *Archives of Sexual Behavior*, 16, 81–4

Conn 1974 Canary Conn, *Canary: the Story of a Transsexual* (Los Angeles: Nash)

Cossey 1991 Caroline Cossey, *My Story* (London: Faber and Faber)

Fallowell 1982 Duncan Fallowell, *April Ashley's Odyssey* (London: Cape)

Feinberg 1997 Leslie Feinberg, *Transgender Warriors: Making History from Joan of Arc to Dennis Rodman* (Boston, Mass.: Beacon Press)

Garber 1992 Marjorie B. Garber, *Vested Interests: Cross-dressing and Cultural Anxiety* (New York: Routledge)

Garet 1991–2 Ronald R. Garet, 'Symposium on Biomedical Technology and Health Care: Social and Conceptual Transformations: Article: Self-Transformability', *Southern California Law Review*, 65, 121–203

Gillies 1935 Harold Gillies, *The Development and Scope of Plastic Surgery*. The Charles H. Mayo lecture for 1934 (Chicago: Northwestern University)

Gumpert 1939 Martin Gumpert, *Hölle im Paradies: Selbstdarstellung eines Arztes* (Stockholm: Bermann-Fischer)

Hartmann 1995 Andreas Hartmann, 'Im falschen Geschlecht. Männliche Scheinzwitter um 1900', in Michael Hagner (ed.), *Der 'falsche' Körper: Beiträge zu einer Geschichte der Monstrositäten* (Göttingen: Wallstein)

Hausman 1995 Bernice Louise Hausman, *Changing Sex: Transsexualism, Technology, and the Idea of Gender* (Durham: Duke University Press)

Hemingway 1964 Ernest Hemingway, *A Moveable Feast* (New York: Charles Scribner's & Sons)

Hirschfeld 1913 Magnus Hirschfeld, *Geschlechts-Übergänge: Mischungen männlicher und weiblicher Geschlechtscharaketere* (Leipzig: Max Spohr)

Hodgkinson 1989 Liz Hodgkinson, *Michael née Laura* (n.p.: Columbus Books) (about Michael Dillon, 1915–1962)

Hoyer 1932 Niels Hoyer (ed.), *Lili Elbe: Ein Mensch wechselt sein Geschlecht* (Dresden: Carl Reissner), translated by H. J. Stenning as *Man into Woman: an Authentic Record of a Change of Sex. The True Story of the Miraculous Transformation of the Danish Painter Einar Wegener* (London: Jarrolds, 1933)

Jorgensen 1967 Christine Jorgensen, *A Personal Autobiography* (New York: Eriksson)

Jung 1995 C. G. Jung, 'Zur Frage der ärztlichen Intervention', in C. G. Jung, *Das symbolische Leben: verschiedene Schriften*, ed. Lilly Jung-Merker and Elisabeth Ruf (Olten: Walter, 1995)

Lévy-Lenz 1954a Ludwig Lévy-Lenz, *Praxis der kosmetischen Chirurgie, Fortschritte und Gefahren* (Stuttgart: Hippokrates)

Lévy-Lenz 1954b Ludwig Lévy-Lenz, *Erinnerungen eines Sexual-Arztes: Aus den Memorien eines Sexologen* (Baden-Baden: Wadi-Verlagsbuchhandlung).

Lopes 1969 Marcelo Lopes, *Meu nome e Marcelo* (Sao Paulo: L. Oren)

Martino 1977 Mario Martino, *Emergence: a Transsexual Autobiography* (New York: Crown Publishers)

Marx 1990 Gary T. Marx, 'Fraudulent Identity and Biography', in David Altheide (ed.), *New Directions in the Study of Justice, Law, and Social Control* (New York: Plenum), 143–65

McDowell 1977 Frank McDowell (ed.), *The McDowell Indexes of Plastic Surgical Literature*, 5 vols (Baltimore: Williams and Wilkins, 1977–81), vol. 5: *The Honolulu Index of Plastic Surgery 1971* AD *to 1976* AD

McLellan 1992 John M. McLellan, 'The Unrising Sun: the Theme of Castration in Hemingway and Sterne', *Studies in English Literature and Linguistics*, 18, 51–61

Menninger 1934 Karl A. Menninger, 'Polysurgery and Polysurgical Addiction', *Psychoanalytic Quarterly*, 3, 173–99

Merlet 1931 Janine Merlet, *Vénus et Mercure* (Paris: Editions de la Vie Moderne)

Money and Ehrhardt 1972 John Money and Anke A. Ehrhardt, *Man & Woman, Boy & Girl* (Baltimore: Johns Hopkins University Press)

Money and Musaph 1977 John Money and Herman Musaph (eds), *The Handbook of Sexology* (Amsterdam: Excerpta Medica)

Money and Tucker 1975 John Money and Patricia Tucker, *Sexual Signatures: on Being a Man or a Woman* (Boston: Little, Brown)

Morgan 1973 Patricia Morgan (as told to Paul Hoffman), *The Man-maid Doll* (Secaucus, N. J.: Lyle Stuart)

Morris 1974 Jan Morris, *Conundrum* (London: Faber and Faber)

Mühsam 1921 Richard Mühsam, 'Der Einfluß der Kastration der Sexualneurotiker', *Deutsche Medizinische Wochenschrift*, 6, 155–6

Mühsam 1926 Richard Mühsam, 'Chirurgische Eingriffe bei Anomalien des Sexuallebens', *Therapie der Gegenwart*, 28, 451–5

Neugebauer 1904 Franz Ludwig von Neugebauer, '58 Beobachtungen von periodischen genitalen Blutungen menstruellen Anschein, pseudomenstruellen Blutungen, Menstruatio vicaia, Molimina menstrualia usw. bei Scheinzwitter', *Jahrbuch für sexuallen Zwischenstufen*, 6, 277–326

Neugebauer 1908 Franz Ludwig von Neugebauer, *Hemaphroditismus beim Menschen* (Leipzig: Werner Klinhardt)

Quadri 1980 E. Quadri, 'Profili Contrattuali e Responsabilità nell'attività del Chirurgo Plastico', *Rivista italiana di chirurgia plastica*, 22, 385–408

Reinhold 1989 Ernest Reinhold, 'Martin Gumpert', in John M. Spalek and Joseph Strelka (eds), *Deutschsprachige Exilliteratur seit 1933, II: New York* (Bern: Francke), 305–20

Rouge *et al.*, 1990 D. Rouge *et al.*, 'Évolution de la jurisprudence en matière de contrat médical en chirurgie esthétique', *Annales de chirurgie plastique, et esthétique* 35, 297–302

Rutherford 1993 Erica Rutherford, *Nine Lives: the Autobiography of Erica Rutherford* (Charlottetown, P. E. I.: Ragweed)

Simmons 1970 Dawn Langley Simmons, *Man into Woman: a Transsexual Autobiography* (London: Icon Books)

Sonnenburg and Mühsam 1903 Eduard Sonnenburg and Richard Mühsam, *Compendium der Operations- und Verbandstechnik* (Berlin: Hirschwald)

Spry 1997 Jennifer Spry, *Orlando's Sleep: an Autobiography of Gender* (Norwich, VT: New Victoria)

Stirling 1989 Peter Stirling, *So Different: an Extraordinary Autobiography* (Sydney: Simon & Schuster)

Sullivan 1990 Louis Sullivan, *From Female to Male: the Life of Jack Bee Garland* (Boston: Alyson)

Volkan and Berent 1976 Vamik D. Volkan and Stanley Berent, 'Psychiatric Aspects of Surgical Treatment for Problems of Sexual Identification (Transsexualism)', in John G. Howells (ed.), *Modern Perspectives in the Psychiatric Aspects of Surgery* (New York: Brunner/Mazel), 447–67

Wade 1963 Carlson Wade, *She-male: the Amazing True-life Story of Coccinelle* (New York: Epic)

8

'Sweet *Hee-Shee*-Coupled-One': Unspeakable Hermaphrodites

Carolyn D. Williams

For over two thousand years, sexually liminal bodies have provoked crises of representation in Western culture. The very words 'androgyne' and 'hermaphrodite' emerge from linguistic contradictions. In Greek and Latin, the end of a name usually indicates its grammatical gender. The Greek 'Ερμαφρόδιτος' (Hermaphroditos) is derived from Hermes, god of virility, and Aphrodite, goddess of love. So is the Latin 'Hermaphroditus': in each case, Aphrodite's termination has been changed from feminine to masculine. 'Ανδρόγυνος' (androgynos) follows a similar pattern: it is formed from 'ανὴρ' (aner: man) and 'γυνή' (gyne: woman), 'a womanish man'. Both words make strongly masculine first impressions, then, just where one would expect the second halves to redress the balance, revert to the masculine. There is also doubt about which word to use. Neither denotes a specific blend of sexual characteristics, despite twentieth-century attempts to establish distinctions: thus the assertion that hermaphrodites were originally ancient Greek kings with artificial breasts, while androgynes were queens with false beards, is unsupported by archaeological evidence (Graves 1960: I, 70). Sometimes hermaphroditism is dismissed as 'an anomalous physical condition', while androgyny is equated with ideal psychological or spiritual harmony (Heilbrun 1973: xii; see also Zolla 1981: 2). Others prefer to 'consider the two terms exactly synonymous' (Büsst 1967: 1). So long as 'androgyne' is not applied to animals, Büsst's rule covers the range of entities discussed in this chapter, which traces the simultaneous depiction and erasure of sexual liminality in such diverse locations as classical and Renaissance literature, eighteenth-century scientific discourse, postmodern critical theory and 1990s Hollywood.

In ancient Greece 'androgyny is at the two poles of sacred things. Pure concept, pure vision of the spirit, it appears adorned with the highest qualities. Incarnate, it is a monstrosity' (Delcourt 1958: 45). Similar ambiguity pervades Judaeo-Christian traditions. Symbolic androgyny represents such exalted abstractions as the all-inclusiveness of God (Mathers 1970: 21–2, 229–40). Yet at the physical level, sexual distinctiveness and rigid gender boundaries are encouraged: the Bible denounces such borderline practices as transvestism (Deuteronomy 22: 5) and same-sex object choice (Leviticus 20: 13; Romans I: 26–7; I Timothy 1: 10); men with damaged genitals are excluded from the 'congregation of the Lord' (Deuteronomy 23: 1; Bible 1611: 215). Marjorie Garber draws a similar dividing line between the actual and the symbolic, though across a different border: she places transvestism among the third ways which act as 'a mode of articulation, a way of describing a space of possiblity', while denying this role to 'an instantiated "blurred" sex as signified by a term like "androgyne" or "hermaphrodite"' (Garber 1992: 11). However, the examples she cites all 'involve moving from a structure of complementarity or symmetry to a contextualization, in which what once stood as an exclusive dual relation becomes an element in a larger chain' (12). This signifying function seems perfectly suited to symbolic hermaphrodites, though not to creatures of flesh and blood.

Figurative hermaphrodites must be set against the persecution and marginalisation of anyone thought to be the real thing. In ancient Greece and Rome, babies with ambiguous genitalia were exposed or drowned, while older children and adults who apparently changed their sex were burned alive or abandoned on desert islands: failing to represent their own sex with adequate clarity, their bodies were read as messages of divine wrath (Livy 1944–76: bk XXXI, ch 2; bk XVII, ch 37; Diodorus Siculus 1888–1906: bk XXXII, ch 12; Pliny the Elder 1601: bk VI, chs 15, 16, 35, 36; bk VII, ch 4). By the first century CE, a more relaxed approach was in evidence: instead of being slaughtered, they were kept as exotic pets (Pliny the Elder 1601: bk VII, ch 3). The growing influence of Christianity, with its ban on infanticide, probably helped to end the practice of exposing hermaphrodite children. In *De Civitate Dei,* Saint Augustine (354–430) not only accepts hermaphrodites as members of the human race, but records, and thus endorses, the practice of giving them the benefit of the doubt by assigning to them the superior, masculine sex (Augustine 1955: 509). Under Roman law, hermaphrodites were considered as men or women, depending on which sex predominated (Justinian

533: I, xi, 16; Gardner 1998: 136–52). This situation prevailed in Europe throughout the middle ages and the Renaissance (Möllerus 1692: 168; Tholosanus 1591: Part II, bk VII, 4–5). Yet the sexually ambiguous still faced destruction *as hermaphrodites*: they could achieve social acceptance only in the guise of 'normal' men or women. Those who acted in a manner deemed inconsistent with their apparent sex faced the penalties for sodomy: burning, hanging, or burial alive (Laqueur 1990: 135–9; Darmon 1979: 54).

The *Symposium* by Plato (c.428–c.348 BCE) abounds with symbolic hermaphrodites, engendering a wide variety of linguistic and sexual embarrassment. This dialogue re-enacts a lively after-theatre party, celebrating the success of Agathon's new play, where the guests compete to give the best account of love. The speech attributed to the comic writer Aristophanes purports to explain the variety and insatiability of desire. Human beings were originally two-headed spherical creatures, with eight limbs apiece. Since their overweening self-sufficiency led them to assail the gods, they were bisected. When they began to pine away, Zeus mercifully moved their genitals to their present position, so that they could reunite themselves, however briefly, with their corresponding halves. This myth gives heterosexual and homoerotic desire equal validity, by including all three sexual permutations, yet none appears entirely respectable, and all occupy sexual borderlines. The all-female couples are hermaphroditic in behaviour, by 'normal' heterosexual standards. The masculinity of the all-male pairing is in doubt: are boys who take male lovers effeminate? Aristophanes claims that such behaviour reveals an affinity for true manliness, and only boys of this type grow up to be successful politicians (192 A). The validity of this argument depends on what the reader thinks Plato thinks about politicians. The double-sexed archetype should surely be honoured by any community where monogamous marriage is the norm. But Aristophanes hesitates to name it: 'androgynon', with its implication that a man has feminine characteristics, has become a 'term of reproach' (Plato 1925: 189 E, 134–5).

The speech attributed to Agathon's lover, Pausanias, implies further complexities in hermaphroditic constructions. Pausanias contrasts two types of love, each represented by a goddess. The younger is Common Aphrodite, child of Zeus, king of the gods, and the goddess Dione. Her devotees 'love women as well as boys', and 'are set on the body more than the soul'. They 'find themselves doing everything at haphazard, good or its opposite, without distinction', because their Aphrodite 'in her origin partakes of both female and male' (Plato 1925: 181 B, 110–11). Heavenly Aphrodite, however, is free of wantonness, since she 'partakes not of the female but only of the male', kindling desire for 'what has a robuster nature and a larger share of mind' (Plato 1925: 181 C, 110–11). As a masculine goddess, Heavenly Aphrodite must be some kind of hermaphrodite, though different from her Common sister. So, too, must Zeus, who produced her without a mother's aid. Yet these apparently all-male hermaphrodites pass unnoticed in the debate.

Hermaphroditus was originally a Greek fertility god, a patron of marriage: 'it is probable that in the beginning he was vigorous and full of meaning, [...] and forcefully represented the richness of the two natures superimposed in him' (Delcourt 1958: 62). The earliest known version of his story appears in the Metamorphoses by the Roman poet Ovid (43 BCE–CE 17); parts of it are probably Ovid's own invention. Hermaphroditus is a wholly masculine boy, who spurns the advances of the beautiful nymph Salmacis, but bathes in the pool which bears her name. She follows him into the water, clasps his body like an octopus, and prays that they may never again be divided. Her prayer is immediately answered, though not as she had expected. The grammatical structure of Ovid's language collapses beneath the impossible task of differentiating between singular and plural:

> *Nec duo sunt et forma duplex, nec femina dici*
> *nec puer ut possit, neutrumque et utrumque videntur.*
>
> IV, ll. 378–9

> [They are no longer two, and they seem a double shape, such that it could not be called woman nor boy, a thing both neither and either.]
>
> (Ovid 1929: I, 204)

Far from doubling his sexual potency, Hermaphroditus is unmanned. His story is presented as a human tragedy: one culture's symbolic perfection becomes another's incarnate monstrosity. This treatment retained lasting popularity: the anguished expression on Hermaphroditus' face in a seventeenth-century illustration still invites specators to pity his terrible plight (Fig. 8.1).

Plato's 'Aristophanic' androgynes enjoyed a respectable afterlife as symbols of Christian marriage, aided by their similarity to the biblical account of Adam and Eve: indeed, Eusebius of Caesaria (fl. 310–16) suspected Plato of mocking the sacred truth of Genesis (Eusebius 1867: 95). Both accounts portrayed marriage as a union of separated halves rather than hitherto unrelated opposites. In 'Le Sixième Jour', his poem on the creation of Adam and Eve, Guillaume de Saluste du Bartas (1544–90) describes their first embrace as an 'amoureux Androgyne', l. 986 (Du Bartas 1581: II, 298). His English translator, Josuah Sylvester (1563–1618), omits the androgyne from the letter, but preserves it in spirit, as 'sweet *Hee-Shee*-Coupled-One', 'The Sixth Day of the First Weeke', l. 1051 (Sylvester 1621: I, 291). The collapse of gender and numerical distinction which, in Ovid, enacted the pitiful obliteration of Hermaphroditus' masculine autonomy, here emphasises the bliss of the first human couple.

Confusion is deliberately confounded in 'Upon an Hermaphrodite' by John Cleveland (1613–58) – one of the first communications to begin 'Sir, or Madame' (Cleveland 1640: 10). Here, if anywhere, one might hope to find a coherent description: this hermaphrodite is not the adaptable, figurative vehicle, but the literal, objectively presented tenor. Disappointment awaits. Cleveland is a learned poet in the metaphysical style, famous for his obscure conceits. He shows no interest whatever in hermaphrodites, except as an occasion for brilliant paradox. The hermaphrodite's function as a symbol of Christian marriage is not forgotten:

> For man and wife make but one right
> Canonicall *Hermophrodite*.
>
> ll. 17–18 (Cleveland 1640: 10)

But it would be hard for the married couple to envisage precisely what they were making. The one fact he establishes with certainty is that his addressee, unlike Aristophanes' primal androgynes, has one head, but only because one head is better than two for juxtaposing contrasts:

> Who would not think that Head a paire,
> That breeds such faction in the haire?
>
> ll. 21–2 (Cleveland 1640: 10)

Sometimes Cleveland's subject appears to be a blend of male and female throughout: 'I finde/In every limb a double kinde', ll. 19–20 (Cleveland 1640: 10). More frequently, it conforms to a common visual pattern, which appears in the picture of Hermaphroditus: male on the right, female on the left. Consequently, 'thy right leg takes thy left to dance', l. 56 (Cleveland 1640: 11). A frisson can also be provided by making lines of demarcation horizontal rather than vertical:

> How many melting kisses slip
> 'Twixt thy male and female lip?
>
> ll. 35–6 (Ceveland 1640: 11)

Finally, the creature's sexual instability is measured by temporal paramaters:

> Thus everie heteroclite part
> Changes gender, but thy heart.
>
> ll. 59–60. (Cleveland 1640: 11)

The unusual word 'heteroclite', a term applied to words which are grammatically irregular, gives the game away: the poet's focus is not on a body, but on language.

The following century witnessed aspirations towards a more enlightened and objective view of the universe. Practitioners of the newly developing scientific and medical discourse, regarding imagery as deceptive and confusing, strove to confine themselves to literal statement: their language was an important tool in their efforts to measure, explain and classify natural phenomena. Abstract hermaphrodites lost their symbolic function, while allegedly real ones were regarded sceptically. Some arguments against the existence of genuine, doubly fertile, human hermaphrodites were carefully researched and medically sound (Home 1799). Others, however, look more like rationalisation than rationality. James Parsons (1705–70) gained widespread respect for his theory that a so-called 'hermaphrodite' would usually turn out to be a woman with an abnormally large clitoris. To say otherwise was to deny the effectuality of God's all-creating word:

> it is impossible that there should be the least Imperfection in the Rudiments of any of the Ova, since they were implanted in Females from the Beginning of Time, by the Almighty *Fiat*, and were under the Restriction of that Law, that every Day's Experience confirms to us as certain; for if there were not so absolute a Law, with respect to the being of one Sex in one Body, we might then, indeed, expect

> to find every Day many preposterous Digressions from our present Standard. (Parsons 1741: 6–7)

While regarding double-sexed bodies as unthinkable breaches of divine law, Parsons acknowledges the existence of other 'preposterous Digressions' from his standards of physical perfection, including the genital abnormalities which led to the belief in hermaphrodites. The uniquely privileged status awarded to sexual dimorphism, upheld by appeals to religion, appears to reflect some deeply personal sense of the fitness of things. At the century's end, Erasmus Darwin (1731–1802), while indifferent to religion, evoked aesthetic standards in his assertion that sexual reproduction, and the associated physical differences, were 'the chef-d'oeuvre, or capital work of nature' (Darwin 1803: 35–6).

Different ideas of beauty, however, might engender different interpretations of natural development. According to Jean-Baptiste Robinet (1735–1820), *philosophe* of the French Enlightenment, mankind, as presently constituted, was not Nature's last word. She served notice of her intentions in the fossil called Histerolithos, which represented male and female organs in combination, so well imitated that they appeared ready for the act of generation (Fig. 8.2). Doubly fertile human hermaphrodites would eventually embody the ideal which generations of artists had striven to represent (Robinet 1768: 222–3). Robinet agreed with the art historian Johannes Joachim Winckelmann (1717–68), who argued that the best Greek sculptors had deliberately mingled the beauty of men with that of eunuchs and women. He singled out for special admiration a bust of such enigmatic appeal that, while he identified it as Bacchus, others believed it represented the beautiful goddess Leucothea, or the young Cretan princess Ariadne (Fig. 8.3).

Complex visual and linguistic depictions of hermaphrodites have continued to flourish. The most influential twentieth-century account of representations of the sexually liminal body is *S/Z* (1970) by Roland Barthes. This modern classic of deconstruction, familiar to all serious students of modern critical theory, is an exercise in multiple readings, based on *Sarrasine* (1830), a novella by Honoré de Balzac (1799–1850). Balzac's narrator tells the story of Zambinella, a beautiful castrato who became an opera star in the middle of the eighteenth century, and who was mistaken for a girl by Sarrasine, a terminally naïve young sculptor. Typical confusions arise when the narrator sees a beautiful young woman standing next to, and apparently incorporated with, a hideous old man (the aged Zambinella). Like Cleveland, he seems uncertain as to whether the hermaphroditic body is divided horizontally or vertically: he describes it as a chimaera (a creature divided at the waist), and reflects that many marriages are equally ill-assorted. The hermaphrodite's symbolic force rotates the line of bisection through 90 degrees (Barthes 1970: 72).

An important feature of *Sarrasine*, closely connected with the sexual ambiguity of its subject, is irony. Neither the narrator nor Sarrasine, whose viewpoint is frequently adopted, is wholly reliable. Sarrasine, for example, finds in his beloved Zambinella all the marvels of the statues of Venus sculpted by the Greek chisel (Barthes 1970: 120). He fails to realise that the beauty he admires has indeed been created by a blade – the *coltello*, or 'little knife', used to operate on a boy's testicles. He fails to make the distinction between natural plenitude and artificial deprivation to which Robinet was so sensitive. Fostered by ignorance and indifference, this irony has extended beyond the text, engulfing Balzc (or at least his narrator), and Barthes, who sees Zambinella's condition solely in terms of lack. To speak of Zambinella's lost phallus makes little sense, either literally, since the penis was always present in eighteenth-century castrati, or symbolically, since the wealthy and influential Zambinella enjoys a full measure of masculine power and authority (Barthes 1970: 169). The only 'lack' that castrati could be supposed to represent 'would be that of masculinity in a performative sense – of the ability to have erections, to penetrate, to ejaculate, to father children' (Noble 1997: 35). But even this lack may have been more apparent than real (Ringrose 1994: 507–18). Barthes' and Balzac's readers have been distracted from flesh-and-blood actualities: Zambinella 'has been treated within *S/Z* (and within the trail of discourse flowing from it) almost entirely as a cultural and psychological symbol – a kind of hallucination' (Noble 1997: 28).

The hallucinatory Zambinella takes many forms:

> The gap between representation and referent is symbolically accentuated by the history of Sarrasine's statue. It is modelled on Zambinella the castrato: it was intended by the artist as the statue of a woman; it is stolen by Zambinella's protector, the cardinal, who has it reproduced in marble, as an image of the ex-male he desires; the copy is itself copied by the artist Vien, but serves as a figure of Adonis (a male), and Vien's Adonis is the model of Girodet's Endymion. (Moriarty 1991: 138)

These portraits are all inaccurate: even the castrato statue is distorted by the spurious femininity with which Sarrasine has contaminated the whole chain of images. The sight of Zambinella has generated many representations, none of which adequately represents Zambinella.

Perhaps this is just as well: if he had been described in accordance with the facts about the physiology of eighteenth-century castrati, Zambinella could not have made such sterling contributions to the subtleties of modern critical theory.

Compared to books, films might seem unproblematical areas for sexually liminal representations, since visual images are always present. Yet, as the following examples of films about animals will show, interaction between words and pictures may obscure already ambiguous subjects, or even create ambiguity where it did not originally exist. The hero of *Babe* (Universal 1995), a plucky little piglet who is consistently referred to as a male in the dialogue, is played by females, to protect viewers' sensibilities from the embarrassing spectacle of porcine testicles and penis. Audiences generally remain oblivious to this cross-sexed performance: since they are expecting to see a male, that is what they tend to perceive. *Jurassic Park* (Universal 1992) also sets up sexual ambiguities, this time by allowing Dr Grant, a professional dinosaur expert, to ignore the fact that all the dinosaurs in the park were created female. When regarding Tyrannosaurus Rex with the detached eye of a scientific observer, he remarks, 'Look how it eats.' When considering the dinosaur's subjectivity, Grant appears to consider 'it' too impersonal, but avoids female pronouns. Instead, he says, 'He wants to hunt.' Grant continues to speak of her as male when she begins to hunt him and his companions: 'He can't see us if we don't move.' The respective mottoes of these two films could be 'See no female' and 'Hear no female.'

Femaleness is obscured again in *Godzilla* (Columbia, 1998), where the dialogue veils the sexual liminality which drives the plot. We see here a true hermaphrodite, laying hundreds of fertile eggs without a mate: a creature with these maternal characteristics should logically be referred to as 'she'. According to well-established scientific convention, even unicellular organisms like *volvox* are considered female when they engage in solitary reproduction: they form a 'mother-colony' (*Encyclopaedia Britannica* 1929: XXIII, 253). Yet throughout *Godzilla*, apart from one snide reference to the 'Virgin Lizard' (where femaleness is implied, though even then not stated), she is called 'it' or 'he'. Godzilla acts in the best traditions of Hollywood motherhood: she carefully selects a nest to lay her eggs, nurtures her offspring with tons of fish, mourns her dead babies with the most convincing display of grief in the film, and pursues their killers with berserk ferocity. Why, then, does the dialogue represent her as neuter, or a male who happens to lay fertile eggs? References to her as 'it' are consistent with normal usage for animals; they need not be understood as allusions to her reproductive physiology, since they begin before it is discovered. The use of 'he' is more problematic. At first, it may be an automatic response to her preternatural size and capacity for mass destruction. What is odd is the failure to change pronouns when the biologist, Nick Tatopoulos, announces that 'He's pregnant.' The script writers should know better. His sole concession to scientific correctness is a remark that Godzilla is 'a very unusual he'.

Is everyone simply being polite, giving a hermaphrodite the benefit of the doubt, as recommended by Saint Augustine? If so, their attempts to elide Godzilla's sexual ambiguity, and especially her femaleness, suggest that female attributes are still regarded as inferior. Their use of male pronouns also reflects an attitude which has been a long-standing grievance for feminists: 'In most natural histories, males are assumed to be the primary members of a species and females their appendages for reproduction' (Elia 1985: 27–8). The film does not necessarily endorse these views: as in *Sarrasine*, the distance between characters' perceptions and actual phenomena offers audiences an ironic perspective. Furthermore, Godzilla, like other hermaphroditic images, illuminates issues which extend beyond her own anatomical peculiarities. Her anomalous reproductive system is one of many mutations caused by nuclear fall-out: as both embodiment and victim of human failure to control and predict natural forces, it is appropriate that she should confront humans who attempt to classify her with an impossible task.

A return to ancient Greece and Rome provides a context, if not a resolution, for these accumulated ambiguities. There is a tradition in classical sculpture that the hermaphrodite should look one way while moving in another: it is probably engaged in 'a magical act whose meaning still escapes us' (Delcourt 1958: 61). Meaning is probably the act in which it is engaged. The last word belongs to that indefatigable antiquarian, Dom Bernard de Montfaucon (1655–1741), confessing his bewilderment at a hermaphroditic image surrounded by an array of inexplicable objects (Fig. 8.4). He decides to share this enigma with his readers, hoping it may yield an answer to some other riddle:

> Such a mysterious piece would puzzle an Oedipus: yet notwithstanding the Difficulties in some parts of such an Image, it is proper to give it to the Publick. For some of these Antique Figures, which may not appear to be of any immediate use themselves, may yet

> prove necessary to explain some other Monuments, which I have very often experienced. (Montfaucon 1724: I, 132)

The versatility of a double-sexed figure, its freedom to move between the opposite poles, even its ontological instability, contribute to its symbolic power. Forced into the position of eternal signifier by societies that will not let it *be*, the hermaphrodite becomes a symbol of representation itself.

Works cited

Augustine 1955 Saint Augustine, Bishop of Hippo, *De Civitate Dei*, 2 vols, *Corpus Christianorum [...] Series Latine*, XLVIII (Turnholti: Typographi Brepols Editori Pontificii)

Barthes 1970 Roland Barthes, *S/Z* (Paris: Seuil)

Bible 1611 *The Holy Bible*, Authorised King James Version (Oxford: Oxford University Press, edn of 1970)

Büsst 1967 A. J. Büsst, 'The Image of the Androgyne in the Nineteenth Century', in Ian Fletcher (ed.), *Romantic Mythologies* (London: Routledge & Kegan Paul) 1–95

Cleveland 1640 John Cleveland, *Poems*, ed. Brian Morris and Eleanor Withington (Oxford: Clarendon, edn of 1967)

Darmon 1979 *Le Tribunal de l'Impuissance: Virilité et Défaillances Conjugales dans l'Ancienne France* (Paris: Seuil)

Darwin 1803 Erasmus Darwin, *The Temple of Nature* (London: J. Johnson)

Delcourt 1958 Marie Delcourt, *Hermaphrodite: Myths and Rites of the Bisexual Figure in Classical Antiquity*, trans. Jennifer Nicholson (London: Studio Books, edn of 1969)

Diodorus Siculus 1888–1906 Diodorus Siculus, *Bibiliotheca Historica*, ed. F. Vogel (Lipsiae: B. G. Teubner)

Du Bartas 1581 Guillaume de Saluste du Bartas, *La Sepmaine (Texte de 1581)*, ed. Yvonne Bellenger, 2 vols (Paris: Nizet, edn of 1981)

Elia 1985 Irene Elia, *The Female Animal* (Oxford: Oxford University Press)

Encyclopaedia Britannica 1929 *Encyclopaedia Britannica*, 14th edn, 24 vols (New York: Encyclopaedia Britannica, Inc.; London: The Encyclopaedia Britannica Company, Ltd)

Eusebius 1867 *Eusebii Caesariensis Opera*, ed. Wilhelm Dindorf, II (Leipzig: B. G. Teubner)

Garber 1992 Marjorie Garber, *Vested Interests: Cross-Dressing and Cultural Anxiety* (New York and London: Routledge)

Gardner 1998 Jane Gardner, 'Sexing a Roman: Imperfect Men in Roman Law', in Lin Foxhall and John Salmon (eds), *When Men Were Men: Masculinity, Power and Identity in Classical Antiquity* (London: Routledge)

Graves 1960 Robert Graves, *The Greek Myths*, 2 vols (Harmondsworth: Penguin)

Heilbrun 1973 Carolyn G. Heilbrun, *Towards Androgyny: Aspects of Male and Female in Literature* (London: Gollancz)

Home 1799 Everard Home, 'The Dissection of an Hermaphrodite Dog, with Observations on Hermaphrodites in General', in *Philosophical Transactions of the Royal Society of London Abridged,* 18 vols (London: C. and R. Baldwin, edn of 1809), XVIII, 485–99.

Justinian 533 *The Digest of Justinian*, ed. Theodor Mommsen with the aid of Paul Kreuger, with English translation, ed. Alan Watson, 4 vols (Philadelphia: University of Pennsylvania Press, edn of 1985)

Laqueur 1990 Thomas Laqueur, *Making Sex: Body and Gender from the Greeks to Freud* (Cambridge, Massachusetts and London: Harvard University Press)

Livy 1944–76 Tite-Live, *Histoire Romaine*, ed. Jean Bayet *et al.*, trans. Gaston Bailet *et al.*, 32 vols (Paris: Société d'Edition 'Les Belles Lettres')

Mathers 1970 S. L. MacGregor Mathers, *The Kabbalah Unveiled* (London: Routledge & Kegan Paul.)

Möllerus 1692 Jacobus Möllerus, *Discursus Duo Philologico-Juridici, Prior de Cornutis, Posterior de Hermaphroditis, Eorumque Jure* (Frankfurt: C. A. Zeitler)

Montfaucon 1724 Bernard de Montfaucon, *The Supplement to Antiquities Explained, and Represented in Sculptures*, trans. David Humphrey, 5 vols (London: J. Tonson and I. Watts, edn of 1725)

Moriarty 1991 Michael Moriarty, *Roland Barthes* (Cambridge: Polity)

Noble 1997 Yvonne Noble, 'Castrati, Balzac and Barthes' *S/Z*', *Comparative Drama*, 31, 28–41.

Ovid 1632 Ovid, *Metamorphosis*, trans. George Sandys (Oxford: Lichfield)

Ovid 1929 *Metamorphoses*, ed and trans. F. J. Miller, 2 vols (London: Heinemann; Cambridge, Mass.: Harvard University Press)

Parsons 1741 James Parsons, *A Mechanical and Critical Enquiry into the Nature of Hermaphrodites* (London: J. Walthoe)

Plato 1925 *Lysis, Symposium, Gorgias*, ed. and trans. W. R. M. Lamb (London: Heinemann; New York: George Putnam's Sons)

Pliny the Elder 1601 C. Plinius Secundus, *The Historie of the World, Commonly Called, The Natural Historie of C. Plinius Secundus*, trans. Philemon Holland, 2 vols (London: Adam Islip, 1601)

Ringrose 1994 Kathryn M. Ringrose, 'Living with Shadows: Eunuchs and Gender in Byzantium', in Gilbert Herdt (ed.), *Third Gender: Beyond Sexual Dimorphism in Culture and History* (New York: Zone), 85–109

Robinet 1768 Jean-Baptiste René Robinet, *Vue Philosophique de la Gradation Naturelle des Formes de l'Etre, ou les Essais de la Nature qu'Apprend à Faire l'Homme* (Amsterdam: R. van Harrevelt)

Sylvester 1621 *The Divine Weeks and Works of Guillaume De Saluste Sieur Du Bartas, Translated by Josuah Sylvester*, 2 vols, ed. Susan Snyder (Oxford: Clarendon, edn of 1979)

Tholosanus 1591 Petrus Gregorius Tholosanus, *Syntagma Iuris Universi* (Frankfurt: P. Fischer)

Winckelmann 1764 Johannes Joachim Winckelmann, *The History of Ancient Art*, trans. G. Henry Lodge, 2 vols (London: Sampson Low, Marston, Searle, & Rivington, edn of 1881)

Zolla 1981 Elémire Zolla, *The Androgyne: Reconciliation of Male and Female* (New York: Crossroad)

9
Indeterminacy in Cyberspace

Francesca Froy

A wealth of discourse has developed surrounding new communications technologies, which suggests that they will transform not only how we communicate, but 'who we are'. Heim has described how technology is most intrusive when it comes to bear on communication, pointing out that where technology touches our language, it touches us 'where we live' (Heim 1993: 66). One of the ways in which the Internet, in particular, has the power to affect us is through changing the presence of our bodies to communication. Many writers claim that we actually become disembodied in cyberspace. The heroes of cyberpunk literature experience 'bodiless exultation' as they negotiate new electronic matrices.[1] Nyugen and Alexander describe how, on the Internet, 'the cardinal points and life's materiality disappear into the weightlessness of cyberspacetime' (Nyugen and Alexander 1996: 102).

The role of our bodies is obviously much reduced in computer-mediated communication. However, it takes a leap of the imagination to call this a 'disembodiment'. This chapter uses a materialist-discursive approach (Yardley 1997: 1) to understanding our relationship to new technologies, emphasising the basic embeddedness of human experience within (discursively interpreted) material conditions. Rather than providing an escape from the body, new communications technologies are understood to provide an extension of the body's operational field, our bodily boundaries and coordinates becoming in flux with the materiality of these technologies themselves. This bodily indeterminacy and extension is a routine aspect of our relationship to technology; however, the relative novelty of the Internet is that this merging occurs in a social space. New communications technologies shift the material context of communication, both negatively affecting the ability of our bodies to participate in the production of meaning and presence, and positively restructuring human communication via the new characteristics of the technology itself. This chapter explores, in particular, how this affects our experience of our own boundaries, asking: where are the boundaries to our 'self' on the Internet, and how do the boundaries change between self and other? In the process, I will look at new forms of indeterminacy and determinacy at the computer interface.[2]

Ideas of cyberspatial disembodiment find full force in the cyberpunk fiction that surrounds the emergence of computer-mediated communications. In cyberpunk, the body frequently becomes characterised as meat or 'datatrash'. As the mind explores the network, the body becomes both redundant and lifeless. But to what extent can computer-mediated communications really be said to disembody their users? While we sit at our terminals, surfing the net, do we really exist in a state of disembodiment? It is apparent that cyberpunk writing, and the theory which draws from it, is influenced by a certain Platonic idealism. However, these ideas do have some basis in the realities of the technologies themselves. Our bodies do appear to become disenfranchised when we communicate on the Internet. The body's physical coordinates cease to have any effect – chatting to someone on the other side of the world becomes as immediate as chatting to somebody in the same room. The Internet incorporates its own particular sorts of spaces and movements that are more abstract than material. Software programmers combine with net users to create virtual spaces, such as 'chat rooms' and on-line gaming environments (MUDs and MOOs) which require negotiation by text rather than by physical action. Our physical appearance and characteristics no longer have any direct impact.[3]

It can be argued, however, that cyberspace merely highlights the everyday ability of our bodily agency to transcend the contingent boundary provided by our skin. Ideas of cyberspatial disembodiment rest on a conception of the body offering a space of containment for the mind, with a firm boundary between what is inside and outside. When our agency is no longer determined by the body's coordinates, the mind is felt to have escaped, leaving the body behind. This idea of the body 'as a container' is a popular one within Western society. Johnson has suggested that it represents a primordial understanding which has acted as a dominant metaphor for our other experiences (Johnson 1987: 21). Lakoff similarly suggests that because we live in bodies we recognise that 'everything is either in a container or out of it' (Lakoff 1980: 272). This way of looking at the body has, however, been extensively critiqued within contemporary theory. Merleau-Ponty describes how our mind and body exist together as a field of operative potential which always projects outwards (Merleau-Ponty 1945: 98–147). Our embodiment is never static, but exists as a movement towards a perceptual and operational horizon. Battersby similarly describes the body as 'an event horizon in which one form (myself) meets its potentiality for transforming itself into another form or forms (the not self)' (Battersby 1993: 33).

Many different technologies allow us to extend our bodily sphere of operationality and action. When we are driving a car or using a pencil, these tools quickly become incorporated into our subconscious sense of bodily extension. Merleau-Ponty describes how objects also become absorbed into our sensory structures, suggesting that, 'The blind man's stick has ceased to be an object for him, and is no longer perceived for itself; its point has become an area of sensitivity, extending the scope and active radius of touch and becoming a parallel to sight' (Merleau-Ponty 1945: 143). Communications technologies are therefore in some ways like any other tool in helping us to extend beyond our bodies. As our engagement with cyberspace involves the negotiation of abstract space, it may be more difficult for us to understand this engagement as a 'bodily' one. However, we quickly become accustomed to using the computer keyboard and mouse to manipulate the software of cyberspace as we would any other practical tools. Also, while only a small fraction of our bodies may seem to be engaged with our negotiation of cyberspace, this disguises the fact that the rest of our body does actually become involved. Merleau-Ponty points to the fact that whatever we are engaged with, our whole body becomes absorbed in each task, no matter how small it is. He notices how, when putting pressure on a table with his hands, 'the whole of my body trails behind them like the tail of a comet' (100). When we type at a computer, likewise, we become completely wrapped up in our task, ceasing often to blink, eat and breathe properly, as our sole point of concentration becomes the computer screen.

Our self-transcendence in cyberspace is made much more apparent, however, because it has such a social impact. As Stone argues, 'inside the box are other people' (Stone 1995: 16). By pushing our boundaries of influence and agency beyond our bodies in a social context, digital technologies make this extension much more obvious, preventing us from experiencing the bodies of the people with whom we communicate. This is a factor relatively new to digital technologies – even the telephone, which also has qualities of being a kind of 'virtual' communication, involves vestiges of human embodiment in the voice. This changing presence of our bodies may be expected to have a dramatic social impact, because in everyday life our bodies are key to our notions of individuality and self. Foucault points to the way in which the body has been implicated in the cultural construction of 'man' – individual subjectivities characterised by interiority and depth (see for example, Foucault 1976). Stone describes how 'it is by the means of this framework that we put in place [...] the "I"' (Stone 1995: 85). The suitability of the body for such a framework is closely bound up with our notions of the boundaries of the body providing a space of individual containment for the mind, as previously discussed. It is also, however, related to the key role the particular physical appearances of our bodies play in constructing ideas of individual identity. The external surfaces of the body become read as clues as to what we are 'inside'. One user on the newsgroup cybermind commented that in everyday life, 'most of what I know about anyone has never been uttered by them or anyone else' (cybermind: Kerry Miller) This knowledge is dependent not only upon physical appearances but also on the way we act and move. It is also constructed by how our bodies are interpreted according to the dominant discourses of race and gender. Butler suggests that we cannot even conceive of human materiality except in relation to these highly politicised terms, which are built into our initial identification processes in the creation of 'culturally intelligible bodies' (Butler 1993: 2). The nature of the body as an object in space encourages us to objectify people as particular sorts of individuals, ignoring the fact that human subjectivity is fundamentally characterised by an indeterminate and changing consciousness which looks and projects outwards.

So what happens when our point of human contact becomes words on a computer screen? Is there any evidence that the invisibility of individual bodies is breaking down our notions of identity and self? One user of the newsgroup cybermind described how in the absence of her body, communicating on the Internet gave her a new feeling of authenticity. She wrote:

> It is this which has held me here. The authenticity. First impressions here are derived from people's own constructed mediation of self. In RL [*real life*], first impressions are more often tainted by social mores, personal prejudices, physical characteristics. We get an impression of people, which is beyond their control, before they ever have a chance to open their mouths. (cybermind: D. L. Richardson)

The fact that people are able to create constructed and mediated versions of their self, however, also creates a social world based on multiple fictions. When we meet other users in cyberspace, we still meet individual characters, as people construct particular identities for themselves. However, we are no longer able to fit these characters easily to 'whole persons'. Large numbers of newsgroups have formed around people's differences of interest to encourage people to explore diverse aspects of themselves and form multiple temporary coalitions. MOOs and MUDs create the most dramatic sense of multiplicity on the Internet, however, as they actively encourage people to develop numerous fictional selves. Turkle describes how Doug, a student, attends three different MUDs and plays four different characters within them – a seductive woman, a macho cowboy, a rabbit of unspecified sex and a sexual tourist (Turkle 1996: 13). Stone suggests that, in the absence of strong notions of body boundaries, the multiple spaces provided by the Internet liberate a natural multiplicity in our subjectivity which is normally constrained by our efforts to make people 'one' (Stone 1995: 42). Some people describe feeling a fundamental 'schizophrenia' in cyberspace, however, as they no longer experience any fixity to their identity over time. One user expressed a growing sense of disconnectedness, which he felt was spilling over into his everyday life. He wrote:

> it has finally dawned on me that 'being online' has an effect on my being offline. Specifically, thought processes which would have gone on 'normally' are truncated, aborted, when the option to drop PL [*physical life*] concerns for imaginary ones is in the offing... That is not to say I don't enjoy or don't feel I gain anything from, the online *portion* of my existence. But if it can't 'find its place' as only a portion, and insists on aggrandising *disconnectedness* as the primary state, then it does start to look like an addiction, and I, I don't need that. (cybermind: Kerry Miller)

Haraway expresses a concern that the multiple spaces of the Internet will leave us feeling that because we can be anywhere, we are 'everywhere' and therefore no longer acknowledge the partiality of our viewpoint (Haraway 1991: 1). She stresses that we still need to accept our location in this 'substantive web of locations' (Csordas 1994: 2). Understanding our relationship to the Internet as an extension of our bodily agency, rather than a disembodiment, is useful here. Our bodies can still be seen to provide a point of continuity over time without necessarily providing any fixity or containment of identity or self. The development of multiple identities may finally force us to revalue the boundaries of our bodies as having importance not for what they contain but for how they extend and connect. Machines are themselves increasingly becoming valued purely for their ability to communicate to other machines – their individual form and structure is becoming less and less important. The value of 'pinpointing' human beings as nodes on a network is already recognised by the technologies that track the movements of individuals on the net in order to target advertising. Human beings become re-understood merely as points where particular consumer preferences find their source.

The Internet may also play a role in altering our sense of identity and self through reducing the boundary we experience between ourselves and other people. One of the ways in which it is doing this is by blurring our notions of the private and the public. Because we are no longer communicating between bodies across public space, the Internet encourages us to externalise private experiences and fantasies in very public news groups. Numerous news groups have been formed around personal issues such as loneliness, sexual fetishes and trauma, encouraging our private thoughts to be effectively transformed into impersonal public discourse. Personal fantasies and problems do of course become externalised in other public spaces within society. However, this most often occurs within specific therapeutic environments which 'put thoughts right' so that they can be re-internalised. On the Internet our private thoughts are aired in groups which are frequently more productive than therapeutic. Seidler describes how the consequences of this can be dramatic. One net user, Sharon Lopatka, arranged her own murder after conversing with a man who responded to an advertisement on a computer bulletin board, where she specifically asked for someone to help her indulge her fantasy (Seidler 1998: 26). 'Private' fantasies become closer to becoming real public events, forcing us to recognise that our most intimate and personal experiences are also objective and impersonal. As Deleuze would say, the inside becomes merely a fold of the outside.[4]

As private relationships become more public on the Internet, public relationships can also become more 'private'. The removal of relationships from their normal performance over space brings hierarchical forms of relationship in particular to a more personal level. Discourse analysis has shown that hierarchical relationships become managed in the particular ways we project our bodies over space and in time, becoming controlled in conversations through bodily expression, movement, and interruption (see for example, Barker and Matts 1982). We manipulate our bodies in ways that alter our boundaries over space, allowing us to gain control over this space and thereby over other people. In the body's absence, the Internet has a dramatic equalising effect. Yancey and Spooner describe how the Internet quickly brings a relationship between a pupil and teacher to a more equal level as, 'through the opaque window of the email, she sees teacher as person' (Yancey and Spooner 1996: 257). Another theorist describes the way in which on meeting somebody in the flesh, 'the emotional boundaries of our encounter seemed to have been much expanded by the email that preceded it' (John Seabrook, cited in Yancey and Spooner 1996: 258). The way the Internet changes the public/private structures within our relationships becomes most obvious with people that we also see 'in the flesh' in everyday life. When we change between one mode of communication to the other, it can have the effect of making relationships seem oddly discontinuous.

The lack of 'bodily posturing' on the Internet may be one of the reasons for the general feeling of intimacy that occurs in chat spaces, and the ease with which new relationships become formed. This intimacy is also amplified by the increased sense of attention we feel as our bodies concentrate entirely on the computer interface. In everyday life our relationships are contextualised within wider ongoing projects and bodily praxis which distract our full attention from the other. However, just as the telephone usually takes all our attention when it rings, so the computer screen also overrides any other presence. As our whole bodies focus in on the computer screen, we can feel as though the other's attention is also completely focused on us, particularly in forms of instantaneous communication such as Internet Relay Chat. Lajoie suggests that this degree of attention creates a m(O)ther-like presence, which is similar to a maternal presence as it is imagined by the infant (Lajoie 1996: 156). Engaging with people over the Internet may perhaps be related to an attempt to 'close off the gap' in a similar way to the couples described by Lesnik-Oberstein elsewhere in this book, who fantasise about doing this through having a child. This feeling of total presence may also expand our egoism, in ways that can only be reinforced by the fact that people's bodies no longer characterise them in terms of particularity and difference, allowing us to imaginatively construct other people as the 'same'. As we project our own characteristics on to others, our sense of self expands, explaining the omnipotence felt by cyberpunk heroes in fictional computer networks. Lajoie indeed describes the Internet as a particularly narcissistic site, calling it a 'spectacular hall of mirrors' (168).

In other ways, however, new computer-mediated communications actually seem to increase the distance we experience between self and other, in ways that can shore up, rather than simply undermine, the boundaries we experience around the self. While my focus so far has been on an increasing indeterminacy at our boundaries in cyberspace, it also becomes interesting to look at ways in which communications technologies can bring new forms of determinacy to our communication, reinforcing ideas about separateness and 'containment'. Blackman describes how the interactivity of Internet spaces helps to reinforce our ideas of self as an independent agent. She argues that the choice and control offered to us within interactive spaces reduces our sense of interdependency and contingency, and thereby reinforces 'the hygienist principles which function within the modern conception of the subject' (Blackman 1998: 142). Blackman asserts a need to reinsert the body and flesh into virtual worlds, 'contaminating and disturbing those discourses that delimit what we take virtuality to be' (140).

Blackman's argument points to the fact that while our bodies no longer provide a boundary between self and other in cyberspace, real boundaries nevertheless exist in the hardware and software of computer technology itself. With its basis in the mutually exclusive 0s and 1s of binary code, digital technology is itself a paradoxically determinate medium. Whereas other building blocks, such as chemical particles, can blend and influence each other to create indeterminacy and flux, the 0s and 1s of binary code are mutually exclusive – the boundary between them cannot be crossed. Dreyfus describes how digital technology is by definition determinate: 'A digital computer – as the word digit, Latin for "finger" implies – represents all quantities by discrete states, for example relays which are open or closed' (Dreyfus 1972: 71). The determinacy of the digital is at the heart of the interactivity that makes computers so popular. Because the binary code is determinate and abstract, it can be easily manipulated. The vast network of the Internet itself arises from the fact that determinate elements can be endlessly and accurately repeated. However, the abstract nature of digital technologies may also mean that the more indeterminate aspects of our communication and our everyday worlds are less easily transmitted. The new digital boundary can bring a sense of distance and separation between us and the 'other', exposing the degree of indeterminacy and interdependency which in fact characterises embodied interaction in everyday life.

In the post below, a cybermind user compares the Internet with the more embodied form of communication that occurs through CB radio, describing how

> CB culture has died out to some extent everywhere, taken over in New York, for example, by late-night racists and just plain lonely people, mixed in with the roar of trucks, sadnesses and consolations. I picked them up; I listened when I first moved to the City, until I couldn't take it any longer, sensing an aural invasion of space. This never happens on the Net, which conveniently remains on the screen – in this sense, unlike CB, the Net is 'object' tied to technology, remote, and out of 'touch'. (cybermind: Alan Sondheim)

Here, a vestige of a human materiality – the voice – is characterised as somehow invasive and abject, illustrating the fact that in most forms of communication our bodies constitute a form of materiality that has a tendency to overflow through its emissions, crossing boundaries in sometimes unexpected and unacceptable ways. Connor describes how, like CB, the telephone similarly incorporates a considerable amount of bodily presence, and thereby creates a 'quasi-controlled collapse of boundaries, in which the listening self can be pervaded by the vocal body of another' (Connor 1997: 206). The contrasting distance of the Internet can partly be explained by the mainly visual nature of the medium, which creates a form of separation as our visual sense depends upon the maintenance of a certain degree of distance. However, it can also be explained by the fact that text-based media are forced to represent rather than transmit bodily expressions and emotions.

The 'aural invasion' described by the mailer above was a particularly emotional one. As appraisals of the world that involve the whole body, emotions are by nature indeterminate, in that they involve states of mind characterised by forces of intensity and flux. While we can partially represent our emotions in language on the Internet, this frequently disguises feelings and attitudes which become 'leaked' at a bodily level. Our emotional behaviour involves a degree of bodily 'posturing' which puts complex demands on other people that are often physical as much as mental, calling us into relationships of interdependency and care. This 'call to care' is also reinforced by the frailty and mortality of the body itself. Because of the possible depth of involvement we can have with other people, embodied forms of communication are risky, as we never know what will be demanded of us next. Talking to people on the telephone or face-to-face can sometimes be tiring as we carry out complex management processes to make sure our communication goes 'the way we want it to go'. On the Internet our relationships are characterised by a much greater degree of control over our reciprocity. Emails in particular provide us with the ability to solidify and reflect on the other and their relationship to us. We can decide when to read our emails, rather than being interrupted by a person's arrival or by the ringing of a phone. We can also keep emails, and refer to them as we wish. Our 'presence' for other people effectively becomes 'presents' which they can possess and manipulate as they would other gifts. This can in effect make computer-mediated communication seem a more controllable and 'safer' form of communication, and as Blackman argues, increase a sense of the automony of self.

The frustration which people feel when they have reason to communicate emotion on the Internet does, however, mean that people are starting to adapt language to compensate for the lack of an embodied presence. Despite fears that the Internet would actually simplify and 'dumb down' language, the use of language in email frequently becomes more 'writerly' as we attempt to convey complex embodied aspects of our experience. One cybermind participant has commented that this requires a real shift in how language is used, being less a question of finding new words than allowing language to 'proliferate in waves'. He writes:

> Perhaps the problem is that one hopes simply to find a word, to tack it on, to do what [...] 'can't be spoken'. But what 'can't be spoken' has a path which has a full body traversing this, and one constituent of that body is speech/writing. The suggestion I'm making is it requires a real shift in how language is used. In its subordination to the 'event' of pain, of comfort, and certainly of violence as well, language does not therefore disappear but rather proliferates and de-emphasised, rambles freely in 'waves', part novel, part chat log etc. (cybermind: Tom Blancato)

This email points to the way in which, in cyberspace, language acts as an intermediary between indeterminate bodies and the determinacy of digital worlds. Digital text may appear safe and homogenised, but it still has a very indeterminate field of reference. Our capacity to use language to hurt each other on the Internet is illustrated by the frequency with which 'flames' (angry and hostile comments) occur. Flaming is perhaps a particularly apt term to describe the peculiarly dry but highly damaging form of personal intrusion and disruption that the Internet enables. The power of language is also demonstrated in the cases of 'virtual rape' which are starting to be taken seriously as assaults upon the person, and are in fact beginning to call freedom of speech into question (see Dibbell 1999). Despite Blackman's argument as to the 'hygienic' nature of the virtual, the Internet is still a risky place to be, and the large number of people who use nicknames and 'tags' on the Internet may perhaps be doing so as much for self-protection as for experimentation.

Beginning to analyse the changing nature of our embodiment on the Internet reveals important implications for our sense of self and presence for others. The Internet creates contradictory experiences. At one point the loss of the body as a visual boundary increases the multiplicity and fluidity of human experience. At another the determinate nature of digital technology itself reinforces ideas of individual autonomy. The ambiguity of our encounter with digital technologies reveals the fact that we experience the materiality of our bodies on several different levels. Much of the increased indeterminacy we experience on the Internet is conceptual, in that it results from a collapse in notions of bodily containment and physical identity that are specific to certain forms of cultural discourse. On a more subconscious level we experience indeterminacy at the boundaries of our bodies throughout our lives. This is not only demonstrated in our engagement with new technologies but in our everyday relationships with other people.

Notes

1 The science-fiction literature which surrounded the emergence of the Internet and predicted the growth of a new virtual world in Cyberspace.

2 The chapter will focus in particular on people's discussion of their experiences on the newsgroup cybermind. It is acknowledged that this material may be particularly self-reflexive due to the nature of this newsgroup as a community that discusses the philosophy and psychology of cyberspace. The quotations stem from a period of research in 1996 into early reactions to the emergence of the Internet as a medium. The original emails can be found within the cybermind archive under cybermind@listserv.aol.com.

3 Short for Multi-User Dungeons and MUDs Object Orientated – on-line 'worlds' created and negotiated through text.

4 Deleuze's use of the concept of the 'fold', was drawn from the philosophies of Leibniz and Spinoza and developed in his analysis of both the baroque and Michel Foucault.

Works cited

Barker and Matts 1982 Ruth A. Barker and Daniel N. Matts, 'A Cultural Approach to Male–Female Miscommunication', in John L. Gumperz (ed.), *Language and Social Identity* (Cambridge: Cambridge University Press)

Battersby 1993 Christine Battersby, 'Her Body/Her Boundaries. Gender and the Metaphysics of Containment', *Journal of Philosophy and the Visual Arts*, 4: The Body, 30–9

Blackman 1998 Lisa M. Blackman 'Cultural Technology and Subjectivity', in John Wood (ed.), *The Virtual Embodied* (London: Routledge)

Butler 1993 Judith Butler, *Bodies that Matter* (London: Routledge)

Connor 1997 Steven Connor, 'The Modern Auditory I', in *Rewriting the Self: Histories from the Renaissance to the Present*', ed. Roy Porter (London: Routledge)

Csordas 1994 Thomas Csordas, *Embodiment and Experience: the Existential Ground of Culture and Self* (Cambridge: Cambridge University Press)

cybermind cybermind@listserv.aol.com: contributions by Tom Blancato, Kerry Miller, D. L. Richardson and Alan Sondheim, Summer 1996

Deleuze 1986 Gilles Deleuze, *Foucault*, trans. Seán Hand (Minneapolis: University of Minnesota Press, edn of 1988)

Dibbell 1994 Julian Dibbell, *My Tiny Life: Crime and Passion in a Virtual World* (London: Fourth Estate)

Dreyfus 1972 Hubert Dreyfus, *What Computers Still Can't Do: a Critique of Artificial Intelligence* (Cambridge: MIT Press, edn of 1994)

Foucault 1976 Michael Foucault, *L'Histoire de la sexualité: I: La Volonté de savoir*, trans. Robert Hurley as *History of Sexuality Vol. 1* (Harmondsworth: Penguin edn of 1990)

Haraway 1991 Donna Haraway, *Simians, Cyborgs and Women: the Reinvention of Nature* (New York: Routledge)

Heim 1993 Michael Heim, *Metaphysics of Virtual Reality* (New York: Oxford University Press)

Johnson 1987 Mark Johnson, *The Body in the Mind* (Chicago: University of Chicago Press)

Lajoie 1996 Mark Lajoie, 'Psychoanalysis and Cyberspace', in Rob Shield (ed.), *Cultures of the Internet* (London: Sage), 70–98

Lakoff 1980 George Lakoff, *Women, Fire and Dangerous Things* (Chicago: University of Chicago Press)

Merleau-Ponty 1945 Maurice Merleau-Ponty, *Phénoménologie de la perception*, translated by Colin Smith as *Phenomenology of Perception* (London: Routledge and Kegan Paul, edn of 1962)

Nyugen and Alexander 1995 Dan Thu Nyugen and Jon Alexander, 'The Coming of Cyberspacetime and the End of Polity', *Body and Society*, vol. 1, 3–4, 99–123

Seidler 1998 Victor Seidler, 'Embodied Knowledge and Virtual Space. Gender, Nature and History', in John Wood (ed.), *The Virtual Embodied* (London: Routledge)

Stone 1995 Allucquere Roseanne Stone, *The War of Desire and Technology at the Close of the Mechanical Age* (Cambridge: MIT Press)

Turkle 1996 Sherry Turkle, *Life on the Screen: Identity in the Age of the Internet* (London: Orion)

Yancey and Spooner 1996 Kathleen Yancey and Michael Spooner, 'Postings on a Genre of e-mail', *Classroom, Computers and Community*, May, 47: 2, 252–78.

Yardley 1997 Lucy Yardley, *Introducing Material-Discursive Approaches to Health and Illness* (London: Routledge)

10
Flaunting the Feminine

Michelle Meagher

> The practices of femininity can readily function, in certain contexts that are difficult to ascertain in advance, as modes of guerrilla subversion of patriarchal codes.
>
> (Grosz 1994: 140)

Cultural constraints imposed upon the ways in which we think of the body have fostered a sense of dualism which separates mind and body, self and other, masculine and feminine. In this chapter, I will explore the body in drag as a challenge to and a reformulation of such a code. The drag body reconceives gender as both surface and depth, learned and innate, public and private. Through its indeterminacy, the drag queen forces us to ask questions about the cultural production of gender. What is of particular interest to me here are the ways in which drag is very much about exaggeration and artifice. Drag queens don't look like women, but instead quote, and perhaps parody, the norms of femininity. In the race to determine sexual materiality (the *truth* of a body), this subtle and yet central point of drag is lost. How else might that aspect of the drag project which exposes the roots of femininity be put into action? Can women use the tools – or the pieces – of drag queens to perform a similar excessive femininity? What would it mean for a woman to perform femininity to excess, to parodically inhabit her own gender? Can such a performance be considered a subversive bodily act (Butler 1990a)?

In addressing these questions, I will explore what Judith Butler calls the compulsory order of sex, gender and desire as well as the processes of gender construction which perpetuate and sustain this order. Drawing from Butler's sense of drag as a subversive bodily act, I will consider the politics of drag as a cultural project. Using examples from the films *Gentlemen Prefer Blondes* (1953) and *Spice World* (1997), I will consider drag as a conceptual tool which might offer women a strategy for over-performing and excessively inhabiting femininity as a mode of 'guerrilla subversion of patriarchal codes' (Grosz 1994: 140).

In *Gender Trouble*, Judith Butler describes gender as performative, 'a stylized repetition of acts [...] the mundane way in which bodily gestures, movements, and styles of various kinds constitute the illusion of an abiding gendered self' (1990a: 140). Indeed, the sense that gender is a construction has been readily accepted by modern feminist theorists. What makes Butler's assertion different is that she also applies constructivist thinking to material sex, in essence, to biology. Her argument is that 'sex', too, is a construct. In *Bodies That Matter*, she asks 'how and why "materiality" has become a sign of irreducibility, that is, how is it that the materiality of sex is understood as that which only bears cultural constructions and, therefore, cannot be a construction?' (1993: 28). Surely sex is also a construct, an ideal to which all bodies are subjected, through which all bodies are made subjects and thereby come to matter. More importantly, the construction and discipline of bodies into two discrete categories serves to perpetuate a system of compulsory heterosexuality. The sexing of bodies has little to do with material difference, and more to do with social organisation and regulatory practices. Butler writes: 'one way in which this system of compulsory heterosexuality is reproduced and concealed is through the cultivation of bodies into discrete sexes with "natural" appearances and "natural" heterosexual dispositions' (1990b: 275).

As Elizabeth Grosz points out, it is this perception of naturalness, of an interior reality of gender identification, which is so strongly created through the regulatory norms and fictions of biological sex, gender, and desire. Drawing on the work of Foucault, she maintains that bodies are produced by culture. It is the disciplinary norms of culture that create 'personalised', 'interior' notions of gendered identity: 'the social inscriptions of bodies produce the effects of depth' (Grosz 1994: xiii). Similarly, Butler writes: 'acts, gestures, and desire produce the effect of an internal core or substance' (1990a: 136). Gender, she explains, is 'a construction that regularly conceals its genesis' (140). In effect, then, gender is constructed in such a way that it seems to arise 'naturally' from an interior sense of femininity or masculinity, a sense which results 'naturally' from a body sexed as female or as male. Furthermore, this 'natural' characteristic is fundamental to identity. Sex (and by extension, gender), considered by Butler to be a construction, is widely perceived as a primary trait and as perhaps the most important defining characteristic of an individual. It is so important a distinction, or in Butler's words, such a fundamental regulatory fiction, that the assignment of sex is the first act performed upon a member of society, and is considered to be a discovery, a reading of the body rather than an inscription upon it. The speech act 'It's a girl' constitutes the girl, it inscribes girlness, and in a sense, humanness, on to a body, marking it as a member of society, and welcoming it with discipline into a highly controlled heteronormative system of sex, gender and desire.

Butler certainly has a clear sense of the body as socially marked, but she does not describe it as an inert mass, nor as a substance which is passively inscribed upon. By arguing that gender is an everyday performance, she opens up a space where we can imagine a sort of permeability or exchange between the ways in which we perpetuate and maintain gender as it is constructed. What becomes clear is that gender is not merely imposed upon a body, nor is it wholly performed or chosen by a subject. In *Gender Trouble,* Butler invokes performance as a means of explaining gender as a repetition of stylised acts; gender is 'a tacit collective agreement to perform' (140). Sexuality, gender and sex are a contingency that is not natural, but rather is produced and constituted through performances that are always also citations. I use the term performance here to call attention to the ways in which Butler's work was taken up as a treatise on purposeful subversive performances. In *Bodies That Matter,* she addresses the vigour with which performance, and in particular, drag performance was taken up. Here, she clarifies the distinction between performance and the more fitting performativity:

> if I were to argue that genders are performative, that could mean that I thought that one woke in the morning, perused the closet or some more open space for the gender of choice, donned that gender for the day, and then restored the garment to its place at night. Such a willful and instrumental subject, one who decides *on* its gender, is clearly not its gender from the start and fails to realize that its existence is already decided *by* gender (Butler 1993: x)

And so, for Butler, there is no genderless subject; there is no subject prior to gender. Rather, we are all, for a variety of reasons, compelled to repeat the various acts of gender. And here is the really important part of Butler's work: if gender is a matter of citations and repetitions, repeated performances of an ideal femininity, an ideal masculinity, it is clear that there might be a real sort of agency inherent in that citing. To return again to Butler:

> 'agency', then, is to be located within the possibility of a variation on that repetition [...] it is only *within* the practices of repetitive signifying that a subversion of identity becomes possible. (1990a: 145)

Butler's project, then, is to look closely at the construction of gender, and within that process, she discovers the possibilities of negotiation. To be gendered means to enact gender, to constantly perform our genders, to repeat. It is the process of repetition – in which we are implicated – that is the source of subversion:

> The task is not whether to repeat, but how to repeat or, indeed, to repeat and, through a radical proliferation of gender, to *displace* the very gender norms that enable the repetition itself. (1990a: 148)

We cannot be rid of gender, but perhaps we can reformulate it, and as Grosz suggests, use the practices of femininity 'as modes of guerrilla subversion of patriarchal codes' (1994: 144).

In considering this question of performing gender as a subversive act, performing femininity excessively and consciously, I want to turn to the example of cross-dressing done by men, and in particular, to drag. Certainly, Butler's work on performance and performativity is of great importance to an understanding of cross-dressing. Indeed, in *Gender Trouble*, she points to drag as an example of a subversive bodily act which, through a dissonance of body and performance, exposes the ways in which gender is not 'natural' but rather performed and, in a sense, arbitrary. By performing femininity upon a body coded and recognised as male, drag displaces the sense of an interior identity which gives rise naturally to gendered performance.

The study of cross-dressing has garnered much attention in recent years. In a book review of two such explorations – Marjorie Garber's *Vested Interests*, and *Crossing the Stage*, edited by Lesly Ferris – Amy Robinson makes clear that the academic field that has grown out of the study of drag as a conceptual tool depends upon 'the oft-repeated claim that cross-dressing poses a systemic challenge to the stability of conventional gender binaries' (Robinson 1994: 197). Indeed, the practice of cross-dressing implicitly challenges the cultural narrative of a natural connection between the body and gender performance. In this way (at least momentarily), it disrupts the finely balanced system. Such performances are enabled by, and indeed prove the point that gender is a performance, that gender is created and enforced by the repetition of stylised acts. Adam Phillips, commenting on Garber's *Vested Interests*, writes: 'The transvestite [*and I would add all cross-dressers*] can make men and women look distinctly odd, peculiar in their "naturalness", absurdly trapped in their codes of difference' (Phillips 1994: 126; parenthesis mine). What they do not appear to do is offer a deep challenge to gender normativity. Michael Moon and Eve Kosofsky Sedgwick say of female impersonation: 'it allows performer and spectator to let off steam without really challenging predominant gender and sex roles for either' (Moon and Sedgwick 1994: 220). Amy Robinson suggests, 'the problem of passing [...] always depends on the intact logic of the binary itself'(197). That is, the body beneath any performance is still considered to be a sign of irreducibility, the source of real sex and by extension gender.

Butler draws upon the work of anthropologist Esther Newton, author of *Mother Camp: Female Impersonators in America*. Newton writes: 'if sex-role behavior can be achieved by the "wrong" sex, it logically follows that it is in reality also achieved, not inherited, by the "right" sex' (Newton 1972: 103). Drag is an instance of gender parody which highlights the dissonance between body and performance, thereby calling into question the naturalness of gender identity. The finely balanced system, what Butler names the compulsory order of sex, gender and desire, is, through drag, exposed as a construction – its genesis is uncovered, the cause is shown to be an effect. Surely, if men can perform femininity as well as women (if men can even out-perform women at femininity), it goes to show that the so-called natural connection between material sex, gender and desire is spurious.

Butler suggests that the source of agency in performing gender is to be found within the system, whereby one might take up the tools of gender binarism and compulsory heterosexuality, finely and fatally reworking gender from within. For indeed, gender is not 'real', but instead a phantasmatic norm which comes to be only in our complicity, in our repeated performances of gender. Certainly then, once the sense that gender is performative is exposed (i.e. by drag) it seems clear that the next step is to perform parodically, to '"cite" the law to produce it differently, to "cite" the law in order to reiterate and coopt its power' (Butler 1993: 15).

Drag has always been an important challenge to gender normativity; drag queens are intimately and proudly connected to questions of sexuality, as well as the system which naturalises sex and gender norms. They were, and continue to be, at the centre of the gay liberation struggle. Stonewall, after all, was about drag queens in New York gay bars. Ian Lucas writes: 'it is the drag queens and cross-dressers who have been at the very centre of debates around sexuality and sexual identity, and who have provided the most daring challenges to conformity and normative practices' (Lucas 1994: 56).

Drag queens revel in pageantry, in artifice, in excess and glamour. Their gender is above all a performance, a conscious and complicated performance. Most importantly, the drag queen is political and noticeable not for an ability to become a woman, but for a *failure* to do so. That is, in citing the phantasmatic norms of femininity to excess, drag queens emerge not as women but as what might be considered monstrously gendered. As that elderly gentleman of indeterminate sex, Quentin Crisp, maintains: 'No one would mistake RuPaul for a woman. He's a thing. They only want to know, "Where does he put it?" And so it was with all great drag artists; they want everyone to know they are men in drag, not women' (Chermayeff et al., 1995: 92). The important point here is that drag performance is not merely a matter of crossing, but of a thicker indeterminacy. That is, through a deliberate highlighting of gender – where gender is performed excessively and monstrously – drag confounds the order of sex, gender and desire and replaces causal connections with an exchange. Drag queens redefine what it is to be a woman, more importantly, what it is to be gendered. Through a thickly theatrical performance, they create a different sort of gender and a different way of conceiving gender altogether.

Using a sense of gender as both performance and performative – a stylised repetition of acts which produces a sense of gendered interiority – I want to consider the ways in which women perform femininity and how we might critically over-perform femininity. How can women take up the tools of gender in such a way that the possibilities for negotiation are revealed? How might women use the performative qualities of gender in order to rework the oppressive ideals of femininity? How might women use drag as a conceptual tool? Does such a performance by women engage more fully with the sense of femininity as constitutive, both inscribed upon and performed by the body constructed as female? Can there be women in drag? In considering these questions, I will turn to two examples of women in drag in film. The first, *Gentlemen Prefer Blondes*, features Marilyn Monroe and Jane

Russell; the second, *Spice World*, features Mel B, Mel C, Victoria, Geri and Emma of Spice Girls fame. Neither film is particularly liberating for women, nor do they explicitly offer subversive commentaries on gender roles. However, in very similar ways, each film offers a glimpse of the female female impersonator.

Marilyn Monroe has become the ultimate symbol of twentieth-century femininity and female sexuality and yet, above all, she is a masquerade. Her representation is utterly artificial, utterly parodic. It is said that Monroe was able to move comfortably in public, for without her mask – the mask of Marilyn – she was unrecognisable. Indeed, Marilyn, with her bleached blonde hair, her distinct bodily habitus, and her dresses reputedly worn two sizes too small, is the height of constructed femininity; she is a symbol of femininity. The mask of Marilyn is so resounding that in retrospect, she is understood as two women: the 'real' Norma Jean Mortenson and the 'constructed' Marilyn Monroe. What is the attraction to Marilyn? Is Marilyn actually Norma Jean in drag? Certainly, Monroe's performance of femininity was purposeful and calculated – she worked with feminine pieces as much as any drag queen might. But the problem is that her performance was taken to represent the pinnacle of femininity – as monstrous or grotesque or foolish as it might appear to us now, it certainly does not have the critical, subversive edge of the drag queen's reworking of gender.

I am particularly interested in an early Monroe film, *Gentlemen Prefer Blondes*, directed by Howard Hawks and released in 1953. In the film, Marilyn is cast as the dumb blonde; she is Lorelei Lee, a cabaret star and gold digger. Playing against her is Jane Russell as her best friend Dorothy. The best friends are an unlikely duo: Lorelei is at once deceitful and naïve, Dorothy is down-to-earth and resourceful. In an attempt to clear her friend's name, Dorothy poses as Lorelei in a French court. In this scene, Dorothy dresses up by wearing a blonde wig, jewels, a fur coat covering showgirl clothes, and affects the silly yet sly stupidity for which Marilyn/Lorelei is famous (Fig. 10.1). In effect, we see the ways in which Marilyn is constructed – Marilyn is a series of accoutrements, a ruse easily enacted. Yet, in this masquerading scene, what is most obvious is that the image does not work for Russell. She seems clumsy in Marilyn's accoutrements. She can't 'do' Marilyn. More than anything, dressing and performing as Marilyn highlights her own body. Russell, in this scene, seems to be performing Marilyn *as a drag queen*. This is the performance of femininity – the contemporary epitome of femininity – on a female body and still, *it does not work*. Similar to the butch who is uncomfortable in high heels, it is Russell's *body* which makes the performance so surreal, so unreal – she seems too tall, too rigid, too (dare I say it) *masculine*. Her inhabitation effects a separation, a glitch, a space between Dorothy and Dorothy as Lorelei, which is also the space between Jane and Jane as Marilyn. In effect, we see the ways in which Marilyn is constructed, but also it is evident that Monroe *is* that construction. When Marilyn *does* Marilyn, or rather Norma Jean does Marilyn, there are no gaps. Marilyn *done* by anyone else becomes a monster, a body out of place.

Just as Marilyn performs what might be considered the height of twentieth-century femininity, each of the five superstar Spice Girls represents one aspect of modern womanhood – Sporty, Scary, Baby, Ginger and Posh – an interesting nineties postmodern twist on feminine roles, allowing a sense of variety yet still severely limited consumptive scripts. Indeed, just as Marilyn is Norma Jean in drag, each Spice Girl has two identities: Posh Spice is Victoria in drag, Ginger Spice is Geri in drag, and so on. Each member of the band defends her differences as unique expressions of her individuality. Yet what becomes clear while watching them interviewed or in video is an engagement in *excessively* feminine behaviour. Watching the Spice Girls, it is never clear whether or not they are engaged in parody. Are they flirting with femininity, or wholly entrapped by it? Is the performance protest or retreat?

Spice World features a scene that is similar to the courtroom scene of *Gentlemen Prefer Blondes*. In a supposed photo shoot, modelling turns to parody when we see the girls dressed up as Charlie's Angels, Elvis, Bob Marley, Marilyn Monroe and, in the end, as each other. What this scene points to is the way in which each persona of womanhood, so cleverly distributed amongst the five Spice Girls, is performed and played out. The photo shoot scene in *Spice World* throws a welcome wrench into the problem of reading the Spice Girls. After dressing up as things they are not, they dress up as each other: Sporty wears Posh's tight dress and high heels, Ginger dons a blonde wig and quotes Baby: 'My mommy is my best friend, shhh ...' Scary creeps up to the camera, fingers in the peace sign and mimics Ginger: 'Girl Power, blah blah blah, feminism, d'ya know what I mean?' Each makes fun of the personae taken on by the others and by extension exposes the performances of femininity as merely mirages, tricks of staging, costuming and make-up. The play within this scene is subtle and it is not until the end of the scene that it becomes clear that they are dressed up in each other's clothes, that they are all in drag.

This drag is ambiguous in a way that drag done by men is not. In both *Spice World* and *Gentlemen Prefer Blondes* femininity is made strange, alien and monstrous on bodies marked and read as female. Indeed, when a man plays at femininity, we can quickly pinpoint what is strange: a male body, a feminine performance. Certainly, such performances offer up a challenge to the structure of gender, but in effect, our reading of materiality – that is, the body – almost always wins out and confirms the system: men in women's clothing look unnatural. However, femininity made strange on female bodies fundamentally shakes up the process by which we come to interpret the sexed and gendered world around us.

Through this sort of alienation, 'the appearance, words, gestures, ideas, attitudes that constitute the gender lexicon become illusionistic trappings that are *nevertheless* inseparable from, embedded in the body's habitus' (Diamond 1996: 47). What becomes clear when discussing the examples of 'cross-dressing' in *Gentlemen Prefer Blondes* and in *Spice World*, is that female female impersonation works at conflicting levels. Jane Russell's attempt to 'do' Marilyn at once points to the way in which Norma Jean's Marilyn is defined by a series of accoutrements and the way in which those accoutrements are hers alone. Baby's youthful naïveté is sabotaged when enacted by Ginger. There is a sense then that gender performance is intimately connected to an individual's way of living in and inhabiting her body – and the body and gender are again connected. Furthermore, we come to a sense that gender is a construction but more than that, it is an individualised performance, repeated and imposed, creating an individually gendered body. Gender then, is a performance – the active repetition of stylised acts – as well as a performative – a repeated act that is also always a citation.

Is *Gentlemen Prefer Blondes* critical of femininity? Is it critical of Marilyn as the pinnacle of femininity? Not likely, but within the film there is a small site in which we can see Marilyn as unreal, as a citation without ground, a phantasmatic performance of an ideal. Similarly, there are glitches in the highly stylised performances of each of the Spice Girls. The alienation effect is momentary – the scenes I have described here are incidental, not central to the films themselves, hardly reflective of any political strategy set out either by Monroe and Russell or the Spice Girls. More importantly, *any* critique offered through a female female impersonator is a matter of a momentary glitch. A woman dressed as a woman – excessive or not – will in some ways always fit into the compulsory order of sex and gender. The subversion of a female female impersonator is found in that moment of indeterminacy when we recognise a thick theatricality, an alienation from what is considered natural. And this is what Elizabeth Grosz alludes to in her assertion that femininity might function as 'modes of guerrilla subversion of patriarchal codes' (Grosz 1994: 140). She goes on to say: 'the line between compliance and subversion is always a fine one, difficult to draw with any certainty' (144). Female female impersonators are, by definition, wrapped up in, defined by femininity as more than merely play, more than merely performance. For women in drag, gender is performed and performative, it is, to use Elin Diamond's terms, both 'a doing and a thing done' (Diamond 1996: 1).

To actually look *at* the female female impersonator is to recognise the thick, critically theatricalised performance of femininity. Compared to transvestism and drag, this is at once a more critical and more volatile form of gender subversion. More critical, because it dislocates femininity, makes femininity alien *on a body marked as female*. The female female impersonator exposes how her own gendered identity is itself a ruse, a masquerade. For female female impersonation does not deny a female body, nor does it deny a feminine identity. Instead, it uses a theatricalisation of femininity to explore the ways in which femininity is both a performance and performative, constitutive of both identity and subjectivity. This is, however, volatile, for the female female impersonator is not performing femininity with the safety of a male body. The male female impersonator is always already removed from his performance by virtue of a physical distance from femininity. For the female female impersonator, there is a potential slippage between the doing and the thing done, between gender as a highlighted performance and gender as an everyday repetition of acts.

Can we really look *at* the cross-dressed figure at all? Amy Robinson writes: 'seeing inevitably turns into reading, and reading is thoroughly invested in the narrative conventions of social intelligibility and legibility' (Robinson 1994: 200). Surely, we cannot remove ourselves from our cultural sex recognition training. Nor can we remove ourselves from the system which produces us as necessarily gendered subjects. The cross-dressed figure – transvestite, transsexual, drag queen, female female impersonator, butch – instead offers a glimpse of a different way of seeing, a different way of conceiving gender. In the moments between seeing and reading, these figures pose a challenge to the ways in which we read bodies, in which we read representations of gender. In that moment, the spectator sees a glitch in the sex/gender system: Is it a man? Is it a woman? Is it a monster? The monstrosity that is the cross-dresser is culturally located in a netherspace: between male and female, between masculine and feminine, between subversion and reiteration. This uneasiness is the subversive strength of the cross-dresser. In exposing the ways in which sex, gender, sexuality, the body and identity are fluid and malleable, the cross-dresser opens up momentary glitches in the system which allow a privileged view into the ways that we construct narratives of sex and gender. Finally, the cross-dresser may not be the most subversive of cultural figures; indeed, as Sedgwick writes, 'the bottom line is generally the same: kinda subversive, kinda hegemonic' (1993: 15). However, it is a figure which engages with some of the most pervasive and encompassing matters of modern Western culture and provokes us to see and read in utterly different ways.

Works cited

Butler 1990a Judith Butler, *Gender Trouble: Feminism and the Subversion of Identity* (New York: Routledge)

Butler 1990b Judith Butler, 'Performative Acts and Gender Constitution: an Essay in Phenomenology and Feminist Theory', in Sue-Ellen Case (ed.), *Performing Feminisms: Feminist Critical Theory and Theatre* (Baltimore: Johns Hopkins University Press), 270–82

Butler 1993 Judith Butler, *Bodies That Matter: On the Discursive Limits of 'Sex'* (New York: Routledge)

Chermayeff et al. 1995 Catherine Chermayeff, Johnathan David and Nan Richardson (eds), *Drag Diaries* (San Francisco: Chronicle Books)

Diamond 1996 Elin Diamond (ed.), *Performance and Cultural Politics* (London: Routledge)

Garber 1992 Marjorie Garber, *Vested Interests: Cross-Dressing and Cultural Anxiety* (London: Penguin)

Grosz 1994 Elizabeth Grosz, *Volatile Bodies: Toward a Corporeal Feminism* (Bloomington: Indiana University Press)

Lucas 1994 Ian Lucas, *Impertinent Decorum: Gay Theatrical Manoeuvres.* (London: Cassell)

Moon and Sedgwick 1994 Michael Moon and Eve Kosofsky Sedgwick, 'Divinity: a Dossier, a Performance Piece, a Little-Understood Emotion', in Eve Kosofsky Sedgwick (ed.), *Tendencies* (London: Routledge), 215–51

Newton 1972 Esther Newton, *Mother Camp: Female Impersonators in America.* (Chicago: University of Chicago Press)

Phillips 1994 Adam Phillips, *On Flirtation: Psychoanalytic Essays on the Uncommitted Life* (Cambridge, Mass.: Harvard University Press)

Robertson 1996 Pamela Robertson, *Guilty Pleasures: Feminist Camp from Mae West to Madonna* (London and New York: Tauris)

Robinson 1994 Amy Robinson, 'Book Review: *Vested Interests* by Marjorie Garber and *Crossing the Stage* edited by Lesley Ferris', *TDR*, 38: 4, 197–200

Sedgwick 1993 Eve Kosofsky Sedgwick, 'Queer Performativity: Henry James's *The Art of the Novel*', *GLQ*, 1: 1, 1–16

11

Shape-shifting and Role-splitting: Theatre, Body and Identity

Lib Taylor

Andrew Parker and Eve Kosofsky Sedgwick propose that 'performative' is a term whose meaning is contested, and that the struggle over its interpretation has been partly responsible for shifts in focus in the field of theatre away from study of 'theatre', its structures and institutions, and towards 'performance' and its focus upon presence and corporeality. They write:

> performativity's recent history has been marked by cross-purposes. For while philosophy and theater now share 'performative' as a common lexical item, the term has hardly come to mean 'the same thing' for each. [...] in its deconstructive sense performativity signals absorption; in the vicinity of the stage, however, the performative is the theatrical. (Parker and Sedgwick 1995: 2)

Postmodernism, feminism and psychoanalysis have theorised identity as performative, perceiving identities as constructed through a process of reiteration (repetition/rehearsal) and citation (reference/quotation). Performativity, in this philosophical sense, entails the incorporation of norms of gender identity into the lived subjectivity of an individual, through a process of unreflected absorption. For this essay, what most significantly marks this definition of performativity is that iterative acts are assimilated imperceptibly and digested unconsciously. At the same time, performativity is fundamental to theatre in that its conventions are developed through a process of citation or reiteration – quotation and repetition – of historical, social and cultural practices. But in theatre, the notion of performativity goes further than describing a denotative/connotative process since the term implies a self-aware theatricality and indicates a theatrical event which foregrounds the representational functioning of the staged event. What most significantly marks this definition of performativity is its conscious use of the practices and conventions of theatre, its deliberate manipulation of citation and reiteration.

This struggle over semantics is at the centre of current debates in the cluster of disciplines which have performance at their core: dance, theatre, film, live art and music. 'Performativity' clearly derives from the same root as 'performance', the activity which distinguishes and links the performing arts, and accordingly is a principal field of interest for performance scholars. Yet, recent reformulations of J. L. Austin's notions of performativity which focus on way the performative of our 'everyday reality' functions to conceal and dissimulate the process of citation and reiteration, has forced live art, dance and theatre performance scholars to re-evaluate their assumptions regarding the nexus of meanings which comprise performative and performativity and the implications for the performing arts (see Austin 1955). As a result, performance, and corporeal elements of performance in particular, have become a locus of the study in theatre. Theatre, with its focus on the split between actor and role(s), and on the manipulation of the liveness of the body, offers a tangible arena for exploring issues of identity and performativity. Transformations and transmutations are the fundamentals of theatre and in its bid to address alternations, shifts, variations and displacements of identity/subjectivity, alternative theatre has placed the exploitation of the performer's body and its potential for disguise, masquerade and impersonation at the centre of practice.

In *Bodies That Matter* Judith Butler focuses on one end of the continuum of meanings when she insists that the process of performativity by which gender identity is produced is not theatrical. She maintains that 'The norm of sex takes hold to the extent that it is "cited" as such a norm' through reiterative and citational performative acts (Butler 1993: 13). These acts are not consciously quoted or repeated but are incorporated into identity through a process of absorption which masks the codes of social performativity being enacted (see Butler 1993: 12). As Geraldine Harris states, 'Butler's notion of sex/gender as performative [...] refers to something the intelligibility of which depends on it having the appearance and the effect of being "real"' (Harris 1999: 175). On the other hand, theatricality, which discloses its mimetic constitution, for Butler, implies a self-consciousness which invokes a 'voluntarist subject who exists quite apart from the regulatory norms' and who can somehow inhabit identities of choice (Butler 1993: 15). Butler, therefore, opposes 'performativity' and 'theatricality' suggesting that performativity 'conceals or dissimulates the convention of which it is a repetition', whilst implying that theatricality is an act of individual, cognizant spectacle (12).

While in no way refuting the distinction Butler makes, what her equation does not take into account is the complexity of the performative dimension of theatrical performance. Harris observes:

> The problem is that, in *theory*, it is very difficult, if not impossible, to distinguish absolutely between performance and Butler's concept of sex and gender as performative, since performativity exists within performance. (Harris 1999: 173)

As I have already suggested, theatrical performance functions through the operation of citation and reiteration, but not only at the conscious level of deliberate reference to a theatrical history or to a regulated set of cultural and dramatic conventions, but also, significantly, at an unconscious level since the theatrical event is circumscribed by the performer whose subjectivity is defined by performativity. The actor's body is a field (or s(c)ite) marked by a set of physical gestures and visual and oral signals which are inseparable from the performance, but which are not part of the voluntary gestus, and which inflect its meanings. Theatrical performance is a kind of palimpsest inscribed upon the body of the actor whose own identity is not erased by the process and, as such, the performer's performativity is part of the performance. It is the presence of the live 'performed' subject who simultaneously both inhabits an absorbed identity and dons an assumed and designated role(s) in the theatrical performance that makes the theatre such an appropriate critical space for deconstructing performativity. While Parker and Kosofsky maintain that the notion of social performativity is deconstructive, I am suggesting that theatre performance has the potential for displaying self-conscious performativity and can become the mechanism for that deconstruction.

In the paragraph above, I coupled 'theatre' with 'performance' in order to attempt to clarify a distinction between the performance of a staged event (intentionally theatricalised performativity) and quotidian performance (Judith Butler's performativity). But the blurring of 'theatre' and 'performance' raises additional contentious questions and the slipperiness of the terminology is further exposed. While theatre sees performance (often rather too unproblematically) as central to its discipline, since the 1960s the term 'performance' has also been used to define an opposition to theatre, whereby performance displaces and destablises the ideologies and authority of illusionist theatre. Influenced by Artaud and his Total Theatre, experiments with performance have rejected traditional structures of theatre with its focus upon text and concealed mimesis, in favour of the plastic, physical dimensions of performance, including the actor's body (see Artaud 1938). Elin Diamond sums up the opposition of theatre and performance as follows:

> Theater was charged with obeisance to the playwright's authority, with actors disciplined to the referential task of representing fictional entities. [...] Performance, [...] has been honored with dismantling textual authority, illusionism, and the canonical actor in favor of the polymorphous body of the performer. Refusing the conventions of role-playing, the performer presents himself/herself as a sexual permeable tactile body, scourging audience narrativity along with the barrier between stage and spectator. (Diamond 1996: 3)

To oppose performance and theatre sets up a kind of binary antithesis in which performance becomes a weapon to defeat theatre. Theatre is thereby reduced to a narrow and sterile definition dependent upon illusionistic mimesis and the (re)constitution of text; and thus it is disconnected from some of its most potent theories of representation and its contribution to the field of performance is disavowed. I would assert that in much current theatre practice there is a strong performance dimension which works in healthy combination with the structures of theatre, both exposing its ideology and drawing upon its interrogative strengths. In contemporary experimental theatre, performance becomes a discourse of intervention, it is not the medium by which the text is channelled unproblematically to a passive audience but an agency that acts upon the text (whatever form that text might take), reconstituting it not as something reinvigorated but as something fundamentally (re)composed and (re)formed. Diamond defines the interdependence of theatre and performance, stating:

> We might observe that if contemporary versions of performance make it the repressed of conventional theater, theater is also the repressed of performance. Certainly powerful questions posed by theater representation – questions of subjectivity (who is speaking/acting?), location (in what sites/spaces?), audience (who is watching?), commodification (who is in control?), conventionality (how are meanings produced?), politics (what ideological or social

> positions are being reinforced or contested?) – are embedded in the bodies and acts of performers. (Diamond 1996: 4)

Theatre proceeds through a process of impersonation and role-play. By adopting forms of theatre which interrogate its means of representation, it can function as a critical site for exploring the constitution of identity through performativity. Susan Bennett maintains:

> In performance practice [...] representations of gender can be produced in a parodic style and offered to the audience for specific recognition of the gaps and dissonances between the received performance of gender positions and the actual performance of those same positions being staged. (Bennett 1998: 267)

Her use of the terms 'audience' and 'staged' suggest that the performance practice to which she refers is theatrical performance. Under these circumstances, theatre becomes a discursive space – a laboratory – in which social performativity, the absorption of reiterated 'acts', can be deconstructed through self-aware theatrical performativity. The 'reiterative or rearticulatory practice' which composes identity is played out and displayed through the formation and reformation, the constitution and reconstitution of corporeal, gestic performance within the regulated and delimited space of theatre (Butler 1993: 15). Judith Butler asks: 'What would it mean to "cite" the law to produce it differently, to "cite" the law in order to reiterate and coopt its power?' (15). Deconstructive theatre provides a space in which the law might be 'cited' differently. Furthermore, deconstruction in theatre advocates the destabilisation of regulated textuality in relationship to theatrical images, thereby dislodging ideologies and disturbing spectator identification. Rather than functioning to enhance the coherence of identity and character roles then, the setting, costume, gesture, bodies, props become a chain of signifiers which attest to performativity (both theatrical and absorbed) and representation. Using the combined resources of theatrical *mise-en-scène* and bodily performance modes, new imaginings of culturally defined bodies can be invoked and proposed, opening up for exploration the ideological currents which determine gendered representations.

While Geraldine Harris cautions against the reification of Brecht's theories as the '"master" discourse for political theatre' and objects to the dominance of his ideas in recent political theatre critical practice, Elin Diamond reclaims the work of Brecht as significant for the performance of gender (Harris 1999: 79). Although anxious to recognise the contradictions in invoking Brecht, who 'exhibits a typical Marxian blindness toward gender relations', in her article 'Brechtian Theatre/Feminist Practice', Diamond proposes that by invoking and reworking his theories of alienation and defamiliarisation, the performative of gender is displayed and critiqued (Diamond 1997: 44).

> When gender is 'alienated' or foregrounded, the spectator is able to see what s/he can't see: a sign system *as* sign system. [...] Understanding gender ideology – as a system of beliefs and behaviour mapped across the bodies of women and men which reinforces a social status quo – is to appreciate the continued timeliness of *Verfremdungseffekt*, the purpose of which always is to denaturalise and defamiliarise what ideology – and performativity – makes seem normal, acceptable and inescapable. (47)

While Diamond argues that reference to Brechtian practice can make theatre an appropriate cultural and theoretical space for deconstructing the process of performativity, Harris maintains that a deference to Brecht 'generate(s) a privileging of a particular set of theatrical conventions as properly political' (Harris 1999: 79). Nevertheless Harris acknowledges that in order for theatre performance to critique social performativity the difference between the two modes must be marked:

> a theatrical performance depends on the legible presence of the quotation marks, which as described by Butler, the process of performativity as citation operates to conceal in 'everyday life'. (76)

Diamond implies that those 'quotation marks', so essential to the critical function of theatre, can be made visible by a postmodern reformation of Brechtian ideas. Strategies of distanciation which draw attention to the apparatus of representation (gesture, pose, costume, the body, proxemics, props) challenge illusionistic iconicity and social behaviour, and contradictory political/historical positions are displayed through the 'gestus' of the performance. In Brechtian terms the alienation of actor from role ensures that the spectator filters their understanding of role through the interpretation of the actor. The disruption of classical mimesis sets up a critical space for the intervention of spectator readings. In postmodern terms, the split of performer from performed identity proposes a performed subjectivity.

The more recent work of the playwright Caryl Churchill and her collaborators, provides a paradigm of a theatre practice which encompasses interrogative performance practices. Working with combinations of actors, dances, choreographers, designers, composers and opera singers, the theatre performances in which she has been involved have explored notions of indeterminacy and identity not only by activating a radical reformation of the performing body but in her challenge to the constitution of theatrical performance itself. The trajectory of Churchill's work traces a path from a more orthodox Brechtian approach to theatre towards a transformed, postmodern epic theatre. Her earlier work like *Vinegar Tom* (Churchill 1982) and *Cloud Nine* (Churchill 1979) for example, deconstructs what Diamond calls 'gender-as-appearance, as the effect [...] of regulatory practices', by focusing upon historical contexts and adopting alienating and defamiliarising theatrical devices to expose class and gender positionality (Diamond 1997: 46). In more recent work, Churchill has developed a carnivalesque set of performative modes for interrogating the politics of constructed roles, exemplifying what Diamond describes as a 're-radicalization' of Brecht's theories for combating 'mimetic linearity' and its ideologies (45). Diamond maintains that, 'Brechtian theory in all its gaps and inconsistencies' continues to be 'a theorizing of the workings of an apparatus of representation with enormous formal and political resonance', and in Churchill's formally more radical plays the cracks in representation and the fractures of coherent identity are revealed through a remade Brechtian focus on the apparatus of performance and the politics of performativity, both theatrical and social (45). In *A Mouthful of Birds* (Churchill and Lan 1986), written with David Lan, choreographed by Ian Spink and directed by Les Waters as a response to Euripides' *The Bacchae* (Euripides 1954), dancers and actors shift between various temporalities and spatialities (past and present; mythic and realist) as well as different gendered and performative modes (androgynous, masculine and feminine; dance and drama). Similar temporal, spatial, performative and gender shifts are exploited in the more recent performance of *The Skriker* (Churchill 1994) which presents a shape-shifting, malevolent creature who induces a spiteful and vicious disruption of corporeal and psychic realities by capitalising on its aptitude for endless disguise and mutation.

A Mouthful of Birds begins with the androgynous and disruptive god of theatre, Dionysus, occupying the centre of the stage space. The play focuses on a single 'undefended' day, 'a day in which there is nothing to protect you from the forces inside and outside yourself', and seven people, infected on this one day by the spirit of Dionysus, experience an overturning of their lives and identities (Churchill and Lan 1986: 5). Each of them is possessed by spirits or passions, 'by forces within as well as without: by memory, by fear, by anxiety' (Churchill and Lan 1986: 6), and these issues are reinforced by the play's explicit borrowings from, and parallels with *The Bacchae*. Concepts of performativity as both self-conscious theatricality and the establishment of gender/biological norms are played out across the field of the performance. First, what might be termed reconceived Brechtian strategies of distanciation discourage spectator identification; the repetition and distortion of speeches and theatricalised gestures and poses attempt to position the audience critically to perceive character/role as fixed in normative, reiterated patterns of everyday behaviour. Second, these established patterns of quotidian performativity in characters are interrupted by their theatrical encounters with mythical and historical figures. Cited deliberately as a threat to regulated norms of social behaviour, these figures incite transformations of performed identities. Third, in being permeated by reference to *The Bacchae*, a key text in the theatrical canon, *A Mouthful of Birds* cites a theatre history, reiterates theatre's emphasis on masquerade and disguise and thereby exposes the self-conscious theatricality of the performance. A form of Brechtian 'literalisation' of the theatre space is produced. For Churchill and Lan (et al.), theatre with its ritualisation of performed gestures and theatrical movement and pose, its self-aware signification through costume, props, and *mise-en-scène*, its reliance upon a performance history and its potential for representing chimerical identities becomes a means of espousing transformation and new imaginings of gender possibilities. Theatrical performance, signalled by *The Bacchae* and a reflexivity of the presentational style, exposes and interrogates the social performativity of the characters and also, by implication, the actors.

Derek, an unemployed man whose gender/sexual anxiety is exposed through his obsession with weight-lifting, embraces his femininity through a theatrical exchange with the nineteenth-century hermaphrodite, Herculine Barbin. This encounter leads to him donning the role of Pentheus, King of Thebes, in *The Bacchae* story, who, like Barbin, masquerades as a woman until exposed as a dissembler. In the imaginary space of the theatre, renewed subjectivities are produced from the death of the body circumscribed by rigid gender division, and from the dismemberment of Pentheus and the suicide of Barbin a re-formed and confident Derek emerges declaring:

> My breasts aren't big but I like them. My waist isn't small but it makes me smile. My shoulders are still strong. And my new shape is the least of it. I smell light and sweet. I come into a room, who has been here? Me. My skin used to wrap me up, now it lets the world in. Was I this all the time? I've forgotten the man who possessed this body. I can't remember what he used to be frightened of. I'm in love with a lion-tamer from Kabul. Everyday when I wake up, I'm comfortable. (Churchill and Lan 1986: 76)

Performed subjectivities are further interrogated through the character of Paul, a businessman who works on the commodity market and who falls in love with a pig, the most degraded of animals. Paul's established identity (language, appearance, social position, career) is overthrown and demolished by his desire for the 'other', the very animal he exploits in exchange for his highly regarded position as a pork futures trader in his 'defended' life. His 'defended' life is shaped and formed by an unconscious performance which ties him to the norms of the business world but in an 'undefended day' a more theatrical performance erupts and dislodges his customary performed identity, inciting new possibilities of multiple subjectivities. The desire for the pig takes the form of an erotic, humorous and charming dance, 'Paul and the pig dance, tenderly, dangerously, joyfully,' displaying the jouissance of the newly forged Paul (46). Both Derek and Paul are transformed within the theatrical performance which enables them to enact new possibilities of identity, ones not circumscribed by narrow social norms or caught within limited citational cycles. The indeterminate bodies which emerge are fluid, multiple and unlimited, no longer only defined by iterated patterns of social behaviour and psychic norms. Within the transcendent world of the theatrical, the reshaping and re-envisioning of images of the self becomes imaginable.

Transformations in *The Skriker* are even more profound than in *A Mouthful of Birds* since the central figure is a shape-shifting creature from a malevolent fairy underworld, who adopts whichever bodily form takes its fancy (see Fig. 11.1). The Skriker is 'a death portent, ancient and damaged', intent on taking revenge on human beings who believe they have transcended the now unseen and inaccessible fairy world (Churchill 1994: 1). Its ever-changing disguises and role-play enable it to infiltrate the world of mortals, threatening its stability and continuity, together with its temporal and spatial realities. In latching on to Josie, who is in a mental hospital, and Lily, who is pregnant and alone, the Skriker attaches itself to those who are most fragile and vulnerable, those least able to resist its seduction. Not bound by the limits of the human body, it is the ability of the Skriker to inhabit all kinds of corporeal shapes and impersonate individuals regardless of age or gender, that make it so dangerous. The play envisions a world radically other to conventional reality, a rotting underworld in which certainties of time, bodiliness and gender are unhinged. Even language is enlisted to reinforce notions of instability and transformation as it becomes a play of associations and games, rhymes and alliterative sounds rather than the conveyance of meaning. Words change shape and disguise meaning along with the creature:

> Heard her boast beast a roast beef eater, daughter could spin span spick and spun the lowest form of wheat straw into gold, raw into roar, golden lion and lyonnesse under the sea, dungeonnesse under the castle for bad mad sad adders and takers away. Never marry a king size well beloved. (Churchill 1994: 1)

What is notable about *The Skriker* is that, although concepts of transformation are central to the play's form and meanings, their critical significance is different from in *A Mouthful of Birds*. While transformation of the body is still presented as a radical form through which to explore identity as performative and discursive, in this play it is no longer the means to achieve or realise a desired identity. Rather, identity transformation is seen as dangerous and subversive, and its challenge to gender and sexual regulation and its transcending of corporeal limitations do not propose idealised identity positions. The Skriker is a symbol of death, perfidious and malignant. Its presence and pervasive influence offers no utopian solution, the 'happy ending' of traditional fairy stories, but rather 'the never ending transformations, the loose chain of signifiers are part of a discourse which perhaps wants to challenge a possibility of resolution' (Manera 1999: 151). In *The Skriker* performativity is to be distrusted and the play's self-conscious hybridity of dance, song, poetry, acrobatics, circus and dialogue exposes its dissembling unreliability.

Although Churchill's work undoubtedly focuses upon performance, social and theatrical, she nevertheless works in the territory of theatre. Theatre is signalled by the presence of written text, the presentation of characters by performers, and a *mise-en-scène* which defines an alternative world in which the fiction is set. She also employs performance in its recently prioritised sense of the self-consciously corporeal and plastic in order to further theatricalise the work, but also to unsettle received notions of theatre. She marks out a theatrical space, and in Harris's terms makes legible the 'presence of the quotation marks' (Harris 1999: 76) around that space, where by developing '"alienation" techniques and deliberate discontinuity in theatrical signification' (Diamond 1997: 44) she can deconstruct social performativity and pose questions of subjectivity, commodification conventionality and politics. As part of this process, iterative performativity is exposed and reconceived through theatrical performance.

Now I am going to focus an example of a theatre performance which I directed, which attempted to foreground the performativity of gender and identity by means of a self-consciously performative theatrical form. In December 1995, I had directed a production of *Mary Stuart* by Schiller (Schiller 1800), in which I aimed to explore the constraints placed on women in positions of authority and the gender and political boundaries which mark the limits of their power. Two years later, in December 1997, I directed a theatrical response to the first production, which I called *The cutting up of Mary S.* This was deconstructed version of *Mary Stuart* using the original performance as a kind of pretext, developing a more abstract version of the material. It was an attempt to refigure the play, foregrounding its structure of gender and questions of representation. Schiller's play compares Mary Stuart of Scotland and Elizabeth I of England as queens who occupied traditional male roles as ruling monarchs at a similar point in history. Both were allowed to be rulers only on the authorisation of the masculine order and only while they consented to masculine values. My interest in the circumscription of women in positions of power was also at the centre of *The cutting up of Mary S* project but now with a specific focus upon the performativity of identity (public and private/political and personal) and on the ways in which the performative is exposed through theatre performance.

Schiller's *Mary Stuart* is concerned with the political and personal conflicts between Mary and Elizabeth. The action shifts between Mary's prison and Elizabeth's court. The dramatic structure of the play has a kind of symmetry as the action swings between the two queens. The theatrical production aimed to use spatial division and *mise-en-scène* to foreground the masculine-defined forces structuring the two queens, who are split between extremes of womanhood, into a self-defeating struggle. Within the patriarchal milieu which they were required to uphold, neither could sustain an identity as both woman and sovereign, both sexualised female and bearer of authority. Elizabeth could not reconcile the possibility of marriage and motherhood with her function as ruler; for Mary, her passion and sexual appetite lost her throne and ultimately her head. In the play, the two queens are defined by each other, both as opposites: the virgin and the whore, and as similar: queens struggling for authority. They are defined as doubles, complementary of one another since only they are able to comprehend fully the other's restricted position, but they are also divided and split, set in binary oppositions as the Protestant and the Catholic; the civilised and the barbaric; the ruler and the deposed; the Englishwoman and the foreigner, the insider and the outsider.

The production indicated historical setting but was not bound by historical data, focusing attention on the structural and critical resources of the play. Costume referred to the Elizabethan period but was not authentic or accurately detailed, aiming to portray the two queens as paradigmatic figures of female authority. The theme of doubling and splitting was structured into the *mise-en-scène*. The end-on stage was divided into two halves separated by a throne of England, threatened by division since it was claimed by both women. Each half of the space represented either the prison of Mary or the court of Elizabeth and was circumscribed by a set of perspex screens, upon which were imprinted the rose or the thistle, floral symbols of England and Scotland (see Fig. 11.2). A single chair directly facing the audience (the only piece of furniture in each half of the performance space) was a modified version of the throne. These chairs placed both women as central to their own space, but juxtaposed with the seat of absolute power signified by the throne. Each queen had a literal 'seat of power', placed in subordination and apposition to the throne of the Law, the masculine centre of authority on the central axis of the performance space (see Fig. 11.3). The similarities between the two halves of the set proposed that Mary and Elizabeth were reflections of one another. This idea was enhanced by the perspex screens which were intended to function as both windows and mirrors, reflecting images of self and other which merged and separated, since occasionally both Elizabeth and Mary could be seen reflected in the screens of their own space while at other moments one queen could be seen through the screen of the other queen's space (see Fig. 11.2 and 11.3).

Although notions of doubling and splitting informed the production, particularly the *mise-en-scène* and gestic systems, there was no self-conscious emphasis on the performance of gender or monarchical identity in this production. While there was an implicit critique of gender norms, there was no explicit exploration of gender (or theatrical) performativity. Schiller's *Mary Stuart* interrogates the compromised positions of authority occupied by both women, but the play's form of romantic melodrama does not allow a link between this and the structured and relentless role-play in which the queens are implicated and which constrains their actions. An essentially mimetic performance style which demands actor/character identification operated against the critical distanciation of the spectator. With neither Brechtian mechanisms for drawing attention to the apparatus of theatre nor the development of a postmodern theatrical performativity, there was no critical frame for exposing and interrogating social performativity and its effects. As soon as the performances were over, I immediately decided to do the play again, or at least to construct a performance which drew on some of Schiller's material but recontextualised it within a more reflexive form of theatre. *The cutting up of Mary S* sought to displace and deconstruct the binary oppositions set up in Schiller's play and to explore not only the political and personal relationship of the two queens but also the ways in which they invaded each other's psychic territory as each became more obsessed and haunted by the other. Using a visual and multimedia form of theatre, the queens were no longer portrayed as coherent individuals, but instead as performed positions, both political and personal.

In this second performance, a range of representational modes, portraiture, music, theatrical action, electronic media and spoken and recorded text, functioned together and in contradistinction. Adopting a fragmented and disrupted theatrical form, the performance focused on the realm of the dreams and desire, fears and nightmares, distresses and anxieties, suggested through a set dominated by pillars holding props indexical of obsessions significant to one, other or both queens, for example a bible, a death warrant, an axe. Each queen was performed by three separate actors simultaneously, and images of the queens proliferated and multiplied across the performance space in slides, portraits and video images, and were endlessly reproduced on the screens around the space (see Fig. 11.4). These sets of images, including live corporeal poses and tableaux, paintings and photographic slides, film clips and video (live and pre-recorded), gesture and movement, were played off against each other to attempt to disrupt binary positionality and narrative linearity. I was interested in how theatrical performance could be used to foreground and analyse the function of historical images and iconographies in establishing, determining and ideologically inflecting the representation of gendered figures, including women in positions of authority. But furthermore, I wanted to focus on the performativity of political and personal identities in physical, bodily action through the ritualisation of repeated, fragmented and distorted gesture, pose, movement and costume.

The self-aware use of representational modes in *The cutting up of Mary S* drew attention to the mechanisms of theatre and framed it as a discursive space. While not adopting obvious Brechtian strategies, the artificial theatricality of the playing space was foregrounded and theatrical performativity was deliberately conspicuous. The theatrical citation and reiteration of images of womanly and queenly behaviour linked the production to issues of gender royal performativity as reiteration and citation. The focus on the psychic in the production showed how citation and reiteration are inscribed and played out both consciously and unconsciously, as performances which the subject both controls and does not control. Received norms of appearance and behaviour both structure the queens' behaviour unconsciously, and are also actively adopted by them consciously as means to exert authority, pursue rivalries and rationalise action. The production aimed to show how reference to and repetition of normative images frame their responses to their similar and different situations and to each other, and also aimed to provide the basis for a critique of gendered norms. Imbricated in the multiple performance text was the previous performance of *Mary Stuart*, which could be traced in the *mise-en-scène*, through the positioning of the two chairs, the placing of the rose and thistle motif among the frames, screens and mirrors which were scattered across the back of the performance space, and through the reappearance in the cast of some of the *Mary Stuart* performers. The issue of citation and reinscription was therefore acknowledged as part of institutional, formal and stylistic situation of the production as a theatre event, as well as part of the substance of the production. As with *A Mouthful of Birds*, the presence of the historical play attested to the theatricality of the event and to the dialectical possibilities of theatre.

Notions of role-splitting and shape-shifting were of considerable significance to the performance of *The cutting up of Mary S.* No single actress embodied either queen, but the roles were divided, shared and deferred across six performers. At any one point in the play the role of each queen was either equally shared between three performers, or one performer might take precedence (see Fig. 11.5). Depending upon which actress or actresses inhabited the role, the physical shape and demeanour of the queen, and thus her identity, was potentially always in question and unstable. At the same time, there was a critical display of reiterative action as each performer was shadowed and copied by the other two, as well as by the mediated images of the actresses and portraits of the queens which proliferated across the performance space. Thus citational performativity was exposed through the processes of theatrical performativity. Furthermore, *The cutting up of Mary S* proposed that the performativity of gender is different to the adoption of modes of behaviour in order to enact state power. The play deliberately separated the performativity of everyday womanliness from the theatricality of the rituals of queenliness. Head of state and woman are both roles, enacted differently but also adopting different modes of performativity. The role of woman is (partially) unconsciously performed, and derives from reiterated and cited norms of behaviour. The role of queen relies upon the theatrical, self-conscious voluntary production of the repertoire of gestures and behaviours which signify the monarch and which are sanctioned by the state. Theatrical performance is thereby deliberately 'coopted' into the social in order to enact politically circumscribed subject positions, in this case to maintain and consolidate state authority.

The significance of theatre for critical practice lies in its simultaneous dependence on, and ability to either dissimulate or deconstruct, performativity. Harris summarises the appeal of theatre as a critical space for examining issues of performativity by suggesting that theatre

> has traditionally been perceived as both quoting the 'reality effects' [theorists] describe as being performatively produced and as simultaneously differing from those 'reality effects' – which is, of course, exactly the effect they seek to achieve as a strategy for subverting identity in the realm of the social. (Harris 1999: 76)

By reference to theories of theatrical representation, performativity as staged theatrically becomes a mechanism which can both demonstrate the ritualised performance of political identities and analyse the quotidian production of personal identity. Indeterminacy in *The Cutting Up of Mary S* depended on the disruption of the signifier–signified relationship between actor and role, redrawing the boundary between character, role and performer. The performance with its multiple representations of the queens and its self-conscious reference to semiotics through gesture, costume, proxemics and props, attempted to expose the theatricality of the performance of positions of power, and propose the performativity of gender.

Works cited

Artaud 1938 Antonin Artaud, *Le Théâtre et son double* (Paris: Gallimard), translated as *The Theatre and its Double* by M. C. Richards (New York: Grove Press, edn of 1958)

Austin 1955 J. L. Austin, *How to Do Things with Words* (Cambridge, Mass.: Harvard University Press)

Bennett 1998 S. Bennett, 'Introduction to Part Eight', in L. Goodman (ed.), *Gender and Performance* (London: Routledge)

Butler 1993 Judith Butler, *Bodies That Matter: On the Discursive Limits of Sex* (London: Routledge)

Churchill 1979 Caryl Churchill, *Cloud Nine* (London: Methuen); first performed by Joint Stock Theatre Group at Dartington College of Arts, 14 Feb. 1979, directed by Max Stafford Clark

Churchill 1982 Caryl Churchill, 'Vinegar Tom', in *Plays By Women. Vol. 1*, ed. M. Wandor (London: Methuen); first performed by Monstrous Regiment at Humberside Theatre Hull, 12 Oct. 1976

Churchill 1994 Caryl Churchill, *The Skriker* (London: Nick Hern); first performed at the Cottesloe Auditorium, the Royal National Theatre, London, 20 Jan. 1994, directed by Les Waters

Churchill and Lan 1986 C. Churchill and D. Lan, *A Mouthful of Birds* (London: Methuen); first performed by Joint Stock Theatre Group in conjunction with Birmingham Repertory Theatre, Sept. 1986, directed by Les Waters

Diamond 1996 Elin Diamond (ed.), 'Introduction', in *Performance and Cultural Politics* (London: Routledge)

Diamond 1997 Elin Diamond, *Unmaking Mimesis* (London: Routledge)

Euripides 1954 *The Bacchae and Other Plays*, translated by P. Vellacott (Harmondsworth: Penguin, edn of 1954); first performed 405 BCE

Harris 1999 G. Harris, *Staging Femininities: Performance and Performativity* (London: Routledge)

Manera 1999 C. Manera, *Carnivalesque Disruptions and Political Theatre: Plays by Dario Fo, Franca Rame and Caryl Churchill* (University of Reading: unpublished PhD thesis)

Parker and Sedgwick 1995 Andrew Parker and Eve Kosofsky Sedgwick, 'Introduction: Performativity and Performance', in Andrew Parker and Eve Kosofsky Sedgwick (eds), *Performativity and Performance* (London: Routledge)

Schiller 1800 Friedrich Schiller, *Maria Stuart*, translated as *Mary Stuart* by Robert David MacDonald (London: Oberon Books, edn of 1987); first performed 1800

Additional performances cited

Mary Stuart by Friedrich Schiller (in a version translated by Robert David MacDonald) was performed at The University of Reading in Dec. 1995, directed by Lib Taylor

The cutting up of Mary S was performed at The University of Reading in Dec. 1997, devised and directed by Lib Taylor

12

Unhomely Bodies and Dislocated Identities in the Drama of Frank McGuinness and Marina Carr

Anna McMullan

The term 'unhomely' derives originally from Freud's *unheimlich*, which he defines as the recurrence of the once familiar which has become 'uncanny and frightening', as the long-ago repressed of the individual or cultural psyche returns to haunt the present. The post-colonial critic Homi Bhabha takes up this concept of the uncanny in *The Location of Culture*, and renames it the 'unhomely'. He explores how the legacies or hauntings of history disrupt the present in such texts as Toni Morrison's novel, *Beloved*. Bhabha emphasises the importance of remembering the past on the part of peoples who have experienced trauma. He writes of the responsibility of the critic and artist to 'attempt to fully realise, and take responsibility for, the unspoken, unrepresented pasts that haunt the historical present' (Bhabha 1994: 12). This essay explores this concept of the unhomely in relation to the work of two contemporary Irish dramatists, Frank McGuinness and Marina Carr, and I will argue that in their work, repressed aspects of personal or communal history are exposed and theatricalised through the bodies of their protagonists.

The unhomely bodies in McGuinness's and Carr's theatre resist unitary images of nation or gender. Their characters' experience of indeterminacy results from their refusal of or exclusion from the borders of a national or gender identity which has been shaped in response to a determining other: the British Empire, Unionist hegemony in Northern Ireland, or a largely male-authored iconography of nation in which women appear as symbols or catalysts for male action. In a climate of historical, economic, cultural and political change in Ireland, these playwrights investigate moments of personal and communal crisis, in order to dislocate the traditional representations of identity and history, to reveal what has been hidden or unrepresented, and to enable alternative modes of identity construction to emerge. In his contribution to *The Making of Political Identities*, Aletto Noval comments: 'The mere fact that the structure is dislocated does not mean that "everything becomes possible". Dislocation always takes place in a determinate situation, that is, one in which there is always relative structuration, and the continuing existence of a symbolic universe of representations. Second, a dislocated structure opens up the space for a multitude of possibilities of re-articulation which are by definition indeterminate. A dislocated structure is thus an open structure in which the crisis can be resolved in a variety of directions' (Noval 1994: 133). For McGuinness and Carr, theatre is a medium through which the divisions and wounds which continue to rupture the Irish body politic and social fabric may be remembered through performance.

Most of McGuinness's recent work is concerned with excavating the wounds of history, whether on a broad historical canvas, as in *Observe the Sons of Ulster Marching Towards the Somme* (1985),[1] or on an intimate scale, in *Baglady* (1985). The two plays by McGuinness which I will be discussing here focus on historical trauma. *Carthaginians*, premiered in 1988 at the Peacock Theatre, Dublin,[2] deals with the impact on the Northern Irish nationalist community in Derry of 'Bloody Sunday', 30 January 1972, when thirteen unarmed civilians were shot dead by British soldiers during a demonstration through the city (a fourteenth died later). *Mary and Lizzie*, developed in workshops and first performed by the Royal Shakespeare Company in 1989, evokes, among other traumas, the Irish Famine. In both of these plays, McGuinness's unhomely bodies are haunted sites where the repressed individual and communal past is played out, so that a revised relationship between past and present may be negotiated. If the past is not remembered, according to Freud, it can either continually re-enact itself in the compulsion to repeat, or the mechanisms of its repression can make the present so fragmented and alienated that it becomes virtually uninhabitable.[3]

In *Heterologies: Discourse on the Other*, Michel de Certeau contrasts psychoanalysis and historiography in their concepts of the relation between past and present: 'Psychoanalysis recognises the past in the present; historiography places them one beside the other. Psychoanalysis treats the relation as one of imbrication (one in the place of the other), of repetition (one reproduces the other in another form), of the equivocal and of the quiproquo (what 'takes the place' of what? Everywhere there are games of masking, reversal and ambiguity)' (Certeau 1974: 4). In *Carthaginians* and *Mary and Lizzie*, McGuinness creates a performative, multi-layered theatrical structure which exposes the trauma of those whose wounds have not been adequately addressed within the traditional discourses of history or nation.

Carthaginians is set in a graveyard or 'burial ground' outside the city of Derry. Since the events of Bloody Sunday, the characters have left their homes and set up camp in the graveyard where they are waiting for the dead to rise. The play evokes several layers of history. The temporal structure parallels the crucifixion and resurrection of Christ during Holy Week. The title evokes the classical city of Carthage, destroyed by Rome, and there are specific references to Virgil's version of the story of Dido, Queen of Carthage, in *The Aeneid*, as well as to Purcell's opera of *Dido and Aeneas*. The central character in *Carthaginians* is Dido, the young, male homosexual Queen of Derry. These diverse temporal layers of history are displayed simultaneously, and the recurring motif of the pop quiz juxtaposes recent and ancient history, high and popular culture, trauma and trivia. The fractured structure of the play mimes the displacement and doubleness of traumatised memory.

Maela, the oldest character, in her forties, refuses to acknowledge the death of her young daughter, who died on Bloody Sunday. However, the daughter was not a victim of the British Army, but died of cancer. Indeed, as the characters' pasts are gradually uncovered, we glimpse a spectrum of wounds which cannot all be attributed to the catastrophe of Bloody Sunday, yet whose lack of healing seems to be connected to the failure of dominant modes of representation to address the source of the characters' griefs. However, the uncovering of the past is a piecemeal and fragmented process, built up through snatches of song or story. Certeau refers to the splits and debris of truth produced by moments of personal and historical crisis 'the forgetting of which organises itself into psychosociological systems and the remembrance of which creates possibilities of change for the present state' (Certeau 1974: 6). Historical trauma is remembered through the corporeal catastrophes of McGuinness's characters. The materiality and functions or malfunctions of the body are constantly referred to: eating, defecation and death, framed by the political context of the Hunger Strikes. There is an emphasis on waste production, both corporeal and cultural, as if identity were being reconstituted from fragments of recycled debris. The pop quiz reproduces and re-sites fragments of cultural or historical knowledge, while parodying what is recorded as knowledge:

> PAUL: Cleopatra died by means of an asp bite. What was the name of the asp? (McGuinness 1996: 363)

Paul is building a pyramid from rubbish through which he hopes the dead will rise, and which he gathers in black plastic bags, also used to wrap the bodies of the dead of Bloody Sunday (McGuinness 1996: 368).

Four of the characters, Greta, Hark, Seph and Sarah, were civil rights marchers walking through Derry city on Bloody Sunday. Although they were not physically injured on that day, each of them has subsequently undergone their own corporeal dislocations. Hark and Seph were interrogated, Hark imprisoned, and Seph released because he informed. Seph has retreated into virtual silence, while Hark's discourse splits under the strain of memory, and often spills over into aggression. Their trauma is expressed through linguistic dislocation: meaning disperses into many-layered clusters of words and images which juxtapose disparate contexts, crossing boundaries, for example, between the public and the private, the personal and the political:

> HARK: Have you ever been picked up, Dido? Picked up, by the army or the police? Will I show you how to pick someone up? (*Hark touches Dido on the face.*) This is how, Dido. And after that, Dido, do you know what they do? (*Hark kisses Dido.*) Does it not turn you on? Answer to your wildest dreams? Me, Dido. (*Hark caresses Dido's face again.*) Answer me. Tell me the truth. Tell me who you're involved with. Give me names, Harkin. Give me addresses. Just names and addresses. That's all we're looking for. You can walk out of here if you just give me one name and address. (McGuinness, 1996: 314)

Greta and Sarah are dislocated both externally and internally, and have difficulty inhabiting their own bodies: Sarah went to Amsterdam and became hooked on drugs, while Greta, in her thirties, underwent a premature hysterectomy. By exposing the multiple wounds and scars in the fractured body of the community, McGuinness disrupts images of a unitary nationalist body or its oppressor. Who is the 'author' of the character's wounds? The British Army? The gendered rhetoric of nationalist republicanism or unionism? Disease (what counts as disease, is it 'natural' or cultural)? The mediating forces of television, ballads or literature?

Discussing the drama of Dumas, Certeau refers to characters who are '"historical theaters" in themselves, or enactments of doubling' (Certeau 1974: 153). Dido is such a character. Like Pyper in *Observe the Sons of Ulster Marching Towards the Somme*, he disturbs gender boundaries. *Carthaginians* features a play within a play, 'The Burning Balaclava', written by Dido, under the identity of a French woman who has in turn assumed the name Fionnuala McGonigle in sympathy with the sufferings of Derry. This is a thinly veiled reference to 'Fiona McCleod', the pseudonym used by a contemporary of Yeats, William Sharp, to emblematise the feminised Celtic soul of the Irish literary renaissance. The masks and substitutions multiply.

'The Burning Balaclava' enacts a parody of the Irish dramatic tradition and its tendency to succumb to a view of history as fatalistic tragedy, doomed to repeat itself. Each of the characters plays a role which forces them to displace themselves into an alternative identity position. Maela is paired with Hark, but Hark plays the long-suffering Mother, while Maela plays the idealistic young revolutionary. Paul plays a female Protestant in love with the idealistic young revolutionary. Seph, who talked too much and is now silent, plays a priest who, in despair at the lack of heed paid to his messages of peace, communicates only through white flags. Dido plays two roles, a local Catholic girl and a British soldier. When the soldier shoots the young Catholic girl's dog, Boomer (the Hound of Ulster), she laments him in a parody of Juno's speech mourning the death of her son in Sean O'Casey's play, *Juno and the Paycock*[4]:

> DIDO: I brought him home in a wee box, tied with string. I had to open it with a razor blade, and I cut my finger. Little did I think that the pain I had bringing him into the house would be anything like the pain I have taking him out of it. (McGuinness, 1996: 338)

In the end, all the characters die, and Dido's soldier has the last lines:

> DIDO: Dead. All Dead. We're all dead. I'm dying. They've got me. It's over. It's over. It's over. (*dies*) That's it. What do you think? *Silence.* Tell me the truth. Isn't it just like real life? (344)

The parodic dislocation of the national 'symbolic universe of representations', while acknowledging the trauma of Bloody Sunday for the nationalist community, becomes an important step towards the possibility of resurrection not of the dead but of the living. References to Carthage are crucial here, as the city that was destroyed, but the Carthaginians of the play remember history. Although the other characters deride Dido's play as 'shite', they nevertheless begin to open up, and tell their repressed stories more freely. As they recognise each other's names, they name the dead of Bloody Sunday, one by one, and distinguish themselves from the dead, finally accepting survival:

> DIDO: If I meet one who knows you and they ask: how's Dido? Surviving. How's Derry? Surviving. Carthage has not been destroyed. Watch yourself. (McGuinness, 1996: 379)

As the sun rises, while the others sleep after their ritual of healing, Dido leaves the scene with the final word 'Play'.

In *Mary and Lizzie*, McGuinness finds a theatrical form to present marginalised histories, in particular the stories of women and Celtic pre-history. He experiments with the symbolic and theatrical paradigm of migrancy, particularly relevant to a culture whose traditional national boundaries are being redrawn through a growing recognition of the Irish diaspora and the increasing numbers of immigrants and refugees residing in Ireland. As in *Carthaginians*, histories are recovered through the corporeal dislocations of the two central characters. This play again uses a fractured, centrifugal structure to tell the tale of two Irish girls, Mary and Lizzie Burns, who lived with and were lovers of Frederick Engels in Manchester.[5] McGuinness places their historically marginalised story centre-stage. The play is structured in nine sections or 'episodes' which flout all concepts of coherent narrative but which do loosely form a quest structure, across the fault-lines of history. Significantly the play was written following McGuinness's translation of Ibsen's *Peer Gynt*.

Mary and Lizzie opens in pre-Famine times, in the City of Women, a community of women who have been banished to the trees after following and being rejected by a regiment of soldiers. This community reflects the countless and nameless women betrayed by and banished from history. The play charts a series of betrayals: by history, by religion and by Mother Ireland, portrayed as a whore-monger, feeding women to her son, a demonic priest, who has embraced 'a killing combination of 2 defunct faiths that can only survive by feeding off each other' (McGuinness 1989: 11). Mary and Lizzie, however, reconstruct their own history as they 'wander through time, through place, for that was their way, their story' (6).

Their world is not bounded either temporally or spatially. They are seen traversing geographical and symbolic spaces: the City of Women, the interior of the earth, Manchester. They meet historical and symbolic people: Mother Ireland, the Pregnant Girl whose womb is a receptacle of relics of the Famine, Marx and Engels, Queen Victoria, a Russian boy. They reveal the hypocrisies and gaps in official versions of history: imperialist attitudes towards the Famine or Marxist theories of history. Mary and Lizzie insist on the material realities of the body, sexuality and gender while Marx and Engels theorise.[6] In one scene, Mary and Lizzie perform oral sex on Engels as he propounds his theory of the inevitable demise of the class structure. Traditional Marxist theory is of little use in the telling of the women's stories. A Russian boy offers a visionary glimpse of waves of migrants and refugees, of 'women walking', as Mary and Lizzie rejoin the women of the camp. They enact a ritual rememoration of their experiences of exile and banishment, yet their articulation does not lead to a return home, but rather to a renewed resignation to wander the earth.

> PREGNANT GIRL: Start again, I suppose. Rough life, eh? No rest, no rest, until the grave. But there's no grave either. Just the earth. Wander it. It is too lonely. (McGuinness 1989: 47)

This can be seen as a rather abstract poetic metaphor of exile, but it is also a sympathetic envisioning of the position of the marginalised, the migrant, the refugee, the itinerant, the traveller, the literally homeless – those who are struggling to find a place in contemporary Ireland and elsewhere. In *Mapping the Subject: Geographies of Cultural Transformation*, Steve Pile and Nigel Thrift argue that 'as the "unhomely" becomes the norm, replacing the sovereignty of national cultures, or the universalism of a human culture, so new subjectivities are needed' (Pile and Thrift 1995: 18). McGuinness presents the female unhomely as a paradigm for the symbolic, imaginative and cultural accommodation of such migrant identities.

*

Marina Carr has been writing for the theatre since 1989, and her work has been presented at the Irish National Theatre, as well as internationally. Her plays since *The Mai* (1994) have featured a central female character struggling to find some place for herself on her own terms. Carr's women remind us of the plight of those whose unhomeliness erupts not in the migrant spaces of the intercultural, but in the cultural hinterlands of Ireland.[7] These characters' experience of indeterminacy arises from their alienation from the traditional domestic roles of wife and mother, intensified by their location in a rural landscape and a small local community, yet their difficulty in defining an alternative identity for themselves. Carr exposes the legacies of an ambivalent cultural iconography which has associated the female body simultaneously with national dispossession and sacrifice, and with the nurturing and reproduction of the nation. By unshackling the female figure from her traditional associations, Carr reveals her lack of place within the culture outside of the maternal function. Her female characters are always defined in relation to an other, whether a husband, brother or mother. Indeterminacy here is both a refusal of expected roles, and a crisis of identity and relation whose only resolution within the world of the plays is the suicide of the central character. Yet through the articulation of this crisis, new paradigms of female subjectivity are forged.

The women in *The Mai*, *Portia Coughlan* (1996) and *By the Bog of Cats* (1998) suffer from an irresoluble conflict between the confines of their location and their 'unhomeliness'. While Carr's earlier work was more abstract in its settings, her recent plays have returned to the Midlands, where Carr herself grew up. The area of the Midlands occupies the centre of Ireland, but it is often marginalised by the cultural dominance of the cities and the West. Carr's women are placed in a setting that is specific, stifling and yet inhabited by mythical, uncanny presences. *By the Bog of Cats* opens with a dialogue between the central character, Hester Swane, and a Ghost Fancier who has come to claim her ghost, but he is 'too previous', having mistaken dawn for dusk. He returns at the end of the play. The family, usually associated with unity and security, is riven with secret histories of incest, inbreeding and even murder.[8] The Mai, Portia Coughlan and Hester Swane are situated in a particular society, they have children, partners, yet they are also dreamers, virtual vagabonds. Their society allows them little imaginative space or agency, so their repressed dreams and desires are figured by the surrounding landscape which seems to possess them or be possessed by them: Owl Lake in *The Mai* engulfs the women in recurring myths of abandonment and literally claims the Mai, who drowns herself after her husband, who has returned after many years' absence, is once more unfaithful; the Belmont river in *Portia Couglan* haunts Portia, till eventually she drowns herself in it, as did her twin brother or lost other self, fifteen years earlier. Hester feels the secret of her identity is held by the bog which she associates with her traveller mother. She cannot leave it, though her common-law husband, Carthage Kilbride, is marrying the daughter of a local farmer, and wants her out of the way. She wanders through the bog night after night; across it she watched her mother disappear when she was seven years old; and by it she waits for her to return.

All of these plays question the idea of the 'natural' mother or the maternal, nurturing body. The Mai is much more absorbed in her hopeless love for her faithless husband than she is in her children, as her Grandma Fraochlán was obsessed by her husband, the nine-fingered fisherman: 'I would gladly have hurled all seven of ye down tha slopes of hell for one night more with the nine-fingered fisherman and may I rot eternally for such unmotherly feelin' (Carr 1999: 182). Portia is more often at the bar or the banks of the river than at home, where she is unable to care for either her husband or her children. In an adaptation of the Medea myth, Hester kills her daughter and herself, when her partner chooses a younger woman from a settled, 'respectable' family. Carr's women tend to be defiant and irreverent, rather than guardians of proper female behaviour or language (see Mayer 2000: 1–24):

> HESTER: And as for me tinker blood, I'm proud of it. It gives me an edge over all of yees around here, allows me see yees for the inbred, underbred, bog-brained shower yees are. (Carr 1999: 289)

However, the gaps and fractures of their identity lead the Mai, Portia and Hester to suicide. It is not only the betrayal of her partner that Hester mourns. The central loss of her life is that of her mother, and she kills her daughter so that she will not wait in vain for a mother who will never return. The French philosopher Luce Irigaray argues that there is a lack of a mother–daughter genealogy within Western culture. She uses the term *déréliction* to describe a kind of exile experienced by women,[9] who have not been adequately represented or 'housed' within culture except through the maternal function, so that they cannot find a place within the dominant currencies of symbolic exchange. Carr gives a powerful voice to the complex crises of subjectivity and genealogy which these unhomely women suffer – where and how can they place themselves?

While there may be a danger in these plays of confirming the unhomely woman as hysteric, the marginalised other in relation to the determining norm of rational (or national) civil society, I would argue that they foreground the limitations and hypocrisies of dominant gender and national identities, emergent as well as historical. In the midst of growing prosperity and cultural confidence for some, the work of McGuinness and Carr reminds us of the reality of those who struggle to find any accommodation with or within the authorised structures of their world. The trauma of this dislocation is figured through corporeal unhomeliness, taken to its extreme in Carr's female suicides. Nevertheless, the unhomely may become a site whose very indeterminacy fuels the production of alternative identities. These plays suggest that, for the contemporary Irish writer, the task is not to celebrate achievements at the cost of forgetting a traumatic past, but to tear apart the historical fabric of our iconography in order to give voice to the multiple repressed stories which, in Bhabha's words, haunt the historical present.

Notes

1 *Observe the Sons of Ulster Marching Towards the Somme* explores questions of loyalty and Protestant identity through the experiences of a group of Ulster soldiers enlisted to fight at the Battle of the Somme, 1916, as remembered by the sole survivor, Pyper. *Baglady* tells the story of an abused daughter through fragmented monologues.
2 The play was subsequently produced by Druid Theatre, and played in Derry as part of Impact 92, in January 1992, twenty years after the events of Bloody Sunday.
3 See Leela Gandhi's discussion of postcolonial trauma and remembering in Gandhi 1998: 9–22.
4 *Juno and the Paycock*, set in the period of the Irish civil war following the partition of Northern Ireland in 1922, premiered at the Abbey Theatre, Dublin, in 1924.
5 See Henderson 1976.
6 In this respect, *Mary and Lizzie* tends to reproduce the gender division of female/body and male/abstract thought which *Carthaginians* disrupts.
7 This section has developed from an earlier article, McMullan 1998.
8 Hester murdered her own brother, partly for the money which her lover Carthage used to buy land, and partly out of jealousy over their mother.
9 The English translation uses the word 'abandonment' for *déréliction*.

Works cited

Bhabha 1994 Homi Bhabha, *The Location of Culture* (London: Routledge)
Carr 1999 Marina Carr, *Plays One* (London: Faber & Faber)
Certeau 1974 Michel de Certeau, *La Culture au pluriel* (Paris: Union générale d'éditions), translated by Brian Massumi as *Heterologies: Discourse on the Other* (Manchester: Manchester University Press, edn of 1986)
Freud 1919 Sigmund Freud, 'Das Unheimliche', translated by James Strachey as 'The Uncanny', in *The Pelican Freud Library*, vol. 14, *Art and Literature* (London & New York: Penguin Books, edn of 1990), 335–76
Gandhi 1998 Leela Gandhi, *Postcolonial Theory: a Critical Introduction* (Edinburgh: Edinburgh University Press)
Henderson 1976 W. O. Henderson, *The Life of Frederick Engels* (London: Frank Cass)

Irigaray 1984 Luce Irigaray, *Éthique de la différence sexuelle* (Paris: Minuit), translated by Carolyn Burke and Gillian Gill as *An Ethics of Sexual Difference* (London: Athlone, 1993)

Jordan 1997 Eamonn Jordan, *The Feast of Famine: the Plays of Frank McGuinness* (Bern: Peter Lang)

Liddy 1995 James Liddy, 'Voices in the Irish Cities of the Dead: Melodrama and Dissent in Frank McGuinness's *Carthaginians*', *Irish University Review*, 25: 2, Autumn–Winter 1995, 278–83

Mayer 2000 Tamar Mayer, *Gender Ironies of Nationalism: Sexing the Nation* (London and New York: Routledge)

McGuinness 1989 Frank McGuinness, *Mary and Lizzie* (London: Faber & Faber)

McGuinness 1996 Frank McGuinness, *Carthaginians*, in *Plays I* (London: Faber & Faber)

McMullan 1998 Anna McMullan, 'Marina Carr's Unhomely Women', *Irish Theatre Magazine*, Issue 1.1, Autumn 1998, 14–16

Noval 1994 Aletta J. Noval, 'Social Ambiguity and the Crisis of Apartheid', in Ernesto Laclau (ed.), *The Making of Political Identities* (London and New York: Verso), 115–37

Pile and Thrift 1995 Steve Pile and Nigel Thrift, *Mapping the Subject: Geographies of Cultural Transformation* (London: Routledge)

Schneider 1997 Rebecca Schneider, *The Explicit Body in Performance* (London: Routledge)

13
Blindness and the Politics of the Gaze

David Forgacs

> What was inevitably found inhuman, one might even say deadly, in daguerreotypy was the (prolonged) looking into the camera, since the camera records one's likeness without returning one's gaze. But looking at someone carries the implicit expectation that our look will be returned by the person to whom it is directed.
>
> (Benjamin 1939: 189–90)[1]

Bruegel's painting of 1568 known as 'The Parable of the Blind' shows six blind men in a line at the moment when their leader, at the right of the picture, has just fallen into a water-filled ditch (Fig. 13.1). To his left the second man is falling on top of him and the third, who is holding on to the stick of the falling man, is about to be pulled off balance too; perhaps he is even starting to fall. The fourth, fifth and sixth men, each with a hand on his comrade's shoulder or his stick, proceed unaware of their imminent fate.

The painting may be compared to others by Bruegel, most directly the small panel in the Louvre dating from the same year known as 'The Cripples' ('Les Estropiés') or alternatively as 'The Beggars' and 'The Lepers', in which five beggars with legs amputated at or below the knee scoot about on crutches and variously shaped wooden prostheses. For educated elites in northern Europe of the late sixteenth century both these images invited, probably, a look not of pity or sympathy but of ironic and humorous contemplation coupled with stoic reflection: a reflection both on the viewer's own human situation (mortality, vulnerability) and on the way of the world, where the larger society does not see these smaller events taking place within it. In 'The Cripples' an able-bodied woman is present at the scene but her back is turned. In 'The

Parable of the Blind' the men are walking in open country and their accident is not seen except by the viewer of the painting. 'Landscape with the Fall of Icarus' (c. 1558) is a more extreme case of the same moralisation: in the most commonly reproduced version of the painting (Musée des Beaux Arts, Brussels) the figure of Daedalus looking down from the sky is absent so that even the viewer barely notices at first the drowning boy's legs jutting out of the waves in the bottom right. W. H. Auden commented sententiously on this version in 'Musée des Beaux Arts' (1938)

> About suffering they were never wrong,
> The Old Masters
>
> (1976: 146)

However, this misses, if not the point, the tone of the painting. 'The Cripples' has been seen by art historians variously as a literal depiction of people with leprosy in a hospital courtyard (foxes' tails were worn by lepers during carnival processions), an allegory of human vanity (the men, despite their low state, have fur tails draped on their backs), a carnivalesque parody of social hierarchy (the beggars are dressed respectively as king, soldier, bishop, burgher, peasant) or an allusion to social protest (the fox's tail, apparently, was also worn as a sign of popular resistance to Spanish rule in the Low Countries). 'The Parable of the Blind' does not seem to be allusive in the same way but it clearly possesses a social meaning too. The painting is a re-literalising of the metaphor, widely disseminated in the Christian homiletic tradition and thence in European popular culture, of 'the blind leading the blind' and as such it is of a piece with Bruegel's other ironic illustrations of proverbs and popular sayings – indeed an earlier image of blind men holding each other's sticks appears in the extreme distance in his 'Netherlandish Proverbs' of 1559. The metaphor was used as a warning against putting one's trust in bad teachers or guides and it has two biblical sources. In Matthew 15: 14 Jesus says of the Pharisees: 'Let them alone; they are blind guides. And if a blind man leads a blind man, both will fall into a pit.'[2] In Luke 6: 39, addressing a large crowd in his first meeting after gathering his disciples, Jesus 'told them a parable: "Can a blind man lead a blind man? Will they not both fall into a pit?"' Shortly after, Jesus remarks on the hypocrite who sees the speck in his brother's eye but not the log in his own (6: 42). In this second passage there is, in other words, a succession of ocular metaphors in which clarity of vision (perspicacity) is equated with wisdom and impaired vision with ignorance or poor judgement. This same metaphorical transfer is at work in the story of the man, blind since birth, whose sight Jesus restores by smearing earth mixed with his spit in his eyes and then telling him to rinse it off. 'For judgment I came into this world,' Jesus tells the Pharisees afterwards, 'that those who do not see may see, and those who see may become blind' (John 9: 35).

With any painting the viewer may choose where and how to look but in this carefully composed picture about balance and destabilisation our attention tends to be drawn away from the centre to the bottom right. The geometric centre, where the diagonals from the corners cross, is at the waistline of the central figure of the group of six, just above his begging bowl. It is at this point in the picture that the group becomes literally upset in that the orderly walk of the three figures on the left turns into the stumbling (perhaps) of the middle figure and the tumbling of the two on the right. These two are separated from the others by a gap, indicated by the long stick and framed by the two diagonal lines which run from just below the top left hand corner, one through the men's shoulders and along the stick, the other behind their knees along the edge of the ditch, and which open up round them like a pair of scissors. The level horizon in the background functions as a reference from which these angles deviate and against which the falling movement in the foreground is graphically displayed. The two figures on the right contrast further with the other four by the wild criss-crossing of limbs and stick, the hat falling, the hand thrust in the air, the swirl of the cloak, the musical instrument plunged in the water.

Within this new centre of attention we find something uncanny. The falling man is 'looking' straight at 'us', but his eye sockets are empty. He is 'staring' without eyes. (Fig. 13.2) The 'gaze' he directs at us is not a real gaze. Of the two derivations of *aveugle* suggested in etymological dictionaries of French one is from *ab oculis*, 'without eyes', and the other is from *albios oculus* or *album oculi*, 'with white eyes', as of a person with severe cataracts – like the other blind men in Bruegel's painting, whose eyeballs are visible between the lids and who possibly have some residual sight. *Aveugle* entered the common language, probably from medical Latin, in the middle ages and by the sixteenth century had displaced the two earlier terms for 'blind': *orb* (L. *orbus*) and *cieu* (L. *caecus*: cf. Spanish *ciego* and Italian *cieco*). In addition, the face of the falling man is like a death's head: the empty eye sockets and toothless mouth are a stripping back of the face to a skull.

Paintings are made for people who can see and this painting uses the blind men as an occasion for a moral statement whose intended recipients are sighted. Like much early modern iconography of blind people, it draws on a tradition of transferred meanings of blindness as lack of knowledge, or of wisdom, judgement or restraint. Even a later tradition, which begins in the Enlightenment and in which blind people's experience is the occasion for scientific analysis, is directed primarily at the community of the sighted. Condillac's thought-experiment in the *Essai sur les connaissances humaines* (1746) is to imagine a senseless statue to which sense organs – nose, ears, eyes, etc. – are added one by one, in order to think how understanding is built up from the experience of the separate senses. The essay extends Locke's *Essay Concerning Human Understanding* (1690) but ultimately reaffirms the equation, central to Enlightenment modernity (consider the tirade of the *philosophes* against the 'darkness' of ignorance, superstition and barbarism) between vision, light and understanding. Diderot's letter on the blind (1749), despite having gone in the last century through several Braille editions in different languages, is a *Lettre sur les aveugles à l'usage de ceux qui voient*. In the Bruegel painting there is a double moralisation: the first is the moral of the blind leading the blind, in which the stumbling beggars function as metaphorical figures for sighted people without wisdom or understanding; the second is the moral generated by the affinity between the blind man and the sighted person looking at him, namely that of their common humanity and therefore their common mortality, reinforced by the image of the skull, the memento mori. But there is also a literal effect of the blind man's 'stare' which remains stubbornly in excess of these two moralisations, a parodic or carnivalesque inversion of the normal order of things.

The 'staring' face in fact condenses three elements which Freud saw as components of the uncanny, by which the repressed familiar returns: blinding by enucleation (gouging out of the eyes), linked to castration (Freud, with his liking for ingenious word associations, pointed out the link between the names of Hoffmann's Sandman who takes out eyes, Coppelius/Coppola, and the literary Italian word for the orbit or cup of the eye, 'coppo'); repetition through doubling (the staring man is a double of ourselves, like a mirror image, but distorted); and the presence of death (Freud 1953: 219–52). It is at the moment of condensation, in the man's face, of blindness, death and the doubling of the viewer's face that Bruegel's painting unleashes its full savage power. This is the same 'deadly' quality that Benjamin identified with early photography and which he associated with the camera's inability to return the gaze of the subject into the lens – so unlike that of the portrait painter whom the studio photographer, shrouded in a black hood, would largely displace. 'The Cripples', by contrast, lacks this uncanny effect and thus this power, and this difference demonstrates that, despite the repeated couplings in the biblical tradition of the blind and the lame,[3] it is not the disabled body as such but blindness specifically which serves to expose and destabilise the normal regime of the gaze.

The point I want to emphasise is this: Bruegel's painting, which 'upsets' classically centred composition and a related form of centred viewing, likewise upsets the 'classical' accounts of the gaze offered by a certain body of contemporary cultural theory. I am thinking in particular of Foucault's analysis of Velázquez's *Las Meninas* (*The Maids of Honour*) in the first chapter of *Les Mots et les choses* (*The Order of Things*) (1966) and the work in art history and film theory that has drawn on it, among other sources. Foucault's chapter functions to some extent as a free-standing essay, but the relation between it and the argument that takes up most of the rest of the book (namely that the same system of synchronic taxonomic classification was shared in the seventeenth and eighteenth centuries by the sciences of living things, languages and the economy), as well as its celebrated ninth chapter on the 'death of Man' as subject, centre or guarantor of scientific enquiry, lies in the argument that Velázquez's painting is at once 'the representation [...] of classical representation and the definition of the space it opens up' (Foucault 1966: 31). This space is constituted by a relay of looks, both within the painting and back and forth between figures in the painting and the viewer, where there is, however, no subject to anchor or centre all the looks, to bring them to rest; rather, the painting is this endless relay or 'dispersion' of looks without a centred and centring subject. The subjects that appear to anchor the painting and give it a perfect reciprocity, namely the royal couple in the mirror, in fact 'stand in for', and therefore push out, two other subjects who would otherwise have occupied their position: Velázquez, the 'author' of the painting (whose image would have been reflected in the mirror had there actually been one in that place in the room) and the spectators in the act of looking at the finished painting (if one were to suppose a real mirror actually in the canvas itself) (Fig. 13.3).

Let us examine in detail Foucault's account of the look in this painting and thence of the look in the system of 'classical representation' in portraiture as a whole, which the painting at once embodies and critically opens up with its baroque tennis game of rebounding gazes which either meet or fail to meet. There are two main propositions. The first is that the look is normally expected to be *reciprocal* or at any rate *capable of being reciprocated*: it comes out from the picture plane to us as viewers and it goes back from us to the painting. We at once are looked at and return the gaze of those who look: in the foreground the painter on the left, the Infanta Margarita Teresa in the centre, the maid of honour and the woman with achondroplasia to the right; in the middle ground and background the two men. All of them look out from the painting as it were at us, but within the fiction or diegesis implied in the painting they are not looking at us at all but at the figures who occupy 'our' position, namely Philip IV and Queen Mariana, whom we see reflected in the mirror just left of centre. It is the possibility of reciprocal looking and at the same time the thwarting of a true reciprocity that engages Foucault and underlies his argument about classical space and the dispersion and decentredness which in fact characterise it. The fact that the gaze of the people in the painting does not reciprocate 'ours' but that of the absent subjects of the painting ousts 'us' from our privileged subject position and instates two other sovereign subjects 'in our place'. The fact that we have no position which we can comfortably occupy gives the painting a disturbing quality, though of a different order from Bruegel's painting.

The second point is the *lack of a single centre* to the gaze within the picture plane itself: figures within it look at other figures; the viewer's look is directed hither and thither by the various axes and curves that traverse the picture plane, and which Foucault takes great care to describe: the large X that crosses on the face of the Infanta, the U that runs through the heads of the central figures with its base, again, in the Infanta's face and which cradles the mirror in the back, which is otherwise off-centre in the painting as a whole; the looping O movement above their heads which takes in the dimly lit paintings of the walls. Foucault's point here is that there is no central axis to the painting but rather a plurality of axes. These reinforce the sense of dispersion or scattering of the gaze. However, they may also be said to stabilise the process of gazing by offering the viewer a variety of centres of attention which all belong to the same stable, enclosed *system* of reciprocated looking. It is an elegant puzzle, a kind of perpetuum mobile of relayed gazing, what Foucault calls (1966: 20) 'a whole complex network of uncertainties, exchanges and feints' ('tout un réseau complexe d'incertitudes, d'échanges et d'esquives') in which someone's gaze is always present and the act of looking is permanently sustained.

In the painting by Velázquez too, then, there is a disturbance of the viewing subject's sense of the familiar. But the look that is not a look in Bruegel has a more profoundly uncanny effect because it so abruptly breaks the pattern of possible reciprocal looking. If someone turns their face directly at me and stays fixed in that position it normally means they are staring at me, and that is embarrassing because it heightens my self-consciousness and makes me wonder how to deal with the stare. Additionally, part of the social meaning of the stare and part of what is considered wrong with it is that it is a form of illicit control, of power over the person stared at. Western children learn the rule that they should not stare at strangers, because it is considered intrusive to their privacy and therefore offensive ('don't stare, it's rude'), but implicitly also because the stare endows the starer with a social power which s/he is not allowed to have, particularly (though not only) if s/he is a child. However, in the case of the blind man I can take pleasure in transgressing this rule with a sort of wilful voyeurism that is closely associated with sadism and the pleasure of the sudden lifting of a taboo. The fact that he cannot reciprocate my look allows me to stare back, to concentrate my gaze on him.

This is part of what I mean by the politics of the gaze, that is to say the social rules which regulate exchanges of looks and the relations of power lying behind these rules. Much film theory since the late 1960s has worked with notions of the politics of the gaze that are more or less explicit. The work on spectatorship informed by Marxism and psychoanalysis, from Jean-Pierre Oudart's pioneering articles on suture (1969: 36–9; in English translation as Oudart 1977/8: 35–47) to the writings of Heath (1976, 1977) and Silverman (1983), the influential essays of Laura Mulvey (1975, 1981), Gaylyn Studlar's work on masochism (1988) and Linda Williams's on pornography (1999), all deals with relays of looking in 'classical' or mainstream cinema and with the power relations of the look. In all these cases the analysis emphasises certain regularities characteristic of dominant forms of cinematic looking. Thus the concept of suture, applied to cinema from Lacanian psychoanalysis, posits a process in which an illusory subject position is created for the spectator by a particular sequence of shots/looks (for example the reverse angle or shot/reverse-shot sequence) in which the 'apparatus' (both the economic institution of cinema and its technical means) effaces itself and the spectator is coopted, 'stitched' as it were, into the film text, as the guarantor and ideological legitimator of its narrative coherence and meaning, by filling in the gaps, supplying presence and plenitude where there was absence or lack. In the work on the gender of the look initiated by Mulvey's landmark essay of 1975 and her 'Afterthoughts' of 1981, which elaborates the original argument and replies to questions and objections, the '"masculinization" of the spectator position' was likewise built into the typical narrative structures of particular film genres (such as the western or thriller) which were based on a narrative dualism of active/acting hero and passive/contemplated heroine. The questions here are those of who controls the gaze, how far its functions are sadistic or castrating in relation to the woman, whether a female spectator can gaze at an image of herself in a way that empowers her and does not control her by fetishising her. All this work, and the discussions of the voyeuristic and narcissistic pleasures of film viewing that have developed with it, is premised on the assumption that looks are always *potentially* reciprocated, i.e. that the object of a gaze can or could become the subject of a returning gaze, but that in fact the reciprocation is thwarted: it is this thwarting that makes it politically objectionable. The gaze in practice only goes one way. Woman is always image and never agent.

One may invoke here as relevant to this work another model of looking, also derived from Foucault, which is the panoptical model of *Surveiller et punir* (*Discipline and Punish*) (1975), where the entwinement of surveillance, knowledge and control is secured by the unidirectionality of the gaze. In the panoptical model, whether in its literal use (as in the prison watchtower or observation post) or in its transferred uses (as in systems of colonial rule or certain forms of anthropological observation), once again the look only goes one way, but once again the power vested in the look lies in the fact that it *might* go the other way if only the reciprocated gaze of those on the periphery were not prevented by those at the centre. In Bentham's Panopticon reciprocation is prevented by the use of a system of shutters or blinds which allow the guards to see the prisoners without being seen, so the prisoners can never be sure at any moment whether or not they are being watched. Thus, although panopticism depends on a monopolisation of the gaze in one direction it is on the *possibility* of reciprocation that its power structure is founded.

These two models of viewing – which we might call respectively the 'classical' and the 'panoptical' – may both find themselves disturbed, knocked off centre as it were, when the system of gazing itself is disrupted by the presence of a person who cannot look and therefore cannot return the gaze. This occurs with the Bruegel painting. It may also occur in films which are about or which contain blind people. Let me give two examples of the latter: one a documentary, the other a fiction.

The first is Werner Herzog's *Land des Schweigens und der Dunkelheit* (*Land of Silence and Darkness,* West Germany, 1971), one of a number of films he made in this period about physical impairment and social marginality – it was preceded by *Auch Zwerge haben klein angefangen* (*Even Dwarfs Started Small*, 1968) and followed by *Jeder für sich und Gott gegen Alle* (*The Enigma of Kaspar Hauser*, 1975). Its main subject is Fini Straubinger, a deaf and blind woman in her early sixties. We learn from her own account that she had a serious fall down a flight of stairs in her apartment block in Munich when she was nine which left her in permanent pain. She went totally blind when she was fifteen and deaf a few years later; she found it difficult to move and was confined to bed for nearly thirty years. She describes this period as one of 'terrible loneliness': 'People promised "I'll come and see you", but they didn't, and even when they sat on the bed they talked to my mother and I stayed silent.' Only when she got herself taken off morphine was she able to get up, go out and interact with other people again (this long isolation from society links her case to that of Kaspar Hauser). When Herzog filmed her she had been working for five years on behalf of the regional association for the blind in Bavaria, visiting other deaf and blind people of all ages in their homes or in residential institutions. She has a network of deaf and blind friends whom we see at her birthday party and on outings with her to the botanical gardens and the zoo.

Fini's past experience as a hearing and sighted person and her present occupation as peripatetic worker for the deaf-blind enables her to serve as a mediator between their world and that of the viewer of the film. Her life has been terrible, but it has become much better: now she travels and her work is valued. When she speaks, the words and the images she evokes engage the viewer's attention and this deflects the potential intrusiveness of our gaze. But in other parts of the film the spectator's gaze is much more raw, voyeuristic, intrusive, aggressive – it is, in other words, a stare – and one of the most unusual things about the film is the way it encourages and colludes with this. The camera lingers 'too long' on deaf and blind people, it observes them when they are unaware of being observed. We see Fini and her friend Julie sitting on a park bench, the camera rolling well after they have stopped speaking. The camera fixes on a blind woman's face in close-up: she is forty-eight-year-old Else Fährer who has been placed, inappropriately, in a psychiatric institution because since her mother's death she has stopped speaking to anyone (Fig. 13.4). Twenty-two-year-old Vladimir Kokol, deaf-blind since birth, is watched for several minutes behaving in a manner typical of those who have been institutionalised and understimulated: he rocks back and forward on his haunches, hits himself in the face with a ball, blows raspberries to himself. The camera follows fifty-one-year-old Heinrich Fleischmann, also so neglected in the past that he went off to live in a stable, as he walks through a garden and collides with a tree branch. Over these shots, for poignant effect, snatches of Bach and Vivaldi are played (as Albinoni is played in the Kaspar Hauser film), but this does not fully contain the sadistic excess of the gaze.

The film, in short, is full of contradictions, and these are embodied in the very form of its photography and editing. Herzog attempts to feel his way into the haptic world of the blind but his film also stays within the tradition of moralisations for the sighted. It is sympathetic to the plight of those in institutions but it also shares the panoptical stare of certain ethnographic films by making the institutionalised seem strangely other. What remains most striking, in all this, are the points when it subverts the classical viewing paradigm, based on a relay of shots between people capable of seeing each other, and forces the viewer into an uncomfortable sense of his/her own intrusive voyeurism.

My second example is *Night on Earth* (1991), an international co-production directed by Jim Jarmusch, each of whose five episodes is imagined as taking place in the same night and has as its protagonist a taxi driver, respectively in Los Angeles, New York, Paris, Rome and Helsinki. The Paris episode makes various satirical disruptions of the normal order of things, and has a biting humour that veers deliberately close to the edge of political incorrectness, playing as it does on differences of gender, race and physical ability. The episode falls into two parts. In the first a black taxi driver (Isaach de Bankolé) has picked up two diplomats, also black Africans, who behave offensively to him: 'Which jungle are you from? Let's take a look at your face. Where are you from?' 'The Ivory Coast', he replies. 'Côte d'Ivoire – c'est un Ivoirien – il voit rien – tout s'explique.' 'You've jumped four red lights and you drive at night without wearing glasses.' The driver gets enraged and throws the passengers out without collecting a fare. The second part begins when a young blind woman, played by Béatrice Dalle, hails his taxi. The driver says 'at least this one won't give me any trouble'. But when he screeches to a halt beside her to pick her up she too is immediately abusive: 'Where did you learn to drive, moron?' There is an alternation of single shots of the woman with two-shots, with the driver on the right of the frame looking in the mirror and the woman seated behind on the left (Fig. 13.5). The driver controls the gaze, but his voyeuristic concentration makes him lose control of the car, which (cut to a single) provokes an angry and racist reaction of the blind woman that momentarily subverts and reverses the power relations. One notes here the disturbance of a 'classical' viewing paradigm based on reverse angles. As in the other episodes in the film we get here a particular kind of two-shot, through the windscreen (cinematographer Frederick Elmes used real taxis with cameras mounted on the front), where the characters are looking the same way and both facing us. The taxi driver is in an ambiguous controlling/subaltern position (he drives/controls the car but his car is hired and the ride paid for by the passenger) but in this case he can see the passenger in his rear-view mirror but she cannot see him.

The most important difference between this and both Bruegel's 'Parable' and most of the shots in Herzog's film is the presence of a sighted person within the frame. The fact that the driver looks at the blind woman and we look at both of them immediately changes the political stakes because the sighted viewer is released from direct involvement in the embarrassed or intrusive gaze. Instead s/he can observe it in the driver from a position of detachment. The distances produced by this triangulation 'release' the audience and enable them to laugh. At the same time the audience are made aware of the complexity of the game in which they are engaged: having been drawn to take the woman's side against the driver's patronising assumptions about the limitations of blindness they are also lured into collusion with her crude racist abuse, which she can disavow because skin colour 'means nothing' to her. What predominates ultimately here is not the troubling of the normal structure of looking but these moralisations. Just as in the earlier traditions, the story of the blind person is directed pedagogically at the sighted person: the driver, the spectator – yes, she can go to the cinema and enjoy it because she *feels* the film; yes, she makes love and does it better because she does it with every inch of her body[4] – but with the added twists to do with race and gender. At the same time part of the nature of the film as play, and part of the particular kind of pleasure it affords, is to do with the audience's knowledge that Béatrice Dalle is not blind and that the film is a fiction. Even so, there is enough even in this case to disturb the normal structure of looking and expose the assumptions on which it is founded.

In conclusion, these films, on the one hand, in breaking out of the closed system of viewing and reciprocity, serve as limit cases which expose how strongly bound up 'classical space' and classical viewing is with the possibility of reciprocation of the look and they therefore oblige us to question the assumption of symmetrical specularity which underlies these paradigms of film studies. Film does not only offer various spectator positions. It can also make the viewer aware of his or her monopoly of the gaze and it can deploy this awareness to produce radical political effects. Moreover sound film, as the Béatrice Dalle character reminds the driver, is also somatic – working directly on the body – and aural: it has dimensions that the ocularcentric model of the cinematic gaze seems to forget. On the other hand, both these films tend to fall back into a moralising discourse about blindness 'à l'usage de ceux qui voient'. This discourse, which draws on a long cultural tradition, not only fails to break the conventional circle of a relay of the film text from sighted (director, apparatus) to sighted (spectators). It also, by the same token, fails to break the powerful cultural connections between seeing, insight and understanding, the very connections which the undermining of the classical paradigm begins to challenge.

Notes

1 I have slightly amended Harry Zohn's translation of this passage against the text in Benjamin 1974: 646: 'Was an der Daguerreotypie als das Unmenschliche, man könnte sagen Tödliche mußte empfunden werden, war das (übrigens anhaltende) hereinblicken in den Apparat, da doch der Apparat das Bild des Menschen aufnimmt, ohne ihm dessen Blick zurückzugeben. Dem Blick wohnt aber die Erwartung inne, von dem erwidert zu werden, dem er sich schenkt.'

2 The text used for biblical quotations in this chapter is the Revised Standard Version.

3 For example 2 Samuel 5: 6; Jeremiah 31: 8; Matthew 11: 5, 15: 30, 21:14; Luke 7: 22, 14: 13, 14: 21; John 5: 3.

4 Compare Diderot's claim (1749: 18) that the Cambridge mathematician Nicholas Saunderson (1682–1739), who was born without eyes, 'saw with his skin' ('Saunderson voyait donc par la peau').

Works cited

Auden 1976 W. H. Auden, *Collected Poems*, ed. Edward Mendelson (London: Faber and Faber

Benjamin 1939 Walter Benjamin, 'Über einige Motive bei Baudelaire', *Zeitschrift für Sozialforschung*, VIII, 1–2, translated as 'On Some Motifs in Baudelaire', in Hannah Arendt (ed.), *Illuminations* (London: Jonathan Cape, 1970)

Benjamin 1974 Walter Benjamin, *Schriften*, vol. I, part 2 (Frankfurt: Suhrkamp)

Diderot 1749 Denis Diderot, *Lettre sur les Aveugles*, ed. Robert Niklaus (Geneva: Droz, 2nd edn, 1963)

Foucault 1966 Michel Foucault, *Les Mots et les choses* (Paris: Gallimard)

Foucault 1975 Michel Foucault, *Surveiller et punir. Naissance de la prison* (Paris: Gallimard)

Freud 1919 Sigmund Freud, 'Das Unheimliche', translated as 'The Uncanny', *The Standard Edition of the Complete Psychological Works of Sigmund Freud*, ed. and trans. James Strachey, vol. XVII (London: Hogarth Press, 1955)

Heath 1976 Stephen Heath, 'Narrative Space', *Screen*, 17, 3, Autumn, 68–112 (also in Heath 1981)

Heath 1977/8 Stephen Heath, 'Notes on Suture', *Screen*, 18, 4, Winter, 48–76 (also in Heath 1981)

Heath 1981 Stephen Heath, *Questions of Cinema* (Basingstoke and London: Macmillan)

Mulvey 1975 Laura Mulvey, 'Visual Pleasure and Narrative Cinema', *Screen*, 16, 3, Autumn, 6–18 (also in Mulvey 1989)

Mulvey 1981 Laura Mulvey, 'Afterthoughts on "Visual Pleasure and Narrative Cinema" inspired by *Duel in the Sun*', *Framework*, 15–17, Summer, 12–15 (also in Mulvey 1989)

Mulvey 1989 Laura Mulvey, *Visual and Other Pleasures* (Basingstoke and London: Macmillan)

Oudart 1969 Jean-Pierre Oudart, 'La suture', *Cahiers du Cinéma*, 211, April 1969, 36–39

Oudart 1977/8 Jean-Pierre Oudart, 'Cinema and suture' (translation of Oudart 1969), *Screen*, 18, 4, Winter, 35–47

Silverman 1983 Kaja Silverman, *The Subject of Semiotics* (New York: Oxford University Press)

Studlar 1988 Gaylyn Studlar, *In the Realm of Pleasure* (Bloomington and Indianapolis: University of Indiana Press)

Williams 1999 Linda Williams, *Hard Core: Power, Pleasure and the 'Frenzy of the Visible'*, expanded paperback edition (Berkeley and Los Angeles: University of California Press)

14

Bodies in Transition, or the Unbearable Lightness of the 'Traditionless' Self

Márta Csabai and Ferenc Erős[1]

The history of twentieth-century discourses about the body is marked by a resolute search for the definitions and 'determinable' features of the body. This project has always gone hand-in-hand with efforts to conceptualise the genealogy and evolution of (post)modern identity and has meant the further fragmentation of the already dichotomic Western view of the human subject. If we take an overview of the major theories of the body, we find at least as many 'bodies' as theoretical approaches and epistemologies. According to the most widespread classification, there are three bodies at three separate but overlapping conceptual and analytic levels (Scheper-Hughes and Lock 1987). The *individual* body is conceptualised in phenomenological theories of the body while the *social* body implies the symbolic, representational uses which are found most commonly in structuralist theories. The third and most widely known in contemporary poststructuralist theory is the body *politic* which is formulated through the regulatory practices and controls of power. The fact that we can find a growing number of 'bodies' in theories of the social sciences reflects both the significance and indeterminacy of the 'body-problem' in contemporary society and also uncertainties in relation to the questions of identity (see for example, O'Neill 1985). Naturally, these 'bodies' also signify the major problems of (the body of) society and its institutions of power which label individuals through their bodies as deviant or normal, impure or clean, needful of control or discipline.

Besides the 'evergreen' controversies of biological essentialism and social constructivism, late twentieth-century discourses about the body have brought together the problems of bodily control, commodity culture, self-expression and narcissism. In poststructuralist theory the human body can no longer be regarded as a given reality but as a product of knowledge. In this sense 'bodies [...] are not born: they are made' (Haraway 1989: 44). At the risk of appearing unjustifiably naïve or pointlessly pompous, we would end the sentence with a question-mark and ask: 'Are bodies born *or* made?' We must do this until we can decide whether the right answer (if an answer can be given to this question at all) or the re-formulation (elimination) of the question would help us to think about the body and its relation to subjectivity differently. It may also help to avoid the further fragmentation of the body and promote our understanding of it as a basis and frame of the identity of the subject.

One of the most common arguments against analyses of the discursive or textual construction of bodies – i.e. how the body is seen and portrayed – states that they tell us little about the body's implication in human agency, of how people experience the 'lived body' (see for example, Turner 1992). Another frequent critique is that the body should not be regarded simply as an object of sociological investigation, but as an inherently sociological and historical phenomenon. Further, there are authors who emphasise that we have to find the place of psychical representations in conceptualising the body not in opposition to the social dimension but as necessarily interactive with it, to create a living subjectivity, a *corporeality* of the body (Grosz 1994). In this regard the body *itself* has to be understood as a 'threshold' or a 'borderline' concept that not only reflects both the diversity and the indeterminacy of its components but also involves the notion of totality. The Janus-faced concept of the border inherently refers to *both* fragmentation and non-differentiation. Does this 'totality' of the body suggest the (re?)unification of the above-mentioned fragmented aspects? Does it mean the desire for the demolition of boundaries between different concepts and theories? Are we fascinated by the indeterminacy of the body or, on the contrary, do we feel embarrassed – even scared – by it?

Today it is often argued that there is a certain nostalgia about the body, a homesickness, a 'not feeling at home' in the body. This is reflected particularly in those contemporary theories of postmodernity which put forward the vision of the 'death' of the body and its replacement by technology. The repeated appearance of the themes of the fracture, instability and fluidity of modern life – and modern identity – in different scientific, popular and lay discourses may reflect a certain nostalgia for the spontaneity and emotional passions often associated with the 'non-disciplined', 'grotesque' bodies of the Other. The wish to 'reconsecrate' the profane could explain the renewed interest in nature, magic, cults and fate, etc. (see Mellor/Shilling 1997). It could also be a possible explanation for the invention of traditions and (new) national or ethnic identities.

Mary Douglas has described the body as a metaphor of social cohesion, differentiation and conflict (Douglas 1966). A widespread concern with the maintenance and purity of bodily boundaries is most present at times of social crisis, when dominant bodies and established identities are threatened. The body has become an intensified object of concern in the last few decades. This has happened in parallel with the processes of globalisation which threaten individual and national boundaries. It is also widely argued that the cleanliness of the body has become a central issue in contemporary discourses about health and illness. As bodily hygiene and also health and fitness have gradually become a moral issue, so the search for a cleaner, harder, more defined body has promoted the strengthening of distinctions, the construction of frontiers between different social groups.

All these points could be connected to more general questions of globalisation and identity (gender, ethnicity, etc.). Responses to the pressure of present-day globalisation processes may be very different, but the most important is the creation of new artificial borders. One significant form of this is *metaracism* which tries to legitimate itself by building up a border around the cultural 'Other' (see Rattansani/Westwood 1994). The creation and disqualification of the cultural Other as an *abject* from society's body is endemic to any creation of group identity, but in excessive forms it may lead to ethnic, gender and other forms of discrimination. All of these raise the question of where the borders of the body start and end, what kind of imagos and – unconscious – fantasies form (and transform) representations about our own and the Other's body.

*

1989–90 was the period of 'transition from dictatorship to democracy' in the Central European communist countries. As part of this historical process, free elections were held in Hungary in the spring of 1990 – this event led to the formation of the first non-communist government for more than forty years. Before the election an extremely heated and exciting campaign had taken place – the parties, most of them newly created, not simply the revitalisations of the old, 'historical' ones, competed for the allegiance of the voters. Naturally, the central issue of the campaign was the evaluation of the past and the delineation of the future. In this respect most of the parties (including the Socialist Party, the ex-communists) agreed, at least on the surface, that a historical period was closing forever and something new had to begin; thus, the elections marked a radical caesura between past and future. Although the transition took place peacefully, constitutionally, through negotiating a consensus between the various groups of the political elite of the country, which was to guarantee a relatively smooth transformation of the political, social and economic system, a genuine revolution had taken place in the *symbolic* sphere. Old taboos collapsed suddenly; repressed, frozen or marginalised identities came to life again; new discourses were set in motion. Many people started to rewrite their life histories and to redefine their identities; 'overnight converts' discovered lifelong democratic attitudes. 'There is a big swarm on the road to Damascus' – the Hungarian writer Péter Esterházy wrote in 1989.

The electoral campaign in 1990 was very rich in visual elements as well – TV programmes, political advertisements, leaflets, posters, grafitti were spread all over the country. Beyond its immediate political messages, this visual propaganda also had a hidden, symbolic structure which appealed not only to the political and ideological attitudes of citizens but to their fantasy structures as well. While the surface of these messages aimed at gaining votes by trying to convince citizens about the rationality and benefits of the realisation of a given party's programme, that is, at a *change of attitude*, the hidden message was aimed at *identity change*, an overall change or redefinition of individual as well as collective identities. In this visual propaganda, the representation of the body had a particularly important role.

The role of body images in political propaganda has become a widely discussed topic since Wilhelm Reich's pioneering work *The Mass Psychology of Fascism* (1933) and, most notably, since Klaus Theweleit's *Male Fantasies* (first published in German in 1978). While most of these analyses are preoccupied with totalitarian propaganda, what we are interested in is the *dissolution* of a totalitarian regime which creates body representations as part of political propaganda.[2]

To illustrate this, we have chosen two political posters from the 1990 Hungarian election campaign. Both posters were celebrated, in Hungary as well as abroad, as the most representative visual expressions of the period of political transition. The first one, which was one of the election posters of the Hungarian Democratic Forum (MDF, the party which finally won the elections) shows the thickset nape of a Russian officer. The man is represented as ugly, disgusting – and the text of the poster contains two Russian words, printed in Cyrillic (but comprehensible to most Hungarians, even those who didn't understand the language): TOVARISHCHI, KONIEC: 'Comrades, this is the end!' (see Fig. 14.1). The surface message of the poster is self-evident: the Soviet military occupation and the Soviet domination of the country must end. It was a direct allusion to one of the slogans of the Hungarian revolution of 1956: 'Ruskies go home!' After 1956, the question of Soviet domination was taboo for more than three decades, but in 1990 the Soviet withdrawal had suddenly become a fact of the very near future rather than a pious hope.[3]

Understandably, 'the Russians' at that time were not particularly popular in Hungary. The inventiveness of the poster was such that it was able to manipulate this unpopularity and concentrate it on the body of a Russian man, a soldier, as the representative of the Russians in general. The soldier-figure has no face, no individuality: it is the Soldier who, as Klaus Theweleit shows in the second volume of his aforementioned book, is the 'phallic weapon'.[4]

It is instructive to take a glance at a similar picture reproduced in Theweleit's book (Theweleit 1977: 83): the Hollywood actor Erich von Stroheim in the role of a German officer (see Fig. 14.2). This picture may have been the source of inspiration for the 1990 Hungarian political poster; however, the roles and the stages have changed. The protagonist of the drama is now 'the Russian'. He is shown in the moment of leaving, before crossing the border. He is still at the peak of his power, his heavy, grotesque neck betraying his bodily strength. However, the Russian word *koniec*, 'the end', also familiar from the last scene of Russian films, suggests that the body might be on the way to becoming a corpse: a shot in the back of the neck (once a popular method of execution in Soviet and Nazi prisons and camps) might transform the body of the Russian soldier into an *abject*. It becomes an abject – not the *object* of an heroic cult over the body of the fallen soldier. According to Julia Kristeva:

> the abject is not an ob-ject facing me, which I name or imagine. Nor is it an ob-jest, an otherness ceaselessly fleeing in a systematic quest of desire. What is abject is not my correlative, which, providing me with someone else as support, would allow me to be more or less detached and autonomous. The abject has only one quality of the object – that of being opposed to. If the object, however, through its opposition, settles me within the fragile texture of a desire for meaning, which, as a matter of fact, makes me ceaselessly and infinitely homologous to it, what is *abject*, on the contrary, the jettisoned object, is radically excluded and draws me toward the place where meaning collapses. (Kristeva 1996: 156)

The implicit aim of transforming the Russian body into an abject is not simply to get rid of the occupying forces – it is the radical exclusion of the former authority from the collective identity, a radical redefinition of this identity which excludes 'foreigners'. This is not the place to discuss the further implications of this poster, namely, its nationalistic overtones, which became evident subsequently in the ideology of the party in whose name the poster was originally issued. Nevertheless, the Russian figure represents here not only the 'invaders' but the filthy, malignant, threatening Other in general. The image puts a finishing touch to the removal of the remains of the Other. As Roland Barthes put it:

> The petit bourgeois is a man unable to imagine the Other. If he comes face to face with him, he blinds himself, ignores and denies him, or else transforms him into himself. [...] Sometimes – rarely – the Other is revealed as irreducible: not because of a sudden scruple, but because *common sense* rebels: a [*sic*] man does not have a white skin, another drinks pear juice, not Pernod. How can one assimilate the Negro, the Russian? There is here a figure for emergencies: exoticism. The Other becomes a pure object, a spectacle, a clown. (Barthes 1957: 141–2)

This poster, however does not tell us what happens after one gets rid of the 'comrades'. What happens after they cross the border? What new power is going to replace the old one, the power of the 'comrades'? What happens after the father or the 'Big (Br)other' has been killed?

The next poster we have selected shows exactly what happens after the father is killed. (see Fig. 14.3). This was the poster of the Federation of Young Democrats (FIDESZ), a party founded in 1988 by radical opponents of the communist regime: young intellectuals, university students, mostly in their twenties, who at that time represented an alternative culture, with a strong emphasis on human rights, liberal values, modernisation etc. This party, despite from time to time enjoying high popularity, remained in parliamentary opposition until 1998, when FIDESZ – in alliance with right-wing parties – won the elections and its leader Viktor Orbán formed a 'centre-right' government, with an agenda and political philosophy very different from the party's public image in the late 1980s and early 1990s.

In the upper part of the poster we see a well-known picture from the 1970s: the leaders of the USSR and the GDR, Leonid Brezhnev and Erich Honecker, greeting each other. The two old men kiss each other on the mouth – which was a gesture unusual even among communist leaders, who generally used to conform to the old Russian custom of men's ritual embracing and kissing on the cheeks. In fact, Erich Honecker was known as one of the most servile communist leaders – but the point here is not simply the political content of the encounter of these two men. The point is the grotesque character of their kissing in the eyes of the contemporary East European viewers who had suffered for several decades under these leaders' hated gerontocracy – in contrast to the picture on the lower part of the poster which shows a pair of young lovers kissing. The slogan says: 'MAKE A CHOICE!' Thus, the FIDESZ poster shows what is going to happen when 'they' leave – for ever. It is 'we' who will then take their place: WE, the young, healthy, *normal*, heterosexual people, instead of the old, disgusting, perverse, homosexual figures. They are the 'abjects' now, and making a choice means an absolute break between the past and the future.

Why does the picture of the two old political leaders kissing call forth such a strong feeling of rejection in fantasy? Why do they become the object of disgust and abjection? It is not only because of the – rather direct – message that these leaders symbolise the hateful and oppressive *ancien régime*. It is (the fantasy-image of) the Leader here who has become comic and impotent since he has lost all of his strength and power. In the past, the Leader was strong even in his death: Lenin's embalmed corpse dominated not only the Red Square in Moscow but the fantasy of Soviet people with the slogan 'Lenin lived, Lenin lives, Lenin will live!' – and, on the other hand, filthy and often obscene jokes about the mummified body and its imagined sexual parts. In the case of the FIDESZ poster this is not simply the pleasure of exposing the mere bodiedness of the powerful but of revealing that they are really members of an easily despised minority, i.e. homosexuals. But the implications of showing them as marginalised, weak deviants are deeper than a simple mockery of the loathed gerontocratic leaders. Beyond the ecstatic feelings of freedom, the 'borderline' state of political transition also had a liberating effect on – existing but hitherto repressed – homophobic fantasies and 'fears of the feminine' (Theweleit 1977). These may be interpreted as symbolic representations of anxieties about uncertainty and 'excessive' freedom: fears of irrationality, loss of control, disorder. Consequently, the 'normal' heterosexual couple is counterpointed as the representation of the need for (a new) 'order'.

The doubling of the Leader in the picture may also mean symbolically that he is turning towards himself – kissing *himself* – in a perverted narcissistic manner. He has lost all of his threatening characteristics. As with the Russian officer on the poster described above, we cannot see the eyes of the Leader, which means that there is no disciplinary gaze monitoring us – the totalitarian leader has lost his authority. 'Big (Br)other' is not watching you any more. His only potential is directed inward, turning to the Self in a deadly manner – he has no capacity to take part in development, is unable to contribute to the sustaining of the Self (the body-self of society) in a creative manner. He can no longer play the role of the Ego-ideal for the group, or for the whole society.

The other possible source of rejection revealed by the picture is the multiplication of objects which, as Freud says, can be regarded as sources of the feeling of the *uncanny* (Freud 1919). The multiplying of objects is uncanny since the Real is lost through doubling, the immobilisation, the freezing of time.

The possibility of change, the chance of (a new) life is clearly marked by the contrast of the two pictures in the poster, which is a perfect image of the 'borderline' nature of transition. The second picture shows a young man and a woman in an idyllic scene, kissing each other in a state of Paradise. The slogan 'Make a choice' – like another FIDESZ slogan from the 1990 election campaign: 'Listen to your *heart*, vote for Young Democrats!' – invites the viewer to follow his/her own desire, promises the possibility of unlimited *jouissance* without the disciplinary gaze of the Leader (Father-God). The slogan of the radical student movement of the 1960s, 'Make love, not war', has arrived in the (ex) Soviet bloc, replacing communist asceticism and totalitarian 'fear of the feminine' with pure *jouissance*.

The strong emotional message of the poster echoes our ultimate desire of being part of the primal scene, remaining there for ever, being man *and* woman, father *and* mother, having the chance of being anything and *anyone* we like. This strongest wish is related to our desire for unrestricted freedom, for non-differentiation, for *indeterminacy*. It is a regressive, infantile desire to remain at the border, *being* the border, not accepting the disciplinary law of the Father. Although this message is very attractive, it contains substantial dangers as well.

*

Identification with the border, 'remaining stuck in' the Oedipal dilemma, ultimately threatens the subject with the loss of identity. As an example, we can cite hysteria, an often-used metaphor for the fragmentation of (*fin-de-siècle*) bodies and identities. The hysteric is someone who is looking for the unlimited possibility of choosing identity but is unable to make any decision. We may suppose that in addition to desire there must be some kinds of anxiety contributing to the ambivalences about 'making a choice'. The hysteric is not able to escape from the Oedipal circle, because s/he is afraid of the suffocating, death-bearing qualities of the 'good' mother (and her womb) but at the same time s/he does not want to leave its safety and warmth, and *simultaneously* s/he is attracted to the world of the father, but scared of the power and dominance it symbolises. So s/he wants to be *neither* mother *nor* father, but desires to be *both* (or *neither*).[5] S/he wants to remain *there*, at the source of beginning, the place of origin. S/he does not want to be either female or male, but wants to be both (or *neither*), to remain *indeterminate*. S/he is struggling for *non-differentiation*, for a 'borderline' body and – as Juliet Mitchell has put it – a *traditionless Self*. S/he wants to be *the* Origin, s/he wants to be the Secret, the ultimate Truth. We know from classical and contemporary cases of hysteria that the hysteric pays the price of her/his never-fulfilled, impossible desire. S/he pays with loss of libido, with mental and physical symptoms – the 'fragmentation' of her/his body and also of her/his Self (see Csabai 1998).

The impossibility of identifying with the border has very similar consequences to occupying it. It will result in the death of desire and also the death of the body. In a Lacanian sense, the total confrontation with *jouissance* is always a fatal act. Non-differentiation and arbitrary, autocratic *determination* are two sides of the same coin.

A good example of this can be seen in Peter Greenaway's movie *The Pillow Book* (1996). As a child, the protagonist, Nagiko, was greeted by her father every birthday with the words: 'When God created mankind, he made the first figure of clay, painted on it the eyes, the mouth and genitals. He was worried that people would forget their names, so he also painted names, one name for each person.' While listening to this declaration we see the father painting four letters on the girl's forehead, cheeks and lips. Nagiko's life is determined by this childhood experience and this is why in her adult life she is able to make love only with men who are willing to write on her body. She also writes on the body of her elderly lover, takes photographs of the inscribed surface, and these photos will comprise her first 'book'. She tries to sell the book to a rich, sophisticated, influential, decadent and homosexual publisher, who sends her away. Nagiko seduces the publisher's young lover, Jérôme, writes her subsequent works on the young man's body and subsequently bombards the publisher with her new books. But the publisher does not want the photos of the 'body-books', he wants to possess the whole body, specifically its borders in both the symbolic and literal senses of the word. One of the most harrowing scenes of the movie is when bored garbage-men dump the inner parts of Jérôme's body in front of the publisher's building. (In a Foucaldian sense, the body has to perish after the inscription of the message.) Then we watch the publisher spread the book made of the young man's skin on his own naked body: he is trying to 'read' it with his own skin. (After occupying the border, he wants to *identify* with it.) At the end of this triangular story (a Holy Trinity, in which the third vertex is occupied by the *woman* – see Kristeva 1979) Nagiko gets back the book, the text, the boundary from the economically-intellectually-erotically powerful publisher. After the two men's death it is Nagiko who owns the textualised surface of the body with its all meanings. She has control over the permeability of the body. But the story does not end here. Nagiko does not remain entrapped by the Oedipal circle. The 'happy ending' of the movie is a satisfactory and 'fair' solution offered by Greenaway. On the first birthday of her daughter – whose father is Jérôme – Nagiko buries the 'leather-bound' book of (Jérôme's) body under a blossoming bonsai-tree. She buries the boundary, closes it away from consciousness, knowledge, rationality and power. The border (of the body) is in a safe place now, there is no one who can occupy or manipulate it. The one-year-old child can live, life can go on, but only under these conditions.

Contrary to great expectations, the Central and East European transition naturally did not create an earthly paradise. It would take us too far afield to make a balance of the 'gains' and 'losses' of transition – it is enough to say here that the young couple portrayed on the 1990 poster had to face various economic and social hardships. Nevertheless, the newly emerged 'consumer society' uses them as the 'ideal couple' at whom the commercials, the advertisements, all the consumer propaganda of the capitalist society is directed. They are no longer the loving, innocent couple who *enjoy* instead of obeying external rules, their young, healthy, fresh outlook and image is 'sold' to the public with the message: *make a choice*, since you *have to* be like them, you have to consume our goods, and only then can you remain young and healthy forever...

Dissatisfaction at the loss of illusions after the transition; the loss of the possibility of remaining young, innocent, and free; losing the possibility of never-ending *jouissance* – all these are portrayed in a caricature, a grotesque photographic montage from 1998 (see Fig. 14.4). This caricature appeared on the front page of a Hungarian magazine *HVG* (Economics Weekly) after the May 1998 parliamentary elections, when the Young Democrats formed a coalition government with a right-wing, populist, agrarian-based party, FKGP, the Smallholders' Party. In contrast to the anonymous young couple in the 1990 poster, both characters – the young 'bridegroom' and the old 'bride' – have a concrete name now, their identity is determined. The 'bridegroom' is the new Prime Minister Viktor Orbán, the leader of the Young Democrats, the 'bride' is József Torgyán, Minister of Agriculture and Regional Development, the leader of the Smallholders' Party. Their unusual, though not unexpected political marriage[6] was widely criticised for a variety of different reasons, especially because of Torgyán's infamous anti-liberal, demagogic views.

The fact that both characters are wearing a disguise in the picture invites the viewer to fantasise, to find a desired object behind the veil. The satisfaction that we find in the new, young, handsome Leader in the costume of a bridegroom is undercut by our feelings about the other character, the bride. The problem is not so much that this bride is too old for the bridegroom – could even be his *mother*, which reveals incest-fantasies – and not even that this bride has an undetermined or androgynous gender identity (and in that way this person could also be the bridegroom's *father*). Nor is the real problem the fact that we do not find the typical object of desire (of a typical young man) behind the veil, nor the fact that we recognise the 'bride' all too well. This recognition again does not provide the well-known satisfactory feeling of success after 'finding out the secret' or 'solving the riddle'. (As in psychoanalytic theories of drag, the satisfaction of the 'revealing shot' proving that it is after all a man under the veil is generally supposed to be *reassuring* to [male] viewers; see Michelle Meagher's article in this volume.) On the contrary, we may have a very similar feeling of the uncanny to the one we had in response to the picture of the two old political leaders kissing. Behind the veil we find *another* leader, who is not the counterpart, not the duplicate of the new young one, but an Other who does not want to unveil his/her real identity. The sad face of the bridegroom in the cartoon suggests that *forced* marriage, with his (and our?) desire of the forced occupation of the border, the desire of both *being* mother and father and possessing them, makes *jouissance* impossible. What makes the whole thing disturbing is that we cannot be sure, but only suspect that it is prohibited by this Other, who – again – in fantasy makes the Leader comic and impotent. (The grotesque may also again be based on the fear of discovering male homosexual desire 'under the veil'.)

At the level of the Ego-ideal (which for a group or society is represented in the figure of the leader) the subject needs the *illusion* of free choice, unlimited possibilities. In order to gain support, to solicit votes at an election, all social systems must offer this illusion to their members. As we demonstrated earlier, these desires can never be totally fulfilled, otherwise the whole system would disintegrate, which would mean a fatal confrontation with *jouissance*, the end of desire.[7] The Ego-ideal derives from the symbolic, the dead, castrated father, the Name of the Father, as Lacan says. He must represent the public Law, in contrast to the hidden, non-written Law connected to the conscience-function of the Superego. This latter comes from the primordial father, the *père jouissance*. This part of the Law, which guarantees the integration of society, bars the subject from the unlimited availability of *jouissance* – always has to remain invisible, otherwise it makes the subject protest (see Žižek 1997a and 1997b). The invasion of this primordial Superego figure into consciousness would mean an autocratic, totalitarian governing of the group (and on the individual level, the Self).

This caricature suggests that the (re-)sexualisation – revitalisation – of the fantasy-image of the Leader after the transition is different from that expected in 1990. It is not only the impossibility of the total abolition of the past – the impossibility of creating a 'traditionless Self' – that causes the frustration reflected in the caricature. It may be much more closely related to the feeling of the uncanny evoked by the obscure figure of the Leader/s. The ambivalences connected to the desired state of indeterminacy are now replaced by anxieties about new boundaries.

Thus the symbolic representations and fantasy-images of the political transition reflect the general contemporary problems of the body and identity that we referred to at the beginning of the paper. These examples may also contribute to our understanding of why the desired fantasy-imagos of neutrality, indeterminacy, corporeality are all shadowed by the *unbearable lightness* of the 'traditionless' Self.

Notes

1 An earlier version of this essay has appeared in the *Journal of European Psychoanalysis*, 8–9 (1999); we are grateful for permission to reproduce it here.
2 Or, more exactly, a post-totalitarian regime: see: Hannah Arendt 1973, especially its last chapter on the Hungarian Revolution.
3 In fact, the last Russian soldier left Hungary in June 1991.

4 The topic of the 'phallic weapon' is also elaborated by the Yugoslav film director Dušan Makavejev in his famous film *W. R., the Mystery of the Organism* (1970) in the scene where the making of a plaster-cast of an erect penis is intercut with the appearances of Mao and Stalin.

5 On the hysteric's ambivalence towards sexual identity Juliet Mitchell writes: 'The hysteric [...] will not acknowledge the Law of the castration complex, will oscillate between the two desired positions of the Oedipus complex – being mother or being father – and will be unable unconsciously to acknowledge that the polymorphous delights of infantile sexuality must be forgotten and repressed if past, present and future – traditions – are to be established in the mind. Not properly internalising the representative of the law (the 'superego') in fantasy, she will be an incestuous Oedipus before his discovery of his origins, a self without a history' (Mitchell 1992: 93).

6 Another possible source of this poster is the American postcard caricaturing Ronald and Nancy Reagan as a cross-dressed couple (see Fig. 14.5).

7 This problem is marvellously elaborated by Dušan Makevejev in his above mentioned film in which he shows how Wilhelm Reich's programme of sexual liberation had been perverted and turned into its opposite: how Reichian 'vegetotherapy' became a violent domination and exploitation of the body and the parallels between this kind of politics of body and the coercive practices of totalitarian regimes and total institutions (like mental hospitals).

Works cited

Arendt 1973 Hannah Arendt, *The Origins of Totalitarianism* (New York: Harcourt)

Barthes 1957 Roland Barthes, 'Le Mythe, aujourd'hui', in *Mythologies* (Paris: Seuil); translated as 'Myth Today', in Susan Sontag (ed.), *Barthes. Selected Writings* (New York: Fontana, 1982)

Csabai 1998 Márta Csabai, 'Her Body Her/Self? On the Mysteries of Hysteria and Anorexia Nervosa. A Feminine Disease', *Replika, Hungarian Social Science Quarterly*, Special Issue, 99–111

Douglas 1966 Mary Douglas, *Purity and Danger* (London: Routledge & Kegan Paul)

Freud 1919 Sigmund Freud, 'Das Unheimliche', translated by James Strachey as 'The Uncanny', in *The Complete Standard Edition of the Works of Sigmund Freud* (London: Hogarth, 1975), vol. 17, 217–52

Grosz 1994 Elizabeth Grosz, *Volatile Bodies. Towards a Corporeal Feminism* (Bloomington: Indiana University Press)

Haraway 1989 Donna Haraway, 'The Biopolitics of Post-modern Bodies: Determination of Self in Immune System Discourse', *differences*, I (1), 3–43

Kristeva 1979 Julia Kristeva, 'Le Temps des femmes', in *Cahiers de recherche des sciences des textes et documents*, 5, translated as 'Women's Time', in Toril Moi (ed.), *A Kristeva Reader* (New York: Columbia University Press), 187–213

Kristeva 1996 Julia Kristeva, 'Approaching Abjection', in Sue Vice (ed.), *Psychoanalytic Criticism. A Reader* (Cambridge: Polity, 1996)

Makavejev 1968 Dušan Makavejev, *W. R: The Mysteries of the Organism*

Mellor and Shilling 1997 Philip A. Mellor and Chris Shilling, *Re-forming the Body. Religion, Community and Modernity* (London: Sage)

Mitchell 1992 Juliet Mitchell, 'From King Lear to Anna O. and Beyond: Some Speculative Theses on Hysteria and the Traditionless Self', *Yale Journal of Criticism*, 5: 2, 87–99

O'Neill 1985 John O'Neill, *Five Bodies: the Human Shape of Modern Society* (Ithaca: Cornell University Press)

Rattansani and Westwood 1994 A. Rattansani and S. Westwood (eds), *Racism, Modernity and Identity* (Cambridge: Polity)

Reich 1933 Wilhelm Reich, *Massenpsychologie des Faschismus* (Copenhagen-Prague-Zurich: Verlag für Sexualpolitik), translated as *The Mass Psychology of Fascism* (New York: Farrar, Straus and Giroux, 1970)

Scheper-Hughes and Lock 1987 Nancy Scheper-Hughes and Margaret M. Lock, 'The Mindful Body: a Prolegomenon to Future Work in Medical Anthropology', *Medical Anthropology Quarterly*, 6–41

Theweleit 1977 Klaus Theweleit, *Männerphantasien* (Reinbeck bei Hamburg: Roter Stern), 2 vols, translated as *Male Fantasies* (Minneapolis: University of Minnesota Press, 1987 and 1989)

Turner 1992 Bryan S. Turner, *Regulating Bodies: Essays in Medical Sociology* (London: Routledge)

Žižek 1997a Slavoj Žižek, 'The Inherent Transgression or the Obscenity of Power', lecture given at the Central European University, Budapest, June 1996; published in Hungarian: *Thalassa* (8), 1997, 1: 116–30.

Žižek 1997b Slavoj Žižek, 'The Big Other Does Not Exist', *Journal of European Psychoanalysis*, 5,. Spring–Fall, 3–19

15

Revolution in Video Dance: the Construction of a Fluid Body

Sherril Dodds

A woman glances outwards hesitantly, her face framed in a black and white close-up. Her hair is a jet black bob. Slowly, she begins to mutter one or two words of French in a Japanese accent. She continues, her gaze growing in confidence as her monologue unfolds. The language is masked by her strong accent, but the unedited close-up captures the venom with which she spits out her words. Fractured sentences develop into a furious diatribe. The sting of each syllable is mirrored by her tormented expression, all of which is caught in this single shot. Against her shouting, the gentle strains of a Monteverdi duet can be heard in the background. Her explosive words shoot from the screen in real time, but the image slips out of synch in fuzzy slow motion. Her furrowed brow, the elasticity of her mouth, the flying spittle and flickering eyelashes can be seen in painstaking detail. At no point does the camera cut away.

The above description is of *Monologue*, a dance work that was conceived and choreographed for the screen. In several ways, this short film draws into question the determinacy of the dancing body. The manipulation of the film speed allows the body to move in ways that could not be achieved in live performance. Consequently, the physical capacity of the dancing body is extended and the spectator is able to see facets of the performer that could not be seen with the naked eye. Not only are physical boundaries called into question, but also conceptual ones. A shouting face clearly challenges accepted notions of dance vocabularies and a single, unedited close-up is a rarity in view of existing televisual conventions. The slippage of sound and image also creates a level of distortion. There is clearly a fluidity or indeterminacy of the dancing body in *Monologue*.

Since the mid-1980s, a new genre of screen dance has emerged that can be characterised by its cutting edge images and innovative filming techniques. *Monologue* is typical of such work. This form, known as 'video dance' (Maletic 1987–8; Rosiny 1994), is dance that is originally conceived for the camera and which explores the creative interface between dance and television. It could be argued that video dance is a 'hybrid site'. It is a fusion of dance and televisual practices through which a creative tension occurs: televisual devices act on dance in such a way that bodies are constructed that transcend the capabilities of the live dancing body; in turn, the codes and conventions of a postmodern stage dance tradition, out of which video dance has emerged, act upon the television medium to produce striking aesthetic images not normally associated with conventional television texts. Thus a fluid body is constructed that transgresses or disrupts established boundaries.

One area of theory that may illuminate the fluidity of the video dance body and its tendency for disruption derives from the work of Julia Kristeva. Kristeva (1977) has developed a theory of signification, characterised by the duality of 'semiotic and symbolic', that can be applied to what she has designated 'poetic language'. The Kristevan notion of poetic language is not the formal patterns of poetic verse associated with certain areas of literature, but those signifying practices that defy the grammatical and syntactical laws of established forms of communication. The concepts of 'fluidity' and 'disruption' are central to this chapter and are purposely employed on various levels.

In opposition to stasis, the notion of fluidity is germane to the mobility of dance. The idea of a fluid moving body, however, transcends the aesthetic realm of dance into other conceptual frameworks. For instance, Shilling (1993) argues that the body is not a fixed phenomenon, but is plastic and unstable. This idea supports the notion of the video dance body as a hybrid entity that perpetually shifts back and forth across different theoretical and aesthetic sites. It is not singular but multiple, inscribed with discourses from the fields of dance, television and other visual, kinetic and technological practices. The sense of motion or fluidity characteristic of dance is also deeply embedded in Kristeva's writing, in which there are numerous allusions to movement as a metaphor for key critical concepts. For instance, she describes the 'semiotic chora' as 'an essentially mobile and extremely provisional articulation constituted by movements and their ephemeral states' (1977: 25). This chapter therefore sets out to examine the fluid or indeterminate character of the body in video dance drawing on Kristeva's concept of 'poetic language'.

In *Revolution in Poetic Language* (1974) Kristeva argues that the semiotic and symbolic are present in all signifying processes. No text is exclusively semiotic or symbolic but the dialectic interplay between them determines the type of discourse that is produced (Kristeva 1977: 24). Kristeva conceptualises the subject as 'en procès' ('in process/on trial'): that is a subject always in the 'process of becoming' (Daly 1992: 244) and constituted through flows, jouissance and energy charges (Lechte 1990: 124). Kristeva refers to the site of drive energies in the subject as the 'chora', an abstract and unpredictable phenomenon. Conceived as a place or receptacle, yet unrepresentable, it is a mobile entity in which drive energies are created and destroyed, articulated and ruptured. Kristeva argues that, although it can never be definitively categorised, it is similar to a kinetic or vocal rhythm (126). It is the chora that forms the basis of the semiotic. The symbolic, on the other hand, represents the laws and structures of social organisation founded on sexual difference and the psychoanalytic framework of the family.[1]

In language, the symbolic refers to the law and order of syntax and grammar, while the semiotic refers to the 'materiality' of language such as rhythm, gesture and timbre (Lechte 1990: 129). Although the semiotic is present in all speech acts, it is the symbolic, or communicative function of language that is generally taken into account. Some discourses, however, draw attention to, or prioritise, the semiotic. Artistic practices are able to explore and manipulate the semiotic through such phenomena as the rhythm and timbre of the voice, the phonetic and graphic aspect of language, or the gesture and movement of the body. This notion is particularly relevant to video dance with its centrality of the dancing body and the televisual image.

The term, 'poetic language', was originally coined by the Russian Formalists who situated it in opposition to spoken language, the primary function of which is to communicate (Roudiez 1984: 2). Kristeva (1977) conceptualises poetic language as disruptive in that it draws attention to the semiotic and calls into question the order of the symbolic. She divides poetic language, and indeed all texts, into the 'genotext' and 'phenotext' (86–7). The former encompasses semiotic processes which are revealed in phonematic and melodic devices and the latter incorporates the social, syntactical and grammatical structures of communication. The strands of the genotext and phenotext can be distinctly seen in *Monologue*. The phenotext is the actual language that she speaks, governed by conventionalised laws and structures, with its own symbolic meaning. It is the genotext, however, that is brought to the fore. As the performer spews out her words in a bitter verbal attack, the language itself is almost incomprehensible and the potential for signification is completely undermined. The subsequent use of slow motion, which further distorts the relationship between word and image, adds to the semiotisation of the symbolic. While in *Monologue* the semiotic effect can be seen through the language, it can also be demonstrated through movement.

Bruce McLean is shot in a stark white studio, with flashes of brilliant coloured objects that invade the space. The movement is located in everyday actions: the performer enters and exits through a door, he looks at his watch, stretches his arm, straightens his bright red tie, holds a lime green watering can and so on. The pedestrian movement could be said to constitute the phenotext in that his actions are recognisable and logical signifiers. Yet the way the televisual apparatus distorts and manipulates the movement suggests a dominance of the genotext. The piece is rapidly edited and jumps from sudden close-ups of various parts of the body, through to medium and long shots that appear to have no logical connection to each other. Split-second images of his face dominate the screen, followed by fleeting glimpses of an elbow or speeded-up exits. A splintered soundtrack of sounds and voices adds further chaos to the frenetic action. Again, due to the lightning-fast camera work and editing, the boundaries and capabilities of the body become fluid and any element of sense is ruptured by the semiotic. It is these poetic distortions that facilitate transformation, subversion and revolution in the text (Kristeva 1977: 81).

Kristeva suggests (57) that aspects of the semiotic can be seen through such devices as rhythm and repetition in language and the distortion of grammar and syntax. These phenomena may also be located in the practices of video dance. It could be argued that video dance has the capacity to disrupt the 'syntactical arrangement' of the body in time and space. Through televisual means, the accepted order and limitations of the body in terms of temporal and spatial possibilities are called into question. For instance, in *Bruce McLean*, by way of television's ability to cut out passages of time, the performer arrives in certain positions or suddenly disappears without any mode of transition. On other occasions the image is doctored so that he executes action at an impossibly rapid pace. Indeed, on screen, the body can be slowed down, speeded up, frozen in time or played backwards. The physical capabilities of the dancing body are both distorted and extended, which can offer new choreographic possibilities and spectatorship experiences.

In addition to temporal indeterminacy, the spatial logic of the body can also be transformed. In a stage setting the spectator views the performance from a static, face-on, upright position and has a clear sense of whether the performer's body is vertical or horizontal. In video dance, however, as the camera is able take up any given position in relation to the performer, it can sometimes disrupt the spectator's sense of spatial logic. In *Waiting* (see Fig. 15.1), three performers, dressed identically in long, red wigs and grey dresses, sit on black chairs that are placed against a white studio setting. As the performers appear to be sitting upright on the television screen, the spectator does not even stop to question whether the performers and the camera are upright, although this is not actually the case. The chairs are built into a frame and are in a parallel position to the ground, while the camera is placed either overhead, so the dancers appear to be sitting upright, or on its side so that they are in profile. At first, the dancers glance around sulkily, clasp their hands and smoke cigarettes. But as they begin to traverse over and around the chairs, their movement is distorted as in actuality they are working against the pull of gravity. Their bright red hair flies out at ninety degrees to their heads and their bodies appear to be weightless. The image is highly disorienting to the viewer.

Another way of conceptualising the distortion of syntax in video dance is in relation to the order of events. Whereas television conventionally employs a linear framework (Fiske 1989), postmodern dance resists the syntactical logic of narrative structures in favour of fragmented, aleatory forms (Banes 1987). What is specific to video dance, however, is that the televisual apparatus can be used to manipulate the logic and order of dancing bodies in ways that could not be achieved on stage. *Kissy Suzuki Suck* is a grainy black and white film and deals with the theme of prostitution. Two women sit in a car wearing peroxide wigs, smoking and chewing gum while the soundtrack mixes a disco beat with women discussing their work in the sex industry. There is no linear order of events, but instead the film cuts from one episode to another: the women climb in and out of the car door, drag hard on their cigarettes, inscribe their arms, necks and faces with lipstick markings and stand on the car roof executing obscene sexual gestures. This fragmented form is facilitated by film's ability to cut from one distinct event to another without any linking transition.

Kristeva (1977) also comments that rhythm and repetition are evidence of the semiotic and this too can be seen in *Kissy Suzuki Suck*. Up to a point, the events of this film are meaningfully linked to the theme of prostitution. The women wear sexy clothes, sit in a car, smoke, chew gum and execute sexual gestures. Yet the symbolic order is ruptured as their actions are performed many times over. The women repeatedly climb in and out of the car or slap their backsides and 'flick a V sign' so that the focus shifts from the logic of the action to the semiotic rhythm of repetition. The materiality of the image is further manipulated through the grainy black and white quality of the film. A similar example occurs when one of the performers says, 'Tuesday's a tacky enough night, and it's cold as a dick's ass, so Dee and I should have let the take go at eighty bucks each'. The second performer repeats the phrase using exactly the same vocal rhythm and intonation. Again, this can be understood as the semiotisation of the symbolic. Although the phrase continues to have the capacity to signify, this is brought into tension through the 'musicalisation' of the language.

Kristeva argues that poetic language subverts the symbolic in that it attacks meaning and denotation (Kristeva 1977: 58; Lechte 1990: 135). This is demonstrated well in *Le P'tit Bal Perdu* in which two performers sit behind a large table in a field of grass, surrounded by cows, and gesticulate the words of a French folk song. In some instances they simply mime the denotation of various words. For example, on the word '*guerre*' (war) the performers point their fingers like a gun, and on '*deux*' they hold up two fingers. In other instances, they begin to challenge the denotation of a word. For example, the words '*qui s'appelait*' are repeated several times throughout the song; on the first occasion, a telephone appears on the table as a literal representation of '*appeler*' (to call). Later, various other props are employed during the refrain, which suddenly bring into question the denoted meaning through a play on the '*pel*' and '*ler*' sounds: several bottles of 'milk' appear as a pun on '*lait*', and this occurs again with '*pelle*' (spade), as a variety of shovels are displayed, and '*laid*' (ugly) on which the man pulls a face. What is perhaps most interesting is that without the words of the song, it is highly unlikely that the spectator would be able to translate the movement back to the lyrics, thus highlighting the instability of meaning in dance. This rupture of meaning is not only typical of *Le P'tit Bal Perdu*, but of the majority of video dance pieces with their incoherent signifiers and semiotisation of the symbolic. Yet this is not to suggest that video dance is meaningless.

Kristeva proposes that the semiotic (the drives and their articulations) is separate from signification (proposition and judgement) and she refers to this positionality as the 'thetic phase' (Kristeva 1977: 43). The thetic phase is a boundary between the semiotic and symbolic, originating in the mirror stage, which would suggest that the semiotic is located prior to meaning. Kristeva states:

> The semiotic can thus be understood as pre-thetic, preceding the positing of the subject. Previous to the ego thinking within a proposition, no Meaning exists, but there *do* exist articulations heterogeneous to signification and to the sign: the semiotic *chora*. (36)

The pertinence of this statement in relation to signifying systems that prioritise the semiotic, such as video dance, is that although the semiotic is pre-thetic it can nevertheless articulate. Kristeva argues that all enunciation is thetic in the sense that the subject must be separate from the object (Kristeva 1977: 43; Lechte 1990: 134). She uses the example of the 'pre-verbal child' whose gestures and vocal sounds are meaningful although the infant does not employ the laws of generative grammar (Lechte 1990: 129). The child's actions represent a judgement or a position of difference. Thus every sign is thetic.

It is possible to comprehend certain articulations within video dance even though they may be fleeting, contradictory and unstable. For example, *boy* follows the activities of a young lad on a deserted Norfolk beach (see Fig. 15.2). The filming style combines distant long shots of the boy set against the coast line, with intriguing close-ups of his private and playful gesticulations. He gambols along the beach like an animal on all fours, punches and kicks, and twiddles his sandy fingers. Low angle shots capture his explosive leaps from the dunes and mobile camera work studies his explorations of the terrain. Although there is a primacy of the semiotic, it is nevertheless possible to read a selection of meanings into the work: images of combat, aggression and threat can be seen alongside notions of isolation, surveillance and escape. The location perhaps makes reference to various 'desert island' texts, such as *Lord of the Flies* (1954) and *Robinson Crusoe* (1719), allowing various readings to be rerouted back into *boy*. There are also notions of a 'make-believe' play friend from the way in which a close-up shot focuses on the child's eyes staring into the distance, to be then followed by a long shot of the boy playing far away, as if a figment of the protagonist's imagination. Although, in each case, it is the same performer, the relationship between subject and camera suggests there are two characters rather than one.

Kristeva conceptualises poetic language as 'text-practice' (Kristeva 1977: 99) and suggests that the human body is part of this dynamic. The subject in process/on trial is said to discover boundaries and laws that are revealed in her/his practice of them. The drive charges are said to burst out, deform and transform the boundaries that society has set (Kristeva 1977: 103). Hence practice is the means by which poetic language takes on the potential for social and political transformation. The video dance piece *Horseplay* lends itself as an illustration of text-practice (see Fig. 15.3). The work follows the playful activities of three young women 'knocking around' on a stretch of wasteland. The piece is structured through fragmented episodes that mark the ordering presence of the symbolic: the women play a kind of leapfrog, emulate great footballing moments, and tease a well-dressed man. This is intercut with sequences of the women trying out 'street dance' moves. The subject in process/on trial is revealed through editing and camera work, which discovers and reveals the boundaries of 'invisible editing techniques' used in realist, narrative television.[2] Whereas realism traditionally minimises the presence of the camera, *Horseplay* employs dynamic, mobile camera work that captures the playfulness of the piece. At some points it draws attention to itself through the shakiness of a 'hand-held' style and, at other moments, it swoops in and around the performers. *Horseplay* also breaks with various editing techniques. In some instances, the edit 'cuts down the line',[3] which creates a jumpy feel to the piece and cuts occur at unpredictable and sudden moments, in stark contrast to the 'seamless editing' of realist television narratives (Fiske 1989).

There are clearly numerous examples of the ways in which video dance matches Kristeva's conceptualisation of poetic language with its dominance of the semiotic; works that are chiefly constituted of symbolic structures are rare. As the analyses in this section suggest, there is a primacy of the semiotic in video dance which ruptures the symbolic in order to create startling and unconventional images. The video dance body is therefore characterised through indeterminacy and fluidity, rather than fixity and closure.

*

Kristeva (1977) proposes that poetic language is revolutionary in form and the 'revolutionary subject' is one that lets the jouissance of semiotic motility rupture the symbolic order. She argues that this process can be seen in the nineteenth-century, literary avant-garde (Moi 1988: 170), which she describes as a challenge to, and transgression of, the historical form of the symbolic (Lechte 1990: 139). What is pertinent is that Kristeva does not regard this as a hermetically sealed occurrence, but instead she argues that it is inextricably linked to the historical context, in particular the rise of French nationalism and the Paris Commune of 1871 (Kristeva 1977: 210). Kristeva is clearly concerned with the social and historical context in any analysis of a text (Moi 1988: 172). Yet she suggests that although capitalism allows the subject to revolt, it reserves the right to suppress that revolt. Hence, revolution must take place within the text (1977: 210).

The late twentieth century is often characterised in terms of a 'technological revolution', which is sometimes referred to as the 'digital' or 'information' revolution (Penley and Ross 1991; Featherstone and Burrows 1995). In this instance, 'revolution' can be used in two of its senses: both in terms of enormous change and in terms of a political uprising (Williams 1988). The sense of change is the result of electronic and digital technologies that have begun to produce, collate and transmit vast amounts of information in ways that alter existing social networks. It is the political facet, however, that is particularly pertinent to video dance. The political potential of electronic and digital technologies lay in the facilitation of access to information for the individual. In television, this democratic notion was rooted in the belief that the television camera ostensibly provided the viewer with an unmediated access to reality (Wyver 1986). This allowed the spectator to witness events not normally accessible to viewers because of certain geographical or social circumstances. Similar democratic aspirations fuelled the early work of the computer hackers of the 1960s who attempted to break into private, corporate and state information; their intention was to make computing technology available for the everyday person, rather than for the selective use of elitist groups, such as the government and militia (Clark 1995; Lupton 1995). It is apparent, however, that the revolutionary potential of these media has been quashed by the mechanisms of capitalism. The hegemonic ideological realism of the televisual form clearly re-presents a highly mediated and distorted framework of reality (Fiske 1989), while digital technologies have been appropriated into the ever-prolific network of consumer culture (Featherstone and Burrows 1995). In Kristevan terms it could be argued that, although the revolutionary potential of television has been suppressed by capitalist forces, the avant-garde status of video dance has facilitated a symbolic revolution within the televisual context. The refusal of video dance to conform to the realist ideologies of televisual conventions disrupts television's purported framework of the 'real'.

Kristeva clearly conceptualises poetic language within a political framework. She suggests that the avant-garde text reveals what has previously been disguised in art: that is, the subject in process/on trial (1977: 211). Kristeva goes on to argue that the 'ethical' or political function of the text must take into account the subject in process/on trial so that signifying mechanisms are called into question. The political function of the text is not to deal with ideology at the level of the symbolic, but to employ the semiotic, which then 'pluralises', 'pulverises' and 'musicates' ossified forms (Kristeva 1977: 233; Lechte 1990: 140). Kristeva suggests that art practices must develop this to the point of 'laughter': 'the practice of the text is a kind of laughter whose only explosions are those of language. The pleasure obtained from the lifting of inhibitions is immediately invested in the production of the new' (225). The possibility of 'lifting inhibitions', or challenging boundaries, is approached from numerous perspectives in video dance, as has been illustrated throughout this chapter. In some instances it is through breaking televisual conventions in terms of the representation of the body, as in the disruptive filming style of *Horseplay* or the use of an intense single close-up in *Monologue*. Or else it may be achieved through constructing bodies that completely transform the boundaries and possibilities of the live body, as in the frenetic performance of *Bruce McLean*. The term 'laughter' provides an astute metaphor for the playful and subversive manipulation of text-practice and the resulting transformation that takes place in the signifying form.

The paradigmatic model of the logical and ordered symbolic in contrast to the unpredictable and disruptive semiotic is evident within other theoretical frameworks. For instance, Barthes's (1990) concept of the 'text of pleasure' and 'text of bliss', and Brecht's notion of a 'dramatic theatre' versus an 'epic theatre', share a similar polarised territory to that of Kristeva's symbolic and semiotic. Another scholar with whom Kristeva's work overlaps considerably is Bakhtin (1965) and his study of 'carnival' (Moi 1986: 34). Bakhtin's theory of carnival is based on medieval carnival, a temporary period of bodily pleasures and inverted social order, and the work of Rabelais, a sixteenth-century doctor and epic poet. Rabelais's writing is scatological in content, it employs a 'grotesque realism', and is intertextual in its appropriation of medical, military and literary discourses (Bakhtin 1984; Clark 1984; Fiske 1991). It is through Rabelais that Bakhtin develops the notion of carnival as a feature of certain texts and it is in this area that Kristeva is indebted to Bakhtin's work.

In *Word, Dialogue and Novel* (1977), Kristeva explores Bakhtin's concept of the 'carnivalesque text', which shares striking similarities with her notion of 'poetic language'. The carnival text is structured in a way that fails to correspond to a coherent, 'scientific' logic (Kristeva 1977: 64) and it evades causality and linearity (Kristeva 1977: 79). This resulting fragmentation is partly to do with the polyphonic, intertextual nature of the carnival text: it is penetrated by 'other voices' (Lechte 1990: 106). This is typical of video dance in that it will always include at least two 'voices' (practices) within itself in that it is constituted through both dance and television.

As with poetic language, carnival transcends the laws of language as they are traditionally understood (Lechte 1990: 111). In the carnival text, repetition does not necessarily lead to tautology, as it would do in everyday communication, but constitutes the rhythmic musicalisation of the text. As a result of the polyphonic, contradictory nature of the carnival text, there is no fixed point of meaning, but rather an intersection of meanings (Kristeva 1977: 65; Lechte 1990: 106). Bakhtin makes a distinction between the 'monological' text and the 'dialogical text' (Kristeva 1977). The former observes the law and follows a single, relatively uniform logic. Realist narratives and everyday communication fall into the category of monological discourse. Dialogical texts, however, demonstrate a carnival, or poetic, logic. They transgress the social and linguistic code by being intertextual, contradictory and open-ended. This polarity is clearly analogous to Kristeva's distinction of the symbolic and semiotic, in that monological texts prioritise the symbolic and dialogical texts privilege the semiotic.

In Kristeva's thesis of poetic language, she propounds a revolutionary potential through the semiotic's disruption of the symbolic framework. There is apparent comparison with both medieval and 'textual' carnival in their temporary disruption of the social order; yet the political effectiveness of this is debatable. It has been suggested that medieval carnival was simply a 'safety-valve' mechanism of the ruling classes that gave the lower classes a misconceived sense of freedom (Clark 1984: 313; Fiske 1991: 100). The fact that this period of disorder takes place within the 'law', suggests a political ineffectuality. Laura Mulvey (1989: 162) questions the subversiveness of phenomena such as carnival that invert the social order. She suggests that dualistic theoretical frameworks are problematic in that the only movement is one of inversion. A binary opposition allows for an 'either/or' strategy, so that in the case of carnival there is either order or disorder. As with the 'safety valve' argument, there is a danger of simply reinforcing a dualist framework. Consequently, this raises the question of how to instigate change in what Mulvey describes as a 'polarised mythology' (168).

The domain in which a dominant order is inverted or disrupted has been referred to as a 'ludic space' (Mulvey 1989: 168). The ludic space is transgressive because the dominant is challenged. It is, however, a domain permitted by the law. The space can easily be reverted back to the norm. Yet in defence of the ludic period, it can be argued that it is a time of resistance and potential transformation. Mulvey characterises the events of carnival within a tripartite structure (172). Firstly a moment of disruption occurs that marks off the following period from the events of normal life. This is followed by a 'liminal phase' in which the norms of everyday are inverted and the people involved are situated in a liminal position to the status quo.[4] Finally, the end of this period is marked by a return to, and reincorporation back into, the everyday. As Mulvey notes, this structure forms the basis of the Oedipus complex and is mirrored throughout the narrative form: an equilibrium is broken, a period of disruption follows, and then is brought to an end with a return to equilibrium (169). It is the middle phase, the liminal position, that interests Mulvey in that it is a domain for action to occur outside the time and space of the dominant framework. The strength of this conceptualisation is that it is constituted in terms of a linear model, rather than the oppositional framework of a polar model (171). It is the liminal stage then that allows for potential revolution. As Mulvey suggests 'it is this liminal phase that suggests imagery of change, transformation and liberation' (174).

Although Mulvey's reading of carnival promotes its revolutionary potential, several scholars critique Kristeva's work in relation to its political framework. Some scholars highlight concern that Kristeva employs a psychoanalytic epistemology (Goellner 1995; Thomas 1996), due to its phallocentric position and the abstract character of the unconscious. Further criticism is directed at her concept of revolution. Moi (1988: 170) states that Kristeva's account of revolution fails to consider the notion of 'agency', in terms of 'who' or 'what' is acting as a revolutionary force. Her emphasis on the semiotic overlooks any conscious and collective decision-making. Notions of organisation and solidarity are disregarded in her concept of semiotic disruption, which is essentially anarchic and subjectivist. Moi asserts that the nineteenth-century avant-garde may have disrupted the structures of language, but had little revolutionary effect elsewhere (171). She cogently argues that although Kristeva provides a detailed account of the social and historical contexts of the nineteenth-century avant-garde, she fails to produce any conclusive proof as to how these writings may have prompted or paralleled social revolutions.

The same critique can be applied to the revolutionary potential of video dance. It may be a disruptive force in terms of dance and televisual practices, but, at present, it continues to hold a marginal position within the mainstream flow of television programming. Yet although there is no evidence that video dance has prompted any kind of social revolution, it has certainly had an aesthetic impact on dance performance. It could be argued that video dance occurs within a 'liminal phase' or a 'ludic space' in that it marks a suspension of both dance and televisual conventions. The hybrid status of video dance constructs a fluid body and this indeterminacy has implications for choreographic practice, spectatorship positions, and the television screen as a context for dance. The notions of 'liminal' and 'ludic' are pertinent in that they parallel Kristeva's characterisation of poetic language as 'marginal' yet 'subversive' (Moi 1986: 35). Video dance is 'marginal' both in the sense that it occupies only a minute space within television programming (Allen 1993) and in that it exists at a threshold of dance and televisual practice. Meanwhile its subversive role can be identified in its playful disruption of existing boundaries: video dance bodies can perform feats that are impossible for the material body to replicate and and its formal properties challenge realist television conventions. One of the strengths of Kristeva's work is the recognition that poetic or carnival texts can be meaningful and that, although such spaces are marginal, they can provide moments of resistance, subversion and transgression. The fluidity or indeterminacy of the video dance body allows it to confront and disrupt the stasis of conventionalised, symbolic boundaries. For the discipline of dance at least, this is a revolution.

Notes

1 For a full exposition of Kristeva's theories on the symbolic and semiotic paradigm in relation to poetic language see Kristeva (1977), Moi (1986, 1988) and Lechte (1990).

2 Metz (1975: 44) argues that in fiction film (and in television texts that employ realist devices), the role of the cinematic (or televisual) signifiers is to erase their presence in order to give the spectator an illusion of reality. That is to say, the various cinematic and televisual codes must be made 'invisible' so that an impression of unmediated reality is constructed.

3 One of the rules of 'invisible editing' is that after a cut, the following shot should be seen from a sufficiently different angle from the previous one

(Monaco 1981: 184). To 'cut down the line' is to keep two or more shots at the same angle, so that a wide shot might be followed by a tighter one, but from exactly the same placement.

4 A detailed explanation of the concept of 'liminality' may be found in the work of Victor Turner (1969 and 1982).

Works cited

Allen 1993 Dave Allen, 'Screening Dance', in Stephanie Jordan and Dave Allen (eds), *Parallel Lines: Media Representations of Dance* (London: Libbey)

Bakhtin 1965 Mikhail Bakhtin, *L'œuvre de François Rabelais et la culture populaire au moyen âge et sous la renaissance* (translated from the Russian by Andrée Robel: Paris: Gallimard, 1970), translated into English as *Rabelais and his World* by Hélène Iswolsky (Bloomington: Indiana University Press, edn of 1984)

Banes 1987 Sally Banes, *Terpsichore in Sneakers* (Hanover: Wesleyan University Press)

Barthes 1973 Roland Barthes, *Le Plaisir du texte* (Paris: Seuil), translated by Richard Miller as *The Pleasure of the Text* (Oxford: Basil Blackwell, 1990)

Brecht 1978 Bertolt Brecht, *Brecht on Theatre* (London: Methuen), edited and translated by John Willett

Clark 1984 Katerina Clark, *Mikhail Bakhtin* (Cambridge Mass. and London: Harvard University Press)

Clark 1995 Nigel Clark, 'Rear-view Mirrorshades: the Recursive Generation of the Cyberbody', in Mike Featherstone and Roger Burrows (eds), *Cyberspace Cyberbodies Cyberpunk: Cultures of Technological Embodiment* (London: Sage)

Daly 1992 Ann Daly, 'Dance History and Feminist Theory: Reconsidering Isadora Duncan and the Male Gaze', in Laurence Senelick (ed.), *Gender in Performance: the Presentation of Difference in the Performing Arts* (London: University Press of New England)

Featherstone and Burrows 1995 Mike Featherstone and Roger Burrows (eds), *Cyberspace Cyberbodies Cyberpunk: Cultures of Technological Embodiment* (London: Sage)

Fiske 1989 John Fiske, *Television Culture* (London: Routledge)

Fiske 1991 John Fiske, *Understanding Popular Culture* (London: Routledge)

Goellner 1995 Ellen Goellner, *Bodies of the Text* (New Jersey: Rutgers University Press)

Kristeva 1974 Julia Kristeva, *La Révolution du langage poétique* (Paris: Seuil), translated as *Revolution in Poetic Language* by Margaret Waller (New York: Columbia University Press, 1984)

Kristeva 1977 Julia Kristeva, *Desire in Language: a Semiotic Approach to Literature and Art* (Oxford: Blackwell, edn of 1984)

Lechte 1990 John Lechte, *Julia Kristeva* (London: Routledge)

Lupton 1995 Deborah Lupton, 'The embodied Computer/User', in Mike Featherstone and Roger Burrows (eds), *Cyberspace Cyberbodies Cyberpunk: Cultures of Technological Embodiment* (London: Sage)

Maletic 1987–88 Vera Maletic, 'Videodance – Technology – Attitude Shift', *Dance Research Journal*, 19, 2, Winter, 3–7

Metz 1975 Christian Metz, 'The Imaginary Signifier', *Screen*, 16, 2, Summer, 14–76

Moi 1986 Toril Moi (ed.), *The Kristeva Reader* (Oxford: Blackwell)

Moi 1988 Toril Moi, *Sexual/Textual Politics* (London: Routledge)

Monaco 1981 James Monaco, *How to Read a Film* (Oxford: Oxford University Press)

Mulvey 1989 Laura Mulvey, *Visual and Other Pleasures* (London: Macmillan)

Penley and Ross 1991 Constance Penley and Andrew Ross (eds), *Technoculture* (Oxford: University of Minnesota Press)

Rosiny 1994 Claudia Rosiny, 'Dance Films and Video Dance', *Ballet International*, 8/9: August/September, 82–3

Roudiez 1984 Leon Roudiez, 'Introduction', in Julia Kristeva, *Revolution in Poetic Language* (New York: Columbia University Press)

Shilling 1993 Chris Shilling, *The Body and Social Theory* (London: Sage)

Thomas1996 Helen Thomas, 'Do You Want to Join the Dance?: Postmodernism/ Poststructuralism, the Body and Dance', in Gay Morris (ed.), *Moving Words* (London: Routledge)

Turner 1969 Victor Turner, *The Ritual Process: Structure and Anti-Structure* (London: Routledge)

Turner 1982 Victor Turner, *From Ritual to Theatre* (New York: Performing Arts Journal)

Williams 1988 Raymond Williams, *Keywords* (London: Fontana)

Wyver 1986 John Wyver, 'Television and Postmodernism', in Lisa Appignanesi (ed.), *Postmodernism: ICA Documents 4* (London: ICA)

Videography

Tights, camera, action! (Channel 4, 1993)

Kissy Suzuki Suck	Choreographer/Director: Alison Murray

Tights, camera, action! 2 (Channel 4, 1994)

Monologue	Choreographer: Anna Teresa de Keersmaeker, Director: Walter Verdin
Bruce McLean	Choreographer: Bruce McLean, Director: Jane Thorburn
Waiting	Choreographer/Director: Lea Anderson
Le p'tit Bal Perdu	Choreographer/Director: Philippe Decouflé

Dance for the camera 3 (1996)

Horseplay	Choreographer/Director: Alison Murray
boy	Choreographer: Rosemary Lee, Director: Peter Anderson

Index